Hi Ms. Elder,

Thanks for all that you do!

Sincerely,

Ron.

The Truth Collector

Being Transformed

Ronald J. Yadusky, BS, MD, FACS

Ronald J. Yadusky MD.

authorHOUSE®

AuthorHouse™
1663 Liberty Drive, Suite 200
Bloomington, IN 47403
www.authorhouse.com
Phone: 1-800-839-8640

First published by AuthorHouse 8/17/2009

ISBN: 978-1-4389-5389-2 (sc)

Library of Congress Control Number: 2009901794

Printed in the United States of America
Bloomington, Indiana

This book is printed on acid-free paper.

Dedication

I dedicate this book to God; and to my dear wife, Margaret, who has stood by me and helped me these many years; and to my five children, living and dead: Mary, Ann, Joseph, William and John; and to their families as well as to mine and to Margaret's.

Acknowledgements

Isaac Newton (English physicist, astronomer, 1643-1727) said that the reason we see so far is because we stand on the shoulders of giants. I thank all the giants on whose shoulders I stand—namely: my wife Margaret, family, teachers, preachers, authors, mentors, and examples that have guided me to this point.

Special thanks to my niece, Stephanie, and her husband, Kit Cessna, without whose encouragement and help this book would never have gotten written and published.

Thanks, also, to my copyeditor Julia Gonzalez, President of Helo Communications, Inc., for all her help and understanding.

Many thanks and heartfelt gratitude, also, to my proofreaders for their caring interest and help with this work:

Mary Galligan, Claire Galligan, Craig and Ann Barta, Christina Barta, Jessica Barta, Jonathan Barta, Joe and Laura Yadusky, Sally Yadusky, Megan Yadusky, Sarah Yadusky, Jacob Yadusky, William (Will) Yadusky, Kaye Yadusky, William and Katie Yadusky, Aleksandra Yadusky, Catherine Staton, Donald and Joan Yadusky, Katie Gold, Kit and Stephanie Cessna, Rachel Cessna, Hunter Cessna, Dan and Julianne Brunson, Anna Katherine Brunson, Peter Yadusky, Scott Yadusky, John Patani, Charles Frederick IV (Chip) and Kim Colvin, Charles Frederick V (Charlie) Colvin, Andrew John Colvin, Grace Margaret Colvin, Sherri and Sabrina Dodd Tumicelli, Nikolas Devon Dodd, Mikhael Gavin Dodd, Catrina Van Diest, Mary (Pete) Troy, Brenda and Joel Clayton, Barnwell Ray and Emma Stone (Rocky) Beard, Cindy and George Patrick, Fay Crouch, Rita Brunson, Marcelo and Nina Alvarez, Gia Alvarez, Jane Black, Paul Bartley, Tom and Grace Hughes.

Special thanks and gratitude, also, to my Pastor at St. Mary Magdalene Church, Reverend Father Donald Staib, who did not find any difficulties with religious matters in this work or any objections that he could see. And he trusts that my words will do much good for others.

Note

Let me explain the letters after my name:

B.S., for graduating from Villanova University with a Bachelor of Science degree in pre-med.

M.D., for graduating from Jefferson Medical University.

F.A.C.S., for going through a surgical residency program and becoming a Fellow of the American College of Surgeons.

My internship was one year at Fitzgerald Mercy Hospital in Darby, Pennsylvania.

My residency program was four years of General Surgery at Lankenau Hospital in Overbrook, Pennsylvania and two years of Thoracic and Cardiovascular Surgery at the Berthold S. Pollak Hospital of Chest Diseases in Jersey City, New Jersey, followed by a year of Cardiovascular Surgery Research Fellowship.

I'm Board Certified in both General Surgery and Thoracic and Cardiovascular Surgery.

Contents

Introduction

Little by little, in the presence of love, you find what it is
that you came, without knowing, to seek.
—*Author unknown*

Knowing without doing is like plowing without sowing.
—*Vernon K. McLellan, contemporary author*

What I know about transformation, I've made the basic content of
this book. It comes from what I've found in my lifelong search for
truth, love, goodness—and all of the other values, virtues, ideals,
and principles—and the transformation that they bring. I want to
share truth that has taken me a lifetime to learn, because I've learned
a lot of truth from my choice of reading, my schooling, and my own
life experiences during my career as a surgeon. Doctors stand by
on call a lot. When you stand by on call in medicine, you can't go
anywhere, which leaves a lot of time for reading. I like to crystal-
lize out the truth and save it in short, wise sayings. To paraphrase
Plato: Wise men talk because they have something to say—I want
to wisely share the truth with you and not just talk. I have found significant nuggets of truth that I have patiently mined out of life, and
I can share my bonanza with you. I want to give you a clear picture
of what transformation is all about. Because I know that by doing
that, it will cause you, by the end of the book, to be transformed in
your *mind, heart, and spirit* by *truth, love, and goodness,* just like I
have been. Because the mind seeks truth, the heart seeks love, and
the spirit seeks goodness and God.

You have to study a great deal to know a little.
—*Charles-Louis de Secondat, Baron de Montesquieu,
French lawyer and writer; and many of his ideas were
incorporated into the United States Constitution, 1689-
1755*

Within these pages is a review of my life and, in that sense, this is like the life review that hospice asks of those who are dying. Elisabeth Kubler-Ross, M.D. (Swiss-born psychiatrist, 1926-2004), in her landmark 1969 book *On Death and Dying,* noted that part of what occurs during a life-after-death experience is seeing your whole life flash before your eyes. If that is what is going to happen to you after dying, then I say, "Why not have the review *before* you die?"

It's said that all that we do can be considered our self-portrait. So, in a certain sense, all that we do is autobiographical. The self-portrait always ends up showing what we love. "The owl flies at midnight" is an old Greek expression. It means that we only really understand something when it's very late or when it's over. In other words, "You cannot appreciate the splendor of the day until it is night." I am old enough to be at that point. After all these many years of my life, I finally feel that I have the truth to share, and I'd like to share it with you. "Knowledge and timber shouldn't be much used till they are seasoned" (Hugo Von Hofmannsthal, Austrian poet, 1874-1929). What I've learned all my life about love may help you to learn about it sooner, rather than later. Such early learning is always to your benefit, because, as an old German expression points out: "We grow old too soon and smart too late." You have to love medicine to choose it as a profession, and you have to love your readers, as I do, in order to write.

This book is also an ethical will to my family, where I share my values instead of my valuables, as in ordinary wills. If something is a burning inspiration in your heart and your life, I think you ought to express it somehow. There's much wisdom in old Grandpas. And I will try to say the truth clearly, because, as Albert Camus (French author, 1913-1960) said: "Those who write clearly have readers."

The inspiration for this work came to me in two ways. It originated from my experiences as a doctor dealing with the heartbreaking circumstances of my many patients, and it has arisen from the sorrows and desolations that have been my own. Outstanding among these was when my son, Joe, was diagnosed with testicular cancer at age 26. With his diagnosis of cancer, he went, symbolically, from the city of consolation with ambition, work, and marriage to the desert of desolation. But from there, he went to a garden of transformation, where he had acceptance and a different attitude toward life. He moved from being cornered by life to being engaged and fascinated with it. He became spiritually refreshed. He seemed to know something intuitively that my wife, Margaret, and I didn't know, because he was at a higher level of thinking and living. He moved beyond the joy of the city and the sorrow of the desert to the garden, to where he was transformed. To our surprise, he had gone from consolation to desolation to transformation.

My wife and I were in a lower level of thinking and living. We were in a desolation of worry and concern for our son, and we needed to be transformed. We wanted to get to the garden where our son had gotten to on his own, which meant that we had to attend cancer support group therapy, do much reading, and attend talks by such eminent authors as Dr. Bernie Siegel (physician, surgeon and contemporary American non-fiction author). We wanted more than just the joy of the city or the sorrow of the desert; we wanted the garden of transformation.

Dr. Siegel gave us hope in telling us that he never knew about any cancer for which someone, somewhere, at some time, did not somehow receive a cure. Slowly, we were able to get into the garden with our son by experiencing the love and concerns of a vast group of medical personnel, family and friends, and many others who were struggling with their own similar medical situations. Also, prayer and having faith helped a lot. We moved into the garden with the help of faith, hope, and love. I believe that love eventually transforms everyone as a "third way" away from the duality of just life's consolation and desolation or joys and sorrows. Desolation includes not only sorrow, but the desolation of anger, fear, and loneliness. Your brokenness is what gives love, and its transformation, a chance to enter into you. Necessity may be the mother of invention, but failure is the mother of success, because in brokenness you can succeed in moving beyond to getting transformed. Little by little, in the presence of love, you find what it is that you came, without knowing, to seek.

"Patience with others is Love, patience with self is Hope, patience with God is Faith."
—*Adel Bestavros, Egyptian deacon and lawyer, born 1924*

Dr. Bernie Siegel, in his 1986 book *Love, Medicine and Miracles,* pointed out that we should expect suffering in our life, especially if we have the blessing of getting older, because we may outlive our loved ones and see them die. In a talk to our cancer support group he said, "To love is to be happy, not to love is to be unhappy. To suffer is to suffer. Not to suffer is to be happy. To love is to suffer. Not to love is to suffer. Therefore, in order to be happy we must either love, love to suffer, or suffer from too much happiness." In other words, we should expect suffering in our life. The premise of this book is to agree with Dr. Siegel and to add that there is more that we should expect, namely, a transformation beyond just sorrow and joy, beyond just desolation and consolation.

To fall in love is awfully simple. Not to fall in love is simply awful. And we shall explore the paradox that even though love may often be a source of our suffering, it is also our way out of suffering into transformation, because we should not allow suffering to determine our future but only let love determine our future.

In one of the cancer support groups that we attended, a lecturer told Margaret and me that life is like an island, rising out of the sea, composed of various-sized rocks representing all the people. A large boulder could be a president or a Pope, lesser ranks could be rocks of various sizes, but most people were just pebbles or even simply small grains of sand on the beach. Those with cancer feel even smaller and more insignificant, maybe only just as big as an atom. However, if you can split that atom symbolically—in other words, by telling your story—you can shake the whole island.

It's certainly true that suffering makes philosophers of us all. Transformation can be found whenever you're attuned to looking above and beyond your present circumstances, towards love and other values. In doing this, you find the transformation that you seek. If you can't seem to find love anywhere else, you can still look to God, who is love. Mother Teresa of Calcutta (1910-1997) said that if you can't find love, put love there, and you will find love. My wife, Margaret, and I learned from experience that cancer cannot corrode faith, shatter hope, cripple love, kill friendships, or destroy peace. And that love conquers all.

Three qualities or values make us all human, and they are truth (mind), love (heart), and goodness (spirit, soul, God). The mind seeks truth, the heart seeks love, and the spirit seeks goodness and God. They, and all the other values, virtues, ideals, and principles, are transforming. You will see examples of this as you proceed through this book.

Transformation is a higher level of thinking and living, where you feel more fully human. And it raises the question, "Are you transformed once and for all or are you always transforming?" The answer to this question will be pursued in this work, where other examples of transformation will be given. I believe that after you read my words, at a minimum, you will feel spiritually refreshed, but I also believe that you, too, will be transformed.

I realize that some of my readers may feel that much of the world does not share the same values. Unfortunately, it will always be true that when it comes to values, some people will be attracted to the bright Christmas lights while they miss out on the care and love for self, family, and others, which spirituality requires. One day, they may understand the full truth: that life is basically our moving away from love and our return to love. The three "R's" are more than just reading, writing, and arithmetic. They are respect for yourself, respect for others, and responsibility for your actions.

The process of life moving from the joy or consolation of the city with ambition, work, and marriage to the sorrow or desolation of the desert with sicknesses and troubles, but ending in the garden of transformation in the presence of love, recalls the story of Moses in the Bible leading the Jewish people from the city into the desert and then toward the garden of the Promised Land. It took time for them to get to where they should be, and it takes time for us to get to where we are going. The words to an old song point out that sometimes miracles hide and God can put some blessings in disguise and it may take a lifetime for us to see it with our eyes.

My son's cancer was found during exploratory abdominal surgery. It had metastasized, or spread, into the lymph nodes of his upper abdomen, which used to be a death sentence in the past. Despite this, I eventually had the consolation of seeing my son cured. At the time of his cure, my son was still living in transformation.

Our cancer support group gave us another example about life. We were told that life is like an apple tree, with everyone who is healthy represented by all of the good apples on the tree. Those with cancer feel like all the rotten apples on the ground, wishing they were healthy and back on the tree. But what can you do with rotten apples? You can throw them at the tree in anger to try to disturb all the good apples. Or you can take what is good from each and every apple and make applesauce, for the benefit of all. In other words, if you are given a lemon in life, make lemonade. Life is more than joy and sorrow. Life is more than health and illness. We must play the hand that we are dealt. We must carry on when the world has not officially ended. When I would break the bad news to my patients that they had a cancer diagnosis, I would put my arm around them and point out that there was plenty of life still left in them, and that they were not dead yet. It's like what people do after a divorce or any serious situation: you carry on. It's not the end of the world, or even the end of the world as you know it.

Cancer cannot suppress memories or silence courage, or invade the soul, or conquer the spirit, or steal eternal life. Transformation is "more," it's an upgrade, a third way beyond joy and sorrow. Gilbert Keith Chesterton (English author, 1874-1936) believed that the story that speaks most directly to our human condition is the story of Robinson Crusoe, where everything from the shipwreck of our lives consists of just the few things that we are able to salvage. And we are each searching to be saved by finding our own "Friday." Symbolically, that "Friday" is love, and we see Friday's (love's) footprints everywhere. Love is to the heart what the summer is to the farmer's year—it brings to harvest all of the loveliest flowers of the soul. Where flowers bloom, so does hope. Where there is a garden, there are always memories. An old Spanish proverb says, "More things grow in the garden than the gardener sows."

> The "Amen" of nature is always a flower.
> —*Oliver Wendell Holmes, American poet, 1841-1935*

> Flowers always make people better, happier, and more helpful; they are sunshine, food and medicine to the soul.
> —*Luther Burbank, Botanist and American horticulturist, 1849-1926*

So does love.

We use symbolism easily and naturally every day. For example, we speak of the early bird catching the worm and the night owls working into the night. And we speak of those in favor of war as hawks and the opposite as doves. Any set of opposites, such as hot and cold, or day and night, or organic and inorganic, is a set of contrasts that I like to call a *duality*. Joy and sorrow constitute a duality (dual, duo, two, binary, polarity or bipolarity) of contrasting opposites. Symbolically, the two are like two mirrors facing away from each other, going in the opposite direction. Like positive and negative. I also know there is more. There is the garden of transformation after the city of joy and the desert of sorrow, after the city of consolation and the desert of desolation.

The third way, trinity, or three, comes out of any duality to lead to transformation. There is always more than two; there is the elevation into three. There is more beyond both joy and sorrow. I am using numbers symbolically to talk about higher levels of thinking and living, namely, the high level called *transformation* that includes truth, love, goodness, and all of the other values, virtues, ideals, and principles. These are invisible, and because they are invisible, they seem as abstract as numbers.

Education is simply the soul of a society as it passes from one generation to another.
—*Gilbert Keith Chesterton, English author, 1874-1936*

An educated mind is, as it were, composed of all the minds of previous ages.
—*Bernard Le Bovier de Fontenelle, French essayist, 1657-1757*

Someone once said that if you look behind, you will be disappointed by seeing your lack of love and your errors; and if you look ahead, you will be discouraged as you see that there will probably be more lack of love and errors; and if you look all around, you will be disappointed by all that you see; and if you look down, you will be depressed—but if you can only look up, you will be delighted.

Two themes, like two chains, intertwine throughout this work. One chain is my lifetime collection of truths in short, wise sayings, each like a link in this first chain. And the second chain is a collection of incidents, from my life and that of my family, that illustrate truths found in the links of the first chain. Each chapter builds on the preceding one to rise and move beyond to a deeper understanding of transformation. The two chains are not left to dangle in space but are moving in escalation to a concluding summary, which is the final chapter and its Postscript.

Thank you for reading, and please enjoy this book.

Chapter 1.

My Story: The Tale of Everyone

As is a tale, so is life: not how long it is, but how good a story it is, is what matters.
—*Seneca, Roman philosopher of the 1ˢᵗ century*

Death leaves a heartache no one can heal, love leaves a memory no one can steal.
—*Found on a headstone in Ireland*

Everyone creates a unique work of art which is their own personal real-life story. Each act is a cut of the chisel or a stroke of the brush. Therefore, since everyone is an artist, and artists must suffer in order to create their greatest work, everyone must suffer. There is an Indian proverb: "Tell me a fact and I will learn. Tell me a truth and I will believe. But tell me a story and it will live in my heart forever." "No narrative that tells the facts of a man's life in the man's own words can be uninteresting" (Mark Twain, American author, 1835-1910).

Life wounds everyone. Besides blood, though, the artist sheds light.
—*Alfred Corn, American aphorist, born 1943*

There is a crack in everything. It's how the light gets in.
—*Leonard Cohen, Canadian poet, born 1934*

What is to give light must endure the burning.
—*Dr. Viktor E. Fankl, Viennese psychologist and physician, 1905-1997*

> The art of living lies not in eliminating but in growing with troubles.
> —*Bernard Baruch, American Presidential advisor, 1870-1965*

> When it is darkest, men see the stars.
> —*Ralph Waldo Emerson, philosopher, essayist, poet, 1803-1882*

The previous quotation matches an old expression: "It's always darkest before the dawn." You can say the same thing by using medical symbolism: "The nearer any disease approaches to a crisis, the nearer it is to a cure" (Thomas Paine, inventor and aphorist; his books and pamphlets helped inspire the American Revolution, 1737-1809).

> Do not go where the path may lead, go instead where there is no path and leave a trail.
> —*Ralph Waldo Emerson, philosopher, essayist, poet, 1803-1882*

In order to give you a clear picture of what being transformed is all about, I begin by taking a series of aphorisms and truisms and matching them with incidents from my life and that of my family. As you progress through this book, chapter by chapter, you will find yourself transformed more and more in your mind, heart and spirit by my words full of truth, love and goodness, because our minds seek truth, our hearts seek love, and our spirits seek goodness and God.

There has been much progress in medicine in just a few decades, since the time I started in medical school in 1953. In surgery we've gone from incisions to puncture incisions of so-called fiber-optic "band aid" surgery, to natural orifice surgery, to robotic surgery. And we have gone from the stitching of wounds to using staples and, from there, to using glue. Actually, there's been much progress in every field of endeavor. We've gone from the first airplane flight to walking on the moon. In 1908, the average American life expectancy was 47 years, and only 8% of homes had a telephone. And here it is 2009, one hundred years later, with an average American life expectancy of at least 76 years and the widespread use of cell phones.

> When did the march of history start breaking into a sprint?
> —*Toon Verhoeven, Dutch aphorist and author, born 1941*

It's said that a hundred years from now, we may have movies in which, by computer, you can put yourself or any other actor into any role. And it may even be virtual-reality movies in three dimensions or holograms. There will be no career for actors and actresses, because everything will be computerized. We shall see. Cities of the future were predicted years ago, and I'm still waiting.

When I was in medical school in 1953, the antibiotics, penicillin and streptomycin, were just starting to get touted as *miracle drugs* because of their effectiveness against infection. I recall that prefrontal lobotomy and electroshock therapy were in vogue then, and now it seems back in the dark ages. Additionally, psychiatry was so relatively primitive that "sham surgery" was in vogue, in which incisions were made and closed without doing anything else, to take advantage of the placebo effect. Over the ensuing years, I would hear stories from a few other surgeons about how they had operated on patients who insisted that another doctor had earlier taken out their appendix or gall bladder, and at their later surgery, an appendix or gall bladder was found. I have never done such placebo surgery myself.

On the other hand, there are some rare patients with Munchausen's Syndrome, who maneuver to be unnecessarily operated upon, repeatedly. And a few other patients who want surgery for anything in order to get some time off from work, or for some other reason. I've had a few patients with extremely acute abdomen pain for which all the tests returned normal. When nothing was found on which to operate, their unexplained severe pain was all gone at the time of their hospital discharge, and these patients apparently were not addicts seeking narcotics.

We've all heard stories about lawyers suing and trying to get the "bad apples" out of medicine, but I have never personally come across any of these "bad apples." Every doctor in my long career was just an honest man or woman trying to do his or her best under difficult circumstances, which can generally be described as overworked, understaffed, and undersupplied. Nevertheless, "bad apples" do exist. One of my daughters had a desolating experience with one doctor who was later found to have a bad record. He recommended amniocentesis, which he performed, resulting in an infection that caused the loss of her premature baby boy, Evan, who was held in the hands of my wife, Margaret, as she witnessed the baby's last breath. And I have been surprised by one nurse in our hospital who was caught trying to kill a patient as a mercy killing by acting as a so-called nurse "angel of mercy." And I've had two mentally and/or morally sick nurses who thought that it's fun to deliberately disturb the doctor to see if they can make him mad. Desolating incidents as these add a pall of darkness to the world and emphasizes to us that it needs more light. It points out that it's certainly true that it takes all kinds to make up the world.

I could make a long list of my sorrows, including those of my immediate family, that would include illnesses, accidents, kidney stones, my wife's miscarriages, family divorces, and estrangements etc., but I'll just pick a few personal sorrows or desolations that have touched me for illustration purposes. I want to illustrate that opposites, such as joy and sorrow in our lives, go together like front and back or buying and selling. This makes us think that this coupling of two may be all that there is to life. This coupling of contrasts or opposites is what I call a *duality* (dual, two). As you progress in this book, you'll see that duality is not all that there is, because there is always a third way. There is always more beyond, which I like to call *trinity* (three, third way). Trinity helps us to get to the garden of transformation, but trinity is not transformation itself, as will be further explained.

I had desolation during my class in Physical Diagnosis in medical school. In Physical Diagnosis class, each student examines another. I was born with a congenital anal polyp that I first noted when it protruded out of my anus during bowel movements as a bright, strawberry-red colored piece of tissue on a stalk. It was removed in medical school by one of my Physical Diagnosis professors, who cut the stalk in front of all my classmates. Talk about desolation: I had to suffer the embarrassment of everyone in my class seeing my pathology—namely, my anal polyp—protruding from my anus, demonstrating to the class its classic strawberry-red color. I had the consolation of being cured of my anal polyp.

One of my classmates during this Physical Diagnosis class was found to have a thyroid nodule for which he underwent surgery to remove it, and he later returned to classes.

In Ophthalmology class, I had an incidental congenital tissue debris free-floater in one of my eyes that everyone in my class had a chance to look at. My consolation is that this free-floater has never interfered with my vision in any way.

Each medical student is given a box of human bones to take home to study in a wooden box, with no lock but just a clasp to close it. My twin brother and I, who had the consolation of being able to go to the same medical school together, would imagine how desolating and embarrassing it would be for the box to fall open as we traveled home on the elevated subway, or "el," from downtown Philadelphia to our home at 69th Street in west Philadelphia, an area called Upper Darby. Our consolation was that, fortunately, our boxes didn't fall open, because we tightly guarded them.

I had the desolation of seeing, when we lived in Pennsylvania, my son, Joe, get Rocky Mountain Spotted Fever from a tick bite that was not obvious because it was hidden in his ear. As a doctor, it is particularly heart-rending to see your young boy's feverish skin covered in small, petechial hemorrhagic spots from head to toe, and watch as he gets weaker and weaker each day, until you know that tomorrow he will probably die. That is, unless he gets the tetracycline antibiotic, which his attending doctor is withholding, because the doctor is awaiting confirmation from the lab of the diagnosis that may take a couple more days. I had to beg the attending physician to give the antibiotic without a confirming diagnosis at hand, and I had to assume the full responsibility. I had the consolation of seeing my son, Joe, promptly cured of Rocky Mountain Spotted Fever by the antibiotic.

I already spoke about Joe being cured, at a later time in his life, of his testicular cancer. In addition to his cures, Joe has the consolation of being married to a wonderful, kind, and compassionate nurse.

I had the desolation of one of my sons becoming an alcoholic.

Part of his recovery required that my wife, Margaret, and I attend four days of rehabilitation sessions at the institution where he committed himself for a month. I learned some things that they didn't teach me in medical school that I'll share with you when I speak of alcoholism in Chapter 13, entitled "Defenses." Alcoholism is a form of self medication used as a defense against the pain that the alcoholic feels in living.

I had the consolation of my son's recovery, which is his daily struggle, because we don't speak of cured alcoholics, only recovering ones.

- Realtors are interested in the inside of things. This is shown by the fact that every now and then you'll see a house for sale with a sign outside saying, "I'm gorgeous inside!" Anyone going into medicine, especially a surgeon, must be interested in the inside of things. Surgeons can see what is gorgeous inside, too.

- I am also interested in inclusions in minerals. An inclusion is basically a crystal that has grown to enclose another crystal inside of it. My interest in minerals may have started with my chemistry set, and then was reinforced by my visits to the Museum of the Philadelphia Academy of Natural Sciences. This museum had an outstanding mineral collection, which they, sadly, sold in 2006. This museum is near the Franklin Institute.

- I'm also interested in mint errors in coins. Perhaps it's because you can find errors more frequently than you can find old dates on coins. But also, perhaps it's because I'm an ACoA: Adult Child of an Alcoholic. They feel that they are a mistake until they learn that God doesn't make mistakes and that God doesn't make junk. And so, maybe as an ACoA, I'm naturally attracted to errors and imperfections in coins.

I had some further desolation and consolation:

I had the desolation of my wife being diagnosed with malignant lung cancer that required the removal of her left lung, followed by chemotherapy and the loss of her hair. She then developed two "leaky" heart valves requiring surgical repair, followed by many years of radiotherapy and chemotherapy to control various areas of her body where her cancer tumor intermittently spread. I have the consolation of her surviving almost nine years with minimal symptoms other than fatigue despite her widespread tumor, and we were able to celebrate our 51st Wedding Anniversary.

After all this time in a marriage, you have the time to hear the sound of each other's sobs and laughs and to know each other's ideas and opinions as well as angers. Yet, in some ways, you hardly know each other at all, and you don't know what is going to happen in the next few minutes, which may be the secret, somehow, to the whole thing of marriage. As Brian Doyle (American screenwriter, comedian, born 1945) said, "Marriage is ultimately an utterly ephemeral thing, a shared idea, a mental and emotional construct that both parties believe in to varying degrees at the same time." The key part is the willingness, because of love for each other, to be together "until death us do part."

I had the desolation of a diagnosis of prostate cancer in myself. And I have had the consolation of being cured by surgery.

I had the desolation of my son John dying suddenly of a heart attack in his 40's, leaving three small children and a devoted wife. And I have had the consolation of knowing that he died as he had lived, helping others at the time. Many have told us that it is not supposed to happen that parents outlive their children. It is at these times that we know that the mind and the heart, the rational and the emotional, are not all that there is, because there is more, and it has to do with love. It has been more than a year now, but in my grief, I am still unable to say more.

Love is triumphant in victory and strongest in loss. That is a powerful duality. But there is always more; love is a sacrament made for a Cross and that is transformation. Suffering, self-sacrifice, and love are transformational. What you have loved you can never lose.

> Earth has no sorrow that heaven cannot heal.
> —*Thomas Moore, Irish poet and singer, 1779-1852*

It's true, that, "Once you think you know, fall in love and you'll immediately know more" (Author unknown). But what is true of *love* is also true of *grief*. Go into grief and you'll immediately know more. After my son's death from a sudden heart attack, I began to think thoughts that I had never thought before. For example, I am a rock hound as my hobby, which means that I am scientifically and aesthetically interested in minerals and crystals, and I collect them. Mineral crystals are beautiful in themselves, as well as scientifically interesting. After my son's death, I was reading a magazine about minerals, and I was drawn to a poem by another rock hound who pointed out that some people are related to claws and fangs, but he is related to rocks, which are serene and fall into the water slowly after being thrown from the hand of a child. The rock settles in serenity to the bottom in silence, and the fish gather around to knock on it. And he wondered if the rock might be hollow, and that maybe the interior can be lighted, since when two rocks are rubbed together there can be a spark. Not the light like the sun, but the light as if from the moon behind a mountain. Just enough light to see the charts and writings on the inner wall showing the way.

Because of this poem, I began thinking how, in a similar way, that in stress and grief we seek solitude and serenity. And we seek comfort in our faith, and we go to Scripture. The Bible refers to Jesus as the "Rock of our Salvation" and the "Cornerstone" of our faith (1-Corinthians 3:11, Matthew 21:42, Mark 12:10, Luke 20:17, Acts 4:11). The fish are what Peter, whom Jesus said he would make a fisher of men (Matthew 4:19), is able to put into the ocean of God's love. When we, that are fish, come to the Rock and knock with our prayers and with our reading of scripture, we get some enlightenment, dim though it may be, to show us the way and to help us continue.

I am well aware of consolation and desolation, but I also know there is more. There is the garden of transformation after the city of joy and the desert of sorrow, after the city of consolation and the desert of desolation. Transformation is the "more" beyond duality and trinity.

I know that there is healing in the communication of truth, love, goodness and all of the other invisible values, virtues, ideals, and principles. They have the power to move, unsettle, and change anyone exposed to them. They are like a destabilizing wave, pulling you out further than you thought that you might want to be into the ocean of God's love.

> One should, after a fashion, welcome and esteem the difficulties one encounters. A difficulty is a lamp. An insuperable difficulty, a sun.
> —*Paul Valery, French poet and essayist, 1871-1945*

> When we are no longer able to change a situation, we are challenged to change ourselves.
> —*Dr. Viktor Frankl, Austrian neurologist and psychiatrist, 1905-1997*

Obstinate political partisanship, with its rigid conflicting opposite points of view, ought to be taught that there is always a way out of stalemate. There is always a third way beyond duality, which this book details, and which they ought to learn.

> By three methods we may learn wisdom, first, by reflection, which is noblest; second, by imitation, which is easiest; and third, by experience, which is the bitterest.
> —*Confucius, 551 B.C. to 479 B.C.*

My twin brother, Don, has his share of life's consolation and desolation, too. He has the desolation of one of his daughters being deaf, but the consolation that she is adept at lip reading and sign language to the degree that she teaches it. And she recently received her Ph.D., with a Doctor in Philosophy degree to follow her Masters degree. She won an Emmy for some television work. This daughter also played a supporting character in the play *Children of a Lesser God* that started as a deaf-theater production in California and went on to tour in London, and the play was also featured in the Spoleto Festival in Italy. Don also has an adopted son, who is a college graduate doing social work. Another son is a male model, and he runs a jewelry business in partnership with a jewelry designer/fabricator. Don also has another daughter who is a college graduate and a homemaker, who works from home sharing information regarding the treatments available for autism. She and her husband have an autistic son who is very handsome looking and a lovely and intelligent daughter.

Don's second wife is an artist who had a stroke that paralyzed her left side permanently after a skiing accident. She was born left-handed, and because of the stroke she now uses her non-dominant right hand. With skill and determination, she is presently an award winning and renowned artist of acclaim. I believe her painting of a child on a carousel is better than the Mona Lisa. The child's innocent and peaceful face dominates the picture with its expression of calmness, serenity, trust, and inner happiness. It shows a quiet strength with great future potential for the child. The picture has a sense of motion, and you can almost hear the sounds of the carousel while viewing the picture. At this point, you may be saying that all pictures are, in a sense, a Rorschach test, in which the viewer shows more of them self than what is shown on the paper, which for a Rorschach test is just an ink blot. But I believe that anyone else seeing the picture *Carousel* will see in it what I have just described seeing.

Life is like coffee that only God can brew. We each have our own cup, each of a different design, but the cup can't add any quality to the coffee. The cup is a symbol of our work or the level of our health or the measure of our wealth, but these are just tools to contain Life. They don't define or change the quality of life that God gives. If we concentrate on the cup, we fail to enjoy the coffee.

Life is like a flower of God's design that only God can unfold. Because we can't unfold a flower, we know that we don't have the wisdom to unfold our lives without the help of God.

Living is like being in a play. Even as you are enacting the part of the fighting character in the play, you are also enacting the will of the author. For the character to refuse to fight because he knows the script, and knows that he will not win, is for him to fight against the author. In the Bible story of Job, when God finally shows up for Job, it is then that Job realizes that Job's the character and not the author of his own story, and Job accepts that. We need truth more than we need comfort. We always need truth, just as we always need love and goodness, because truth, love, and goodness are three of the attributes of God. And we always need God.

Our lives are either selfish, little, solitary stages surrounded by darkness, or else our lives and all of the world (and the universe) is a stage, and all of our stories and all of our spots of darkness and suffering are in the plot. If we accept the latter, then suffering is our part, our gift, our task, our work, and our cross.

> Life is misery, loneliness and trouble, and it's all over much too soon.
> —*Woody Allen, American film director, actor, author and comedian, born 1935*

We are each an ember of the mind of God and we are each
sent to illumine the other through the dark passages of life
to sanctuaries of truth and peace
—*Sister Joan Chittister, OSB, contemporary author*

This is the true joy in life, the being used for a purpose
recognized by yourself as a mighty one…Life is no "brief
candle" for me. It is a sort of splendid torch, which I
have got hold of for the moment, and I want to make it
burn as brightly as possible before handing it on to future
generations.
—*George Bernard Shaw, Irish playwright, 1856-1950*

Vincent Van Gogh (Dutch painter, 1853-1890) said, "I prefer painting people's eyes rather than cathedrals, for there is something in the
eyes that is not in the cathedral, namely, a human soul, be it that of a
poor beggar or of a streetwalker." As an artist, he could see beyond
the mind and the heart to the soul. He could see the three qualities
that make us all human, namely, truth (mind), and love (heart), and
spirit (goodness)—all three of which help to make us in the image
of God. These three qualities of being human are invisible things,
therefore, to get a clearer idea of what transformation is, the next
chapter will explore how to see invisible things.

Chapter 2.

Seeing Invisible Things

A rock pile ceases to be a rock pile the moment a single person contemplates it, bearing within them self the image of a cathedral.
—*Antoine de Saint-Exupery, French author and aviator, 900-1944*

Climb the mountains and get their good tidings. Nature's peace will flow into you as sunshine flows into trees. The winds will blow their own freshness into you, and the storms their energy, while cares will drop off like autumn leaves.
—*John Muir, Scottish-born American naturalist author, 1838-1914*

So much of what we experience is intangible, inexpressible, and invisible, like truth (mind), and love (heart), and spirit (goodness). This chapter will help you to see invisible things.

In his 1984 book *The Song of the Bird*, Anthony de Mello (Jesuit priest and psychotherapist, 1931-1987) tells a story of a master-teacher who, when his students start complaining, says to them that we listen to the words of the scholar because those words are to be understood, but we listen to the words of the master-teacher like we listen to the sound of the wind in the trees, or the water in the babbling brook, or the song of the bird, because just like these sounds his words are meant to awaken something in our hearts that is beyond knowledge. I also want to awaken something in your hearts by touching them with the invisible truth that is beyond the visible world of symbols. I want you to see the truth of the existence of values, virtues, ideals, and principles, and the transformation that is beyond life's consolation and desolation, beyond life's joy and sorrow. As this book's subtitle says: *Being Transformed.*

> Man reading should be man intensely alive. The book
> should be a ball of light in one's hand.
> —*Ezra Pound, aphorist, 1885-1972*

The invisible things, such as faith, hope, and love, and the qualities that make us fully human, such as truth (mind), love (heart), and goodness (spirit) are a part of transformation.

There is a goodness, or a benevolence, in life that can't be explained other than by the existence of God. We speak of "luck" for good things happening all the time, but we have no opposite term to suggest bad things happening all the time, and so we have to use the term "unlucky."

All invisible values, such as awe, wonder, worship, wisdom, meaning, purpose, mercy, spirituality, etc., constitute the "more" that is transformation as distinct from and beyond just joy and sorrow, consolation and desolation. These values are part of the higher things in life and constitute higher thinking and living. They are the gold nuggets that remain when the stream of time moves everything else away. Anyone in possession of this spiritual gold is spiritually rich. They are living transformed, as the chart below shows. Notice in the chart that transformation is having all the values, virtues, ideals, and principles and living in the garden in happiness, as distinct from only having just joy and/or sorrow in life.

1. Pleasure	City	Joy/Comfort	Consolation
2. Pain	Desert	Sorrow/Suffering	Desolation
3. Happiness	Garden	Values, Virtues, etc.	Transformation

Chart 1. Transformation Characteristics

The material world that we see is always teaching us truths about the invisible things that we can't see. What we are thinking can make a world of difference in our lives. When something material that we can see symbolizes something of importance that we can't see, there is the chance of transformation from higher thinking.

Some people can't see the woods for the trees, which means that some people can't see the big picture. It seems invisible to them. I learned that very early as a surgeon. When a patient comes to the emergency room with a gunshot wound, the surgeon can picture in his mind everything the patient will need, from blood to x-rays to surgery to convalescence. Others just see that the patient needs blood.

It's the difference of the floodlight versus the spotlight approach to life. The floodlight, or big-picture, approach helps you to see just what it is that what you see is telling you about something that you can't see. A person with the floodlight or big-picture approach to life can see not only the visible, but also the invisible that is being pointed to beyond the visible.

For example: "When it rains it pours," means that when trouble comes, it often comes as a lot of trouble. And "Don't jump out of the frying pan into the fire," means that we should be careful not to go from a bad situation into a worse one.

I know there is more to life, because the material world is always teaching us symbolic lessons about something signified that is immaterial and invisible And it's at these times that we know in our hearts, without words, that spirituality exists and God exists. Just as the act of loving explains without words to us why we are male and female, so too, the act of living explains to us without words why this particular universe exists. It exists for you and for me to live. And truth exists in it, because life would not be worth living without truth. Without the existence of truth we would never be able to ask any questions. Our inner self and the outer world are related.

> I only went out for a walk and finally concluded to stay out
> till sundown, for going out, I found, was really going in.
> —*John Muir, American naturalist and writer, 1838-1914*

> Our life is a faint tracing on the surface of mystery.
> —*Annie Dillard, American author and 1975 Pulitzer Prize
> winner, born 1945*

The love of a man for a woman is just a wave on something more, namely, the ocean of God's love. The best proof for the existence of water is not just our thirst but the quenching of it. And the best proof for the existence of God is not just love, spelled with a small "l" (the love of a man and a woman) but something more (that ocean), which is love spelled with a capital "L." Our current concept of love is inadequate; it's like having seen a glass of water but not the ocean. The ocean refuses no rivers. We are like fish surrounded by an ocean of truth, love, and goodness, searching for water (truth, love, and goodness).

We sense an invisible higher power that we can't see and enter into transformation:

- when we fall in love;

- when we become bonded after years of marriage rather than just mated as when first married;

- when things make sense to us and everything just seems to fall into place;

- when we are transformed by higher thinking and living; and

- when we suffer in grief so much that we realize the great extent to which we loved in life. It is then that we know that the duality of the height of love and the depth of grief is not all that there is to life; there is more, something eternal. And gaining the knowledge of that is more power to us than to any deceiver who would try to tell us that there is only just joy and sorrow.

After 51 years of marriage, mated for life, you enter into an eternal bond of love. You are living in the ocean of God's love. This state is much different than when you were first just married. My wife lovingly told me that she feels it's worth the taking of her daily chemotherapy in order to spend one more day of life with me. She takes her medicine despite the severe fatigue she gets and the risk of possible anemia, infection, bleeding, and liver damage that chemotherapy entails. We live one day at a time in our love, not worrying about any future travel or plans. We enjoy our family and our grandchildren. We are blessed to have most of them live nearby. We go to restaurants, go shopping, and attend their activities of ballet, movies, etc.

The first symptom that tumor had spread from Margaret's lung to somewhere else in her body was paralysis of the left side of her tongue, which made her talk with a lisp. The paralysis was due to nerve involvement by the tumor's spread into the bone at the base of the skull into the left occipital condyle, which is at the joint between the skull and the start of the spine. She received radiotherapy to this tumor area, wearing a rigid face-mask molded to her head and face so the beam of the radiotherapy could be focused precisely on the tumor. Since then, she has undergone many magnetic resonance imaging scans, called MRI studies, and Computer Axial Tomography x-ray scans, called CT-scans or CAT-scan studies. Even though she has claustrophobia with the machines, she gamely closes her eyes and toughs it through. She required speech therapy for her left tongue paralysis and lisp. I told her I thought the lisp was cute. After prolonged daily tongue exercises she now speaks normally.

Margaret has required radiotherapy for pain in the right chest and back, due to tumor in a rib and in the nearby spine near the spinal cord. And also radiotherapy to her right clavicle bone which had a tumor in it, causing a painful swelling. Additionally, she had so-called "Gamma Knife therapy" to a few metastatic brain tumors. This therapy employs focused radiotherapy, using a head frame that is temporarily screwed to the head for the precise focusing of the treatment beam of radiotherapy. And she later had, also, whole-brain radiotherapy. She has persistent hair loss and fatigue. But she is generally pain-free and enjoying life, even though she has been through quite a lot. The truth is that love is all.

Silently we are born because of the love of our parents, and silently we die, surrounded by our friends and loved ones, and in between is nothing but silent love, for those who can see it, for those who can feel its fire, and for those who can hear love as the loudest sound on the other side of silence. Love is born and lives in the silence of our hearts. We also silently suffer when our loved ones suffer.

> Love one another and you will be happy. It's as simple and as difficult as that.
> —*Michael Leunig, Australian cartoonist, born 1945*

We can't materially explain the presence of the spiritual any more than we can explain love. What is mind? No matter. What is matter? Never mind. A human being is more than rational and emotional. A human being is worshipful. A human being is mind, heart, and spirit. A human being is truth, love, and goodness.

Belief in an invisible higher power (God) is mandatory for recovery in 12-step recovery programs. This belief is part of such programs as Alcoholics Anonymous (AA), or Adult Children of Alcoholics (ACoA), or Al-Anon (spouses of alcoholics and family recovery program), or Alateen (Teens of alcoholics).

My twin brother and I knew that our future depended on our ability to get an education so that we could be free of our family and live on our own.

There are functioning and non-functioning alcoholics.

- The functioning ones go to work every day and drink, mostly at night, but they "have to have it every day." They cannot say that they will only drink just for today.

- The non-functioning alcoholic cannot work every day, as they are impaired.

My father was a functioning alcoholic. Therefore, my family was dysfunctional. And because of that, it was hard for anyone in my family to say, "I love you," or to give a compliment. You are only as sick as your secrets. Therefore, I believe that writing this book is a form of therapy for me, as I reveal secrets and move further to my recovery from my dysfunctional upbringing, even at this late stage of my life. And I pray to God that I am honoring my parents by using the story of our family to help others.

My mother was quiet and didn't talk much, and she didn't give her opinion about much of anything, especially about what she was feeling. She drew people to herself who were depressed and had other problems, because she couldn't say "No." And she was known as a "good listener." In retrospect, that may have been because she was in a state of chronic congenital depression (from her genes), just like her two sisters, who were also severely depressed. My mother's long-suffering demeanor, which may have attracted others who were suffering, may also have stemmed from the chronic verbal and physical abuse she received from her alcoholic husband, my dad. She could sympathize with others, because she knew of suffering. My father tended always to be critical and complaining about something or someone with a "down-in-the-mouth" or depressive demeanor. As children, of course, my brother and I thought all of this was normal, because as children, we couldn't know any better.

To embrace each other in love and to weep is to recognize, at once, that all things are bound together in a single book of love, designed by God, of which creation is the scattered pages. The consolation of love and the desolation of weeping can bring us to the transformation of recognizing our being bound together in love, with all designed by God. An 18th-century French Jesuit priest, Jean-Pierre de Caussade (1675-1751) said that every moment is given to us from God and so bears God's will for us. Thus, when we "accept what we cannot avoid, and endure with love and resignation things which cause us weariness and disgust," we are following the path to sanctification. He also said that faith "tears aside the veil so that we can see the everlasting truth." If we do not live by such light, "we shall find neither happiness nor holiness, no matter what pious practices we adopt…" The everlasting truth that we can see is Jesus ("the way, the truth, and the life"—*John 14:6*), and His self-sacrifice of carrying a Cross. And each of us must bear our own. You can see by my desolations what my cross is. Someone once said that if we all could get together in order to exchange our cross for someone else's cross, we would soon be satisfied to carry our own. I am satisfied to carry my own.

The imperfection of human nature means that in reality, there is no "perfect partner" or "perfect community." Always seeking better options will make us not happy but dissatisfied. Only by committing to where we find ourselves out of our own free choices, and keeping our vows and promises, can we find the happiness we seek.

Whenever you find an opportunity to suffer with God, you will find that is an expression of love and an opportunity to be happy. Wherever you find love is where there is transformation and an opportunity to be happy.

> Happiness is nothing but the conquest of God through love.
> —*Henri-Frederic Amiel, Swiss philosopher, 1821-1881*

> Don't wait until everything is just right. It will never be perfect. There will always be challenges, obstacles, and less-than-perfect conditions. So what? Get started now. With each step you take, you will grow stronger and stronger, more and more skilled, more and more self-confident, and more and more successful.
> —*Mark Victor Hansen, American author and motivational speaker, born 1948*

The philosopher priest, Pierre Teilhard de Chardin, S.J. (1881-1955), pointed out how we are shaped by what we do and also by what we endure. What we do is our self-portrait, but what we endure is God's portrait of us and our cross. And our cross is an invisible thing. The "whole cup" with all the joy and all the sorrow is the way to happiness. Because, through joy and sorrow, we are led to see the third way that leads to transformation—namely, a whole cup containing its double contents of joy and sorrow. The whole is greater than the sum of its parts and leads to transformation, which is "more," and which is a higher level of thinking and living. This will become clearer to you as this book proceeds.

Experience is an invisible thing.

> There is nothing so easy to learn as experience and nothing so hard to apply.
> —*Josh Billings, American humorist, 1818-1885*

The question is not "Why do we die?" but "Why do we live?" And out of that duality of life and death, it is not the dying, but something else, a third thing—deadness of life—that we should fear. In life, there is a way of dying (self sacrifice) that leads to a more authentic life, a life that includes God and that includes ethics and morals, for a full spirituality. Deadness of life does not include any of that. Someone once said that the greatest spiritual question is not about life after death. The greatest spiritual question of all is: "Is there life before death?" This question involves invisible things.

Self-sacrifice takes will and moral courage. Ronald Reagan (former actor and 40th President of the United States, 1911-2004) said, "Above all, we must realize that no arsenal or no weapon in the arsenals of the world is so formidable as the will and moral courage of free men and women. It is a weapon our adversaries in today's world do not have. It is a weapon that we, as Americans, do have. Let that be understood by those who practice terrorism and prey upon their neighbors." Our enemies have to be told about our will and moral courage, because these are some of the invisible things.

Everyone, as children, must think that they're living in a parallel universe. I certainly did! After all, everyone seems to know much more than you do, and compared to your own family, there are so many others who on radio, in movies, and on television exhibit more enviable talents, gifts, and accomplishments. And to top it all off, no matter what you attempt to do, there's always someone else who's better.

If you ever feel that you're living in an isolated and separate parallel world, take heart, because we're all united and living with the rest of the world by experiencing love and experiencing life's consolation, desolation, and transformation—the invisible things.

> The greatest danger for most of us lies not in setting our aim too high and falling short, but in setting our aim too low and achieving our mark.
> —*Michelangelo Buonarroti, Italian artist, 1475-1564*

Goals start out as invisible things. My brother, Don, and I had jobs when we could in the summers. We worked part time for a couple of years delivering mail for the Upper Darby post office. In order to work at the post office, you have to take a written test. The test mainly involves quickly matching addresses and street numbers. A sample pre-test is given first to show you how the exam works. Some applicants didn't pay too much attention to this pre-test instruction and the practicing of it. Later, as you start the real test, you're told that the sample pre-test is an actual portion taken from the real test. I paid close attention to everything and I seemed very adept at doing the test, so I finished several minutes before everyone else. That gave me time to check my work. Those conducting the test seemed surprised that I finished so quickly, and I got a good score, which gave me the job.

My twin brother and I have had the singular blessing of always being together through school and with work, until we got married, and then we separated. That kind of camaraderie is priceless and a cherished memory. Camaraderie is an invisible thing. It is felt in the heart.

- We worked one summer as bus boys cleaning tables at a fish-food restaurant on the boardwalk while living in an apartment at the beach.

- We worked as car-hops serving food to cars for Howard Johnson Restaurant on 69th Street.

- We worked as servers in a local swimming-pool fast-food booth.

- We worked as bus-boys in a Swedish smorgasbord restaurant.

- We worked as inventory counters, or map data collectors, for the local telephone company.

- We worked as night watchmen, carrying a time clock that was "punched" at various stations in the apartment house that we lived in.

All of that work is good experience for life, and it makes you feel a part of the real world. It gave us real hope for the future.

> Pay attention to what you do, because what you do doesn't just proceed from who you are; it also makes you who you are.
> —*Gilbert Keith Chesterton, English author 1874-1936*

> Opportunity is missed by most people because it is dressed in overalls and looks like work. Genius is one percent inspiration, ninety-nine percent perspiration.
> —*Thomas Alva Edison, inventor, entrepreneur, 1847-1931*

> You can't build a reputation on what you are going to do.
> —*Henry Ford, automobile manufacturer, 1863-1947*

In the 1984 book: *Is It Worth Dying For?*, Dr. Robert S. Eliot and Dennis L. Breo relate a story about a patient who saw a movie about prehistoric life called: *Quest for Fire.* The patient, after seeing the movie, noted that she never realized it before, but her work was her fire. "Without it I would never have discovered who I am, what I can do, and what I want to do," she said, "Without it, my life would be very cold." Without finding fire, her life would not have been so vastly improved.

Love does the same thing with its fire. We always put our money where our heart is. All of us are on a quest for love's fire, because there is nothing like finding love to tell you who you are, and what you can do, and what you want to do. Love is transforming.

It's certainly true that you should not go into medicine if you don't love it. That love is an invisible thing. In the summers during medical school, the medical students apply for hospital jobs. I spent a summer in a Gynecology operating room, prepping the patients for surgery. One day, a patient on a stretcher came into the operating room for surgery wearing full makeup, which was against the rules. She looked somewhat like Elizabeth Taylor, but of course, she wasn't. The family doctor was holding her hand and talking to her very solicitously, to reassure her. She seemed tearful and agitated as she was being wheeled into the operating room. She seemed so glamorous compared to the usual patient that everyone stared. We usually don't think of glamorous people needing to have surgery, except plastic surgery.

Another summer I was assigned to the Pathology lab to help cut the tissue specimens removed at surgery and prepare them for the crew that made the tissue-pathology slides. One advantage was that a doctor in training could get some teaching tissue slides for his own, of rare tumors or interesting tissue specimens.

In 1988, a book came out called *The Signs of Our Time: The Secret Meanings of Everyday Life* by Jack Solomon. This illustrated quite well how there is a lot that is invisible behind the visible. He speaks of the science of *semantics*, which studies the meaning of words as signs or symbols, and *semiotics*, which studies the hidden meaning of everything else, such as dress codes, gender codes, codes behind our choices of foods, hidden agendas in television advertising, etc.

We are surrounded by non-verbal communication. Consider the known fact that "sex sells." Sex is presented to us non-verbally, verbally and visually in three ways:

1. Subliminal suggestion, subtle (hidden);

2. Innuendo, double meanings, double entendre, or double talk (indirect)

3. Blatant, vivid, in your face (direct).

Following the suspected use in the 1950's by cinemas of subliminal advertising during previews to encourage people to buy from the concession stand, the advertising associations took the position that it is unethical to secretly embed commercial messages or images.

Jack Solomon (Semiotician and English professor at CSUN), also talks about the field of *proxemics*, which specializes in interpreting spatial organization, which is architecture, because architectural structures are a system of signs, or a non-verbal language, by their special configurations and by their colors, sizes, decoration, etc.

Communication of any kind is healing whenever there exists the possibility to call attention through symbolic convention to something invisible of importance that lies behind the visible. In other words, healing seems to take place whenever there is contact with the invisible things of beauty, truth, love, goodness, wisdom, wonder, humor, etc.

Whenever something in us gets healed, we get changed. I call that being transformed.

> Vision is the art of seeing things invisible.
> —*Jonathan Swift, Anglo-Irish writer, 1667-1745*

> Where there is no vision the people perish.
> —*The Bible KJV: Proverbs 29:18*

The truth is that to be as much as you can be, you must dream of being more, and in order to achieve all that is possible, you must attempt the impossible. And to see all that there is to see, you must see the invisible.

> If we attend continually and promptly to the little that we can do, we shall ere long be surprised to find how little remains that we cannot do.
> —*Samuel Butler, British author and aphorist, 1835-1902*

The impact by truth on our hearts and the overlooking of invisible things that are seen only by the eyes of the heart are illustrated by the words of Robert F. Kennedy (U.S. Senator and Attorney General, 1925-1698) in a speech in March 1968. He said, "The gross national product...does not include the beauty of our poetry or the strength of our marriages, or the intelligence of our public debate, or the integrity of our public officials. It measures neither our wit nor our courage, neither our wisdom nor our learning, neither our compassion nor our devotion to our country. It measures everything, in short, except that which makes life worthwhile."

Ronald Reagan made moral leadership visible when he said, "I will not stand by and watch this great country destroy itself under mediocre leadership that drifts from one crisis to the next, eroding our national will and purpose. We have come together here because the American people deserve better from those to whom they entrust our nation's highest offices, and we stand united in our resolve to do something about it."

Another example of truth and invisible things is Antoine de Saint Exupery (French writer and aviator, 1900-1944), who said: "If you want to build a ship, don't herd people together to collect wood and don't assign them tasks and work, but rather teach them to long for the…endless immensity of the sea." In other words, when you want to accomplish something that is visible, get people looking to see things that are invisible.

Ingenuity is another invisible thing.

> Never tell people how to do things. Tell them what to do, and they will surprise you with their ingenuity.
> —*George S. Patton, United States General during World War II, 1885-1945*

Outer things point to inner things.

> I have seen the sea when it is stormy and wild; when it is quiet and serene; when it is dark and moody. And in all its moods, I see myself.
> —*Martin D. Buxbaum, Virginian poet, born 1912*

Poets are always seeing the invisible that is being symbolized by the visible. Similar to these poets, I often see symbolically with the eyes of my heart and not with my physical eyes, because everything in the material world seems to me to symbolize something in the immaterial or invisible world.

- It is only with the heart that one can see rightly. What is essential is invisible to the eye.
  —*Antoine de Saint Exupery, French writer and aviator,1900-1944*

- "The eye sees only what the mind is prepared to comprehend."
  —*Henri Bergson, 1927 Nobel Prize-winning philosopher 1859-1941*

- The real voyage of discovery consists not in seeing new

landscapes, but in having "new eyes." (By "new eyes," he meant "eyes of the heart.")
—*Marcel Proust, French author 1871-1922*

- Life without love is like a tree without blossom and fruit.
  —*Khalil Gibran, Lebanese American author 1833-1931*

- Knowing trees, I understand the meaning of patience. Knowing grass, I can appreciate persistence.
  —*Hal Borland, American author and Journalist 1900-1978*

- The day the Lord created hope was probably the same day (the Lord) created spring.
  —*Bern Williams, British philosopher and Oxford professor*

- Plenty of people miss their share of happiness, not because they never found it, but because they didn't stop to enjoy it.
  —*William Feather, American publisher and author, 1889-1981*

Two entwined chains go throughout this book. The next chapter will explore the first chain, namely the pithy aphorisms and truisms to which incidents from my life and that of my family are attached to become the entwined second chain. The second chain illustrates the truths found in the first chain. The two chains are not dangling in space but rise with each chapter to the concluding summary, which is the last chapter, followed by the Postscript.

Chapter 3.

Aphorisms, Truisms

Someday, after mastering the winds, the waves, the tides,
and gravity, we shall harness for God the energies of love,
and then, for a second time in the history of the world, man
will have discovered fire.
*—Pierre Teilhard de Chardin, Jesuit philosopher priest,
1881-1955*

If we had keen vision and sensitive feeling for all of
ordinary life, it would be like hearing the grass grow and
the squirrel's heartbeat, and we should die from that roar,
(that loud sound), on the other side of silence.
—Author unknown

Love is the loudest sound on the other side of silence.

**An *aphorism* is a tersely phrased statement of truth or opinion,
and a *truism* is a self-evident, obvious truth.**

Would you like to know the truth? I'm happy to share the truth with
you, because I'm a truth collector. I've been collecting truth all my
life, because I know that if you have the truth, then:

- you not only taste life, but you also savor it;

- you not only see, but you also observe;

- you not only know, but you also understand; and

- you not only understand, but you also are wise.

In short, with the truth, you not only feel, but you also feel alive.

In other words, truth makes you: enlightened, insightful, illuminated, awakened, open, inspired, touched, contacted, moved, and changed. And to be so moved and changed is to be healed and transformed. It is an elevation into a higher level of thinking and living, and so having the truth is very worthwhile.

But if you want the truth, be prepared for a shock, because truth is an unexpected surprising shock! Henry David Thoreau (naturalist philosopher, 1817-1862) said, "Truth strikes us in the back of the head and in the dark," which means that *truth* is the *sudden, unexpected opposite* of what we're thinking or the sudden awareness of what we're not thinking and should be thinking. This striking impact by the insight of truth has the same effect on us as something said from the heart reaching the heart. So, truth is not just an education that teaches you, but truth is an experience that changes you. Truth is transformational. Education that supplies you with truth is not just filling a bucket but lighting a fire.

> A man's mind, stretched by a new idea, never goes back to its original dimensions.
> —*Oliver Wendell Holmes, Jr., American novelist, poet, and aphorist, 1841-1935*

Johnny Carson (American television entertainer, 1925-2005) said that people will pay more to be entertained than to be educated. Don't you find this to be true? We always put our money where our heart is, not where our mind is. It's as if we don't want to hear the truth.

Hearing the truth gives us an unexpected, surprising shock. This shock is not the same experience as the reading of a Japanese haiku poem that simply evokes associations out of the richness of your own memory, like a pebble thrown into the pool of your mind using three lines and 17 syllables. The truth is, symbolically, like a defibrillation of the brain, which brings it back to life again.

A thought is a thing as real as a cannonball.
—*Joseph Joubert, French aphorist, 1754-1824*

The truth is a trap: you cannot get it without its getting
you; you cannot get the truth by capturing it, only by its
capturing you.
—*Soren Kierkegaard, Danish philosopher and author,
1813-1855*

Communication occurs not when something is said but when something is "heard." Truth makes itself heard when it strikes us in the
back of the head and in the dark, by being the shocking, sudden,
unexpected opposite of what we're thinking or a sudden realization
of what we're not thinking, giving us a moment of truth.

I was given a moment of truth in school when I heard, for the first
time, what St. Augustine said. He was bishop of Hippo in the 5th century and is considered a Church Father. He said: "What good does it
do you to gain the whole world if you lose your own soul?"
—(Matthew 16:26) And "Seek not to understand that you may believe, but seek to believe that you may understand."

Some things have to be believed to be seen.
—*Ralph Hodgson, British poet, 20th century*

Truisms:

- Someone once said that our life is not made up of years that
  mean nothing but rather, moments that mean all.

- The butterfly counts not minutes but moments, and has time
  enough.
  —*Rabindranath Tagore, Indian poet, 1861-1941*

- Moments and years do not come to be counted; they come
  to count.

- Real living is not measured in the number of our breaths but in the number of our breathless moments; not in moments of time but in our timeless moments.

- Real living means, don't just bury another year but plant one.

- Time isn't measured by length but by depth.
  —*Isolde Kurz, German author, poet, aphorist, 1853-1944*

- Not everything that counts can be counted, and not everything that can be counted counts.
  —*Albert Einstein, German theoretical physicist and 1921 Nobel Physics Prize winner, 1879-1955*

- God is truth.

- The impact God has planned for us doesn't occur when we're pursuing impact. It occurs when we're pursuing God.
  —*Phil Vischer, American creator of present-day Veggie Tales, born 1966*

I believe that you get a shock from the truth not only when you hear it and when you then get it, but you also get a shock from the truth when you miss it. For example, as I was growing up, each summer we would visit my mother's brother, Uncle Jimmy. His wife was thin and nervous, with bulging eyes and a face that some would call hatchet-faced. She always struck me as anxious, active, and easily agitated. It was while I was in medical school that I heard that a local doctor finally had diagnosed her hyperthyroidism. The truth of it had been before my eyes for years, but I was not yet educated enough to see it. I was surprised and shocked both on hearing the truth and realizing I had missed the truth.

Truth is often presented to us in the form of aphorisms, analogies, axioms, maxims, adages, wise sayings, truisms, slogans, anecdotes, parables, symbolisms, metaphors, similes and mottos, etc., and I collect them, because I'm interested in the truth and nothing but the truth. In modern time, we might call them sound bites of truth or concentrated truth or crystallized truth or smart remarks. The truth gives us "eureka!–epiphanies" that cause us to feel enlightened, euphoric, exhilarated, vital, liberated, dynamic and authentic—in other words, struck to the heart and, on some level, healed. The truth to me is a miracle of consolation or, better yet, a miracle of transformation.

> The difference between the almost-right word and the right word is really a large matter—it's the difference between the lightning bug and the lightning.
> —*Mark Twain, American author and critic, 1835-1910*

> Defective language produces flawed meaning
> —*Confucius, Chinese thinker and philosopher, 551 B.C.-479 B.C.*

> Great literature is simply language charged with meaning to the utmost possible degree.
> —*Ezra Pound, American expatriate poet, critic, and intellectual 1885-1972*

The truth is, we can all list some miracles that have happened in our lives and that have given us great consolation or transformation. These miracles give us a chance for special celebrations. I call them *God-incidences*, as there is no such thing as coincidences. We are all blessed. But unless you believe in miracles you will never have one, because even if you did have a miracle, you would not recognize it as a miracle, because you don't believe in miracles.

My daughter, Mary, heard about a contest to win a car at a car dealership in Fayetteville, North Carolina, where we were living at the time. She had a hunch that if she entered the contest she would win. And she did! It was a reconditioned, white Volkswagen that had the number 53 on its side to imitate *Herby, the Love Bug*, which was a car made famous about that same time in a movie of that same name by Walt Disney. As we slowly drove away, Mary and I couldn't believe that they were letting us drive off the dealership's lot with the car, because it was so hard to believe that she had won a car that was just being given away. She was a winner, and the car was a great blessing for our children in their teenage years. It was a great consolation to us and it transformed our lives. It was a miracle.

My daughter, Ann, was admitted to the medical school of her choice. And that caused us to dance with joy to a song that is sung in Charismatic prayer groups. The words of the song are: "Joy is the flag flown high from the flagpole of my heart." While singing these words, you raise your hand high and wave it to symbolize a flag flying. Ann and I were hopping up and down with joy with our "flags" flying. Ann's achievement was a great consolation to us, and it transformed our lives. The rest of the song's words are, "To show that the King (Jesus) is in residence there!"

The truth is that in addition to the consolation of miracles that we all can list and that have happened in all of our lives, we can also list the opposite, or the desolations. There is a strong depression gene in my family, as my mother and her two sisters were severely depressed, but it was never recognized early by the family. Depression was diagnosed very late in my mother's life, and only in retrospect in both of her sisters after their deaths. I am, also, the child of an alcoholic father, who has self-medicated with alcohol all his life in order to relieve his pain of living. He suddenly just stopped smoking and drinking too late in his seventies when he had emphysema, chronic bronchitis, and lung cancer.

Because I am the child of an alcoholic, I have certain traits that are common to all children of alcoholics: I am an overachieving, impulsive, introspective-loner, and I use humor to relieve stress and to keep people from getting too close so that they cannot see my real feelings and the real me. It's hard to be real because all alcoholic families contain the unwritten rules of don't talk, don't trust, and don't feel. You don't talk because of the secret that dad is an alcoholic; you don't trust because you can't rely on the alcoholic; and you don't feel because then you would hurt too much. There are lifelong feelings though of inadequacy, guilt, anger, and hurt. Some of the dysfunctions, such as overachieving, can be blessings in disguise, as they may help you succeed in life, but you still are damaged and dysfunctional.

The dysfunction in a dysfunctional family can be like a bird always flying over your head, because it has built a nest in your hair. Being an overachiever is a defense, and there are other defenses that are useful to a child in growing up, but they need to be discarded and changed as an adult. I'll go into greater detail in Chapter 13, entitled "Defenses."

There's a lot of truth that I don't have to tell you, because you already know:

For example, isn't it true that you automatically know that truth exists; otherwise you would never ask any questions?

What would be the point in asking anything, if answers were not the truth?

Consider these truths that you already know automatically or intuitively:

- Because you are a thinking person, it is unreasonable to think that a person who can *think* would be put into a crazy, empty world in which there is nothing to *think*.

- And it is unreasonable to think that a person who can *love* would be put into a crazy, empty world in which there is nothing to *love*.

- And it is unreasonable to think that a person who can be *good* would be put into a crazy, empty world in which there is no *goodness*.

You can put into that sentence all of the values, virtues, ideals, and principles. For example, it is unreasonable to think that a person who can be trustworthy, loyal, helpful, friendly, courteous, kind, etc., etc., would be put into a crazy, empty world in which there is no such thing as trust, loyalty, helpfulness, friendliness, courtesy, kindness, etc., etc., especially since you find all of these in yourself. You are capable of being trustworthy, loyal, helpful, friendly, courteous, kind, etc., etc.

When I was in the Boy Scouts, I learned that a scout is: trustworthy, loyal, helpful, friendly, courteous, kind, obedient, cheerful, thrifty, brave, clean and reverent. I knew those qualities were all in me, and so I automatically knew of the existence of all of the values, virtues, ideals, and principles. So do you. "We only understand that which is already within us" (Henri Frederic Amiel, Swiss author, 1821-1881). There is an old African saying that you don't have to grow taller in order to see the moon.

We all know what we ought to be doing, because it's the right thing to do. The hard part is to do it. Abraham Lincoln (16th President of the United States, 1809-1865) said, "When I do good, I feel good. When I do bad, I feel bad. That's my religion. You have to do your own growing no matter how tall your grandfather was."

When I was in bacteriology lab in medical school, our professor lost track of a Petri dish that contained plague bacillus. We weren't told at the time that this was the reason that we were all told to put all of our Petri dishes out on the tables, which were the tops of our lockers, and to keep our locker doors open. We each had a series of Petri dishes growing various bacteria so that we could become familiar with how those bacterial colonies looked growing in a Petri dish, so that we could learn to identify them. I suspected that one student in our class didn't fully comply with the instructions, and this student eventually ended up in a mental institution. When our class visited the regional mental institution for our psychiatry study rotation, that former student from my class was shouting "Hi! Remember me!" out of the window at us, because he was a patient there.

Not doing the right thing can be dangerous and perhaps even crazy.

Thomas Barry (contemporary impressionistic artist) said, "What happens to the outer world happens to the inner world. If the outer world is diminished in its grandeur, then the emotional, imaginative, intellectual, and spiritual life of the human is diminished or extinguished. Without the soaring birds, the great forests, the sounds and coloration of the insects, the free-flowing streams, the flowering fields, the sight of the clouds by day and the stars at night, we become impoverished in all that makes us human."

Modern mankind is becoming less than human as we live in artificial environments away from nature. Children are nature-deprived when they play computer baseball instead of baseball outdoors. And that's the truth. We have gone from landscapes to the sterile landscapes of cityscapes to plastic futurescapes.

Without the truth, we are less than human. Without love, we are less than human. Without spirituality and goodness, we are less than human.

How could a creature without a mind desire knowledge and truth?
How could a creature without a digestive system learn to desire food?
How could a creature with no capacity for love desire love?
How could a creature with no capacity for God desire God?

We have a capacity for God. It's part of what makes us human.

Knowledge is there, truth is there, food is there, love is there, and God is there.

Margaret had a seizure after her Gamma Knife radiotherapy. It occurred while I was driving her home from the hospital in our car the next day, and I was holding her from falling over with one hand and driving with the other, while looking for the hospital on strange roads. I thought she was going to die in the car, and I cried out to

God for help. I saw a policeman who was stopped at the side of the road because he had pulled someone over. I pulled up behind and started honking my car horn. The policeman walked over angrily to my car window and when he saw my wife in a seizure and that I needed to get to the emergency room of a hospital he changed his expression from one of anger to one of compassion and understanding and said; "Follow me!" I felt that God had answered my prayer. I felt that web of connection of truth, love, and goodness that makes us all human.

Another time that I felt that web of connection was by a lake. There comes a moment of truth in every life, when all that we have learned to be true is tested: When my family and I were living in New Jersey during my residency in Thoracic and Cardiovascular Surgery, Margaret and our five children and I went to a local lake for swimming and a picnic. I thought that there was some reluctance to let us enter because we had five children. But they did let us enter. We settled in on the shore near the water. It was then that I saw a pretty girl in the distance, talking with one of the lifeguards, and the girl was pointing out into the water. The lifeguard looked like he had a bottle of beer in his hand. Suddenly, the lifeguard ran into the water of the shallow lake for about 30 yards, and while standing waist-deep in the water, he started frantically searching around until he finally touched something with his foot and he shouted, "Here he is!" He lifted an unconscious boy, about 6 years old, out of the water. He carried the limp body to the shore and collapsed in fatigue.

As he was heading for shore, I ran to meet him, first asking Margaret to watch our children. I shouted: "I'm a doctor! Is anyone else here a doctor?" No one was. Then I instructed the lifeguard to hold the boy upside down by his ankles. A large volume of water poured out of his mouth and nose. The mother handed me a towel to wipe the boy's face. Then I listened for a heartbeat with my ear on the boy's chest and it sounded fast and regular. I said loudly, "His heart's still beating." I then gave three breaths into the boy's mouth while I pinched his nose closed. The boy was still upside down and held by his ankles by a tired, and tiring, lifeguard. And on the third breath into the boy, I felt some resistance, as if the boy was trying to take a breath on his own. We lay the boy down with his head on my lap and I lifted his jaw angle to keep his airway open for breathing. We saw the boy taking rapid and pathetically shallow breaths that were gradually increasing in depth with every breath. The boy was coming back, and I said, "He's going to make it," and the lifeguard jerked back in relief and perhaps quiet tears. I was choked up myself. I asked that everything be taken off the boy's chest to allow freedom of movement to his chest that he needed to breathe. A portion of a towel and the lifeguard's hand touching the boy were removed. Just then, suddenly and unexpectedly, someone tossed a heavy folded blanket onto the boy's chest, causing the lifeguard and I, and those standing around, to shout, "No!" The person throwing the heavy blanket seemed confused saying, "But you're supposed to keep them warm."

As the breathing got gradually deeper and stronger, the child seemed to wake up. He started to cry immediately with consciousness. His mother took him and held him upright in her arms as the child kept crying, while we waited for an ambulance. The boy cried a long time. As the only doctor around, I accompanied the boy and his parents to the hospital in the ambulance for their son's further evaluation and a chest x-ray. I didn't stay once they were in another doctor's hands. I came back to the lake with the ambulance. Later, I heard that the doctors at the hospital were reluctant to do an x-ray, as they felt that everything was all right now, and the lungs sounded clear.

The lifeguard came up to me later and said, "Thank you for saving the boy's life; when I got to the shore, I was too tired to do anything." I said, as we shook hands, "You're the one who saved his life. You pulled him out of the water." We both smiled as our handshake became stronger.

There is more to life than meets the eye, and that something more is what meets the inner eye. The next day at our hospital, I related the story while we were operating, and another resident with us at the surgery said that I should have asked for a season pass to the lake.

But that was not anything I would say, as it was the farthest thing from my mind.

My life was very busy, and we never had a chance to go back to that lake again. I often wondered what if my family and I were not allowed into the lake because they thought we had too many children. Margaret has had a couple of sad miscarriages, and a severe case of mumps has made me sterile, so our family size ended with five children.

When I was in the Boy Scouts learning first aid, we all dreamt of being heroes by saving someone with what we learned. The technique I used that day was very different from the first-aid teaching in the Boy Scouts when I was young, but still it was a nice feeling to save a life. It's a feeling that can't be put into words. It feels a lot like gratitude. It helps balance all those times when, as a doctor, I couldn't save a life, no matter how hard I tried. We gradually learn the truth that there are times when words are not sufficient.

No one can quench their thirst on just the word "water." And no one can ever explain color to a blind man. You can't explain the taste of any food. You can't put into words the music you have just heard. The truth is that it is a mistake to think that a thinking mind and a non-thinking brain are all that there is to a human being. There is something more noble, moral, and ethical. There is truth, love, goodness, humor, compassion, etc., because of the presence of *ideals* and not just *ideas*.

Simone Weil (French philosopher, 1909-1943) said, "The danger is not that the soul should doubt whether there is any bread, but lest, by lie, should persuade itself that it is not hungry." This can be paraphrased to say: The danger is not that the soul should doubt the existence of God, but that it should lie to itself that it has no need for God or that there is no God. The truth is that from the beginning of time, people have found that a belief in God is essential, as evidenced by the fact that a belief in God is present in all cultures all over the world and throughout all time. Coincidence is God's way of remaining anonymous.

There is no such thing as coincidence; it is all God-incidence.

> Coincidence is a God-scheduled opportunity.
> —*Scott Hamilton, American figure skater, Olympic gold medalist and cancer survivor, born 1958*

I once performed a bronchoscopy on a patient who had a hoarse voice, and I saw a large tumor on one of his vocal cords. I am very familiar with the appearance, through the bronchoscope, of a tumor, having seen and biopsied hundreds in my lifetime. I prayed with the patient and sent him to a distant hospital to an ear, nose, and throat specialist for treatment. Some time later, the patient was admitted again for treatment of another ailment, and he hurried toward me in the hallway. He was very happy to see me. And he related that after we had prayed, he went for his consultation and he was examined and nothing wrong was found, no tumor. I noted that his voice was now normal in conversing with me. Miracles do happen with prayer, and that's the truth of my experience.

Because of the many intense years of schooling that the life of a surgeon requires, which makes any spare time precious, I decided very early in my life not to use up my time by following sports or reading novels. I like reading serious books that interest me on philosophy, religion, psychology, and psychiatry. I became a student of human nature. I wish, at the present time, that education wouldn't devote so much time and treasure to sports and expend as much on education as it does on sports. I wish soccer moms would push for the teaching of mathematics as much as they do for sports. The American educational system is already falling behind Europe by over a year in what American students are taught about mathematics compared to what Europeans are taught. Unless our American educational system changes, eventually the Europeans will get the jobs, and Americans will be left out.

To be a reader first and a writer second seems natural to me. If you're a writer and you're not doing too much reading, that's like playing a sport you don't even watch.

41

As I've said, I want to share crystallized truths that have taken me a lifetime to learn. I want to share wise words of truth that have become part of who I am, because I believe that all communication of truth on some level is healing. Truth has a way of comforting the afflicted and afflicting the comfortable.

> We must learn to live off the happiness of each other and not off the misery of each other.
> —*Charlie Chaplin, American comedic actor, 1889-1977*

We also must learn to live off the wisdom of each other.

After Anatomy class in medical school, I was told that half of what I was going to be taught was false but that my teachers didn't know which half. This added to my ongoing search for the truth; a search which has been going on since I was a little boy. As a child, I can recall seeing, at a lottery in Shenandoah, Pennsylvania, a sign that read: "Winners never quit, and quitters never win." I thought that was a pretty smart and clever way to say something, and a smart and clever way to induce people to keep gambling. I didn't realize it at the time, but at an early age I was attracted to these invisible truths that I would continuously collect.

My parents were not highly educated, and we didn't have erudite conversations. Culture came later in my going to school and as a teenager visiting the museums in Philadelphia with my twin brother, Don. My parents did, however, use old proverbs and sayings, such as, "All that glitters isn't gold" and "Don't take any wooden nickels," which means to keep your eyes open for what is genuine or not, or for what is of true value or not. And I was always fascinated by the truth found in these sayings.

My parents used such expressions as, "Make hay while the sun shines," which means take advantage of opportunity while it's here, and "Haste makes waste," which means that hurrying through a job leads to mistakes and starting all over again, which is a big waste of time and materials. And I learned a lesson the hard way, "If you play with matches, you'll get burned." And I learned that "A poor workman blames his tools." I was being introduced to letting something that you can see point me to something of truth that you can't see, because it's invisible, and it can only be seen by the inner eye. I could read some of these short truths in the daily newspaper, too. "If the winds won't serve, use the oars," which means that if you can't do it the easy way, you can still do it the hard way. I became fascinated with the truth of these pithy sayings.

Robert Southey (English Poet, 1774-1843) said, "It is with words as with sunbeams—the more they are condensed, the deeper they burn." I believe that they burn because that is the impact of truth striking you in the back of the head and in the dark, as pointed out by Henry David Thoreau (naturalist philosopher, 1817-1862). In other words, the truth in these condensed sayings has an impact, because the truth in them is very often the sudden unexpected opposite of what you've been thinking or it's truth that you hadn't thought about before. My appreciation and fascination may have stemmed from my innate ability, like most folks, to recognize and value truth and wisdom, in addition to my need to know more in order to catch up with the rest of the world.

The science-fiction book The *Hitchhiker's Guide to the Galaxy* (Douglas Adams, 1952-2001) points out that an editor on a piece of celestial real estate called Ursa Minor Beta has left his office one morning, possibly to go to lunch, and has never returned. Einstein's ideas of time passing slowly for some and faster for others, and the possibility of wormholes, space travel, time travel, and other speculations make the editor's staff believe that their editor will eventually return, but it may take some time. So all subsequent editors are designated "acting" editors. His desk is left untouched, going on 100 years, and a sign is placed stating: "Editor missing, presumed fed." This is a play on the words, "presumed dead." Plays on words and intelligent insights are almost as fascinating to me as concentrated truths in short sayings, mottoes, slogans, aphorisms, truisms, wise sayings, quips, etc..

Always, as I went through school, I continued to be fascinated by the truth found in stories, poems, and in wise sayings, such as: "We hit what we aim at," which means that you need a goal in order to reach one, or you only can get to where you are seeking to go. "Talking without thinking is like shooting without aiming" (Zbigniew Herbert, Polish poet, 1924-1998). Brief sayings remind us that what we see is always telling us something about what we don't see. Another example is: "Birds of a feather flock together," which means that people of similar interests congregate together. Some visible thing is related, by using words, to some invisible thing, such as a desire in the heart to be together.

I just knew that there is much more to life than what I was living, namely, my life of just joys and sorrows. And I kept following the clues of truth that I kept finding, such as: "Once you think you know, fall in love and you'll immediately know more." I knew the truth of that saying when I fell in love for the first time. The experience was an eye opener, an inner eye opener. And I certainly found that short statement held a lot of truth, because I immediately knew more after I fell in love. I was able to verify the truth of the saying by my own experience of falling in love, as you probably have verified the truth of this saying from your own experience of falling in love.

Ralph Waldo Emerson (philosopher poet, 1803-1882) said that the only true doctor is the poet. He said that because the poet is sensitive to insight and is able to put into words the truth, which is difficult for most of us to express. And all truth, on some level, is healing. Therefore, the reason that I write is because I want to be a doctor enough to give you the truth so that it will cause some level of healing in you, as it does in me. When Albert Schweitzer was asked why he wanted to become a doctor he said: "I wanted to be a doctor that I might be able to work without having to talk…this new form of activity would consist not in preaching the religion of love, but of practicing it." I started out as a doctor, and now I am reaching out in words; nevertheless, it is all done in the spirit of love, because doctors know that it is not enough to heal the body; the soul needs healing, too. And in the presence of love, everything is healed. And love is not love unless it is given away. This means doing something with your love. The ability of the poet to express himself or herself is done without an "impediment to speech" that the rest of us have, so the poet is able to gaze, record, diagnose, and prophesy truthfully without impediment. And like the doctor, the poet is "healthy," and everyone else by comparison seems "sick" with their "speech impediment."

If truth is symbolized by flour, then a sack of flour compressed into the size of a thimble is an aphorism or a truism. The collecting of concentrated truth condensed into short, wise sayings, truisms, and aphorisms that strike me to the heart with their truths and which give me timeless moments has been on some level healing to me, and I know it will be healing to you as I share them with you. Let one after another short truth wash over you until you sense the existence of something that is there all the time but is invisible, and it is named "love and goodness," a lot of which is needed in order to tell the truth.

What I have collected has touched me personally and profoundly over the years. It has held great meaning and instruction for me personally. However, in talking with people over these years, they have told me that by using these pithy words, I wasn't sharing anything personal about my life. This always surprised me, because what I was sharing was how I deeply thought and felt about life, and I was convinced that the ideas in these pithy words truly represented me. They were the best words that I could use in my attempt to say something quickly in a condensed way and to the point, and letting the truth give its own timeless moments, its own touches of accompanying love and goodness. Since truth strikes us with unexpected surprise, "To ignore the unexpected (even if it were possible) would be to live without opportunity, spontaneity, and the rich moments of which life is made" (Stephen Covey, contemporary author and teacher on leadership, born 1932). In other words, to ignore the truth, even if it were possible, would be to live without rich moments.

Man reading should be man intensely alive. The book
should be a ball of light in one's hand.
—*Ezra Pound, American expatriate poet, critic and
intellectual, 1885-1972*

The next chapter, Science, will explore how science tends to study
only two of the three qualities that make us human. This will aid in a
better understanding of the up-coming Chapter 8, Duality (Polarity
and More) as we move to a clearer understanding of transformation.

Chapter 4.

Science

The real voyage of discovery consists not in seeing new landscapes, but in having new eyes.
—*Marcel Proust, French author, 1871-1922*

A loving heart is the truest wisdom.
—*Charles Dickens, English novelist, 1812-1870*

Human beings are so constituted that if they *see* something, they have to *say* something. And since they are always seeing invisible things, such as all of the values, virtues, ideals, and principles, then they are always talking about these invisible things, which are immeasurable. For example, people are always talking about truth, love, and goodness.

Scientists, on the other hand, upon seeing something, have to measure it. So they are always talking about what they have measured. For example, scientists tell us that the duodenum, which is a portion of the proximal intestine, is approximately the same length as the width of 12 fingers, and that's what duodenum means. Our world or planet is habitable, and inhabited, by conscious human beings with both scientific measurability and spiritual ability to see invisible things.

We must always tell what we see. Above all, and this is more difficult, we must always see what we see.
—*Charles Peguy, French poet and aphorist, 1873-1914*

When you can measure what you are speaking about, and express it in numbers, you know something about it; but when you cannot measure it, when you cannot express it in

numbers, your knowledge is of a meager and unsatisfactory kind. It may be the beginning of knowledge, but you have scarcely in your thoughts advanced to the stage of science.
—William Thomson or Lord Kelvin, Irish-born, British mathematical physicist and engineer, 1824-1907

In the Introduction I pointed out how, when my son, Joe, was diagnosed with cancer at a young age, my wife, Margaret, and I were able to move from the joy of the city through the desert of sorrow to be with our son in the garden of transformation. Slowly we were able to get into the garden with our son, by experiencing the love and concerns of a vast group of doctors, medical personnel, family, friends, and many others who were struggling with their own similar medical situations. Also, prayer and having faith helped a lot. We were moved into the garden with the help of faith, hope, and love. We were in the realm of spirituality, having moved from the hell of desolation to the heaven of transformation. The poet, Emily Dickinson (1830-1888), said, "Hope is the thing with feathers (and wings and things) that perches in the soul and sings the tune without the words, and never stops at all." In addition to hope, as we moved into the garden, we also had faith and love. Someone once said that you can't know all about a bird simply by listening to the song that it sings. There is more to being human than rational and emotional; there is also being spiritual.

Science, with its secular approach to life and its secular philosophy, avoids mentioning anything about spirit or soul as part of being a human being. Nevertheless, human beings have a mind, heart, and spirit. The mind seeks truth, the heart seeks love, and the spirit seeks goodness and God. There is something about us all that is mental, emotional, and spiritual. We are always thinking truth, feeling love, and seeing, with our mind's eye the invisible things, such as goodness. If you avoid the spiritual, you miss seeing and knowing a lot.

An education isn't how much you have committed to memory, or even how much you know. It's being able to

differentiate between what you do know and what you don't.
—*Anatole France, French novelist and 1929 Nobel Prize winner in literature, 1844-1924*

I believe in Christianity as I believe the sun has risen: not only because I see it, but because by it I see everything else.
—*C.S. Lewis, Irish author and scholar, 1898-1963*

There are a lot of things that science can't explain, such as visionaries; seers; prophets; pre-cognition; foretelling; premonitions; paranormal; clairvoyance; correct hunches; correct rapid do-or-die decisions; snap judgments; first impressions; intuition; instant dislikes; love at first sight; luck; serendipity; unexplained healings; benevolence; miracles; insights; pattern recognitions; gut feelings; unconscious choices; internal radar; animal instinct; 6th sense; extra sensory perception (ESP); mental telepathy; spot diagnosis; power of the glance (coup d'oeil); rapid cognition; mind reading; eidetic images (seeing images in the patterns of clouds or images in the patterns in linoleum, wallpaper, rugs etc.); finding answers in a blink instead of a long think; stigmata; etc. The simplest and best explanation for so many of these is the existence of God.

Blaise Pascal (French mathematician, physicist, and religious philosopher, 1623-1662) argued that it literally was a good bet to believe in God, when he used probability theory to mathematically analyze a gamble containing value, or the expectation of getting a value, in the bet.

Albert Einstein (physicist, 1879-1955) said that the most beautiful thing that we can experience is the mysterious. The most beautiful and mysterious thing in the world is to love and to be loved. God is love. To quote Einstein: "To know that this love really exists, manifesting itself as the highest wisdom and the most radiant beauty, which our dull faculties can comprehend only in their most primitive forms—this knowledge, this feeling, is at the center of true religiousness."

Very shortly I will continue with Albert Einstein, but first I have to interpose two short paragraphs relating to innocence and guilt:

There are times when you get accused of doing something wrong, and you are completely innocent. For example, my brother and I thought it would be fun, as an experiment, to put a fuse into flash powder tied below a helium-filled balloon, just to see the sparks shoot high into the sky. We did it in the courtyard of the U-shaped apartment house in which we lived. The balloon went up as high as the fourth floor, but it drifted to an area of a window. And before we could pull the balloon away, and before the balloon could go higher, the sparking went off. A man passing by grabbed my arm, and accused us of trying to scare someone. I protested vehemently that all we were doing was an experiment. He repeated his accusation, and at that point I asked him loudly, "Who are you?" I persisted in maintaining that we weren't doing anything to scare anybody, just an experiment. I thought he could be a plainclothes detective passing by and coming upon the scene. At that point, he quickly walked away, leaving us to wonder. It's said that it takes a village to raise a child. As far as I'm concerned, no, it doesn't. It just takes two parents.

There was another time, when my brother and I were blamed for something, and we were totally guilty. We were just youngsters, and we thought it would be fun to throw pebbles from the roof of the apartment house where we lived, which was four stories high, onto passing cars. Then we would duck like two Mr. Innocents and giggle. One car stopped and the driver came up to the roof and told us that what we were doing was quite wrong. We forever stopped throwing pebbles—on the spot!

Some people blame Albert Einstein (physicist, 1879-1955) for modern man's attempts to create a new and supposedly improved philosophy about life, which may have led many to become lukewarm in their faith. These new philosophies are taking the ashes from the old altars, instead of the fire, and the new thinkers are thinking that they have something new. Many people may subconsciously feel compelled to bring out any and all ideas that are non-traditional and to call them truth, simply to mimic Einstein's ideas. Their new ideas, which seem so counterintuitive and nontraditional, are brought out simply because some of Einstein's counterintuitive and nontraditional speculations have ended up being proved true. Einstein studied the behavior of systems in motion relative to the observer. However, in the earlier time of Isaac Newton (English physicist astronomer, 1643-1727), space, matter, and time were separate from each other, and our three dimensions were height, width, and depth, with time as a fourth dimension. One of Einstein's ideas is that distance (space) and duration (time) are not absolute but are affected by one's motion, and he postulated such things as curvature and ripples of space-time. If time, space and matter (mass) were in motion, an observer in one system, in reference to an observer in another system, "would note a slower passage of time, a contraction of distance, and an increase of mass of objects in the other system." This becomes more pronounced as velocities of motion are closer to the speed of light.

Einstein's formula of energy equals mass times a constant squared, describes mass as having an enormous amount of energy because "c" (the constant) is a very large number, namely, the speed of light (in a vacuum) squared. The speed of light being 186,300 miles per second. Note that this is in one second and not in one minute or in one hour. Another part of the theory is that energy has mass. If you heat an object, the mass, or its weight, increases. This weight (mass) increase, however, is so tiny that its measurement is outside the scope of current technology, because the formula used for that measurement is mass=E/c, where the amount of energy "E" is divided by the very large number "c."

Einstein has shown us that the universe is more wonderful and mysterious than we thought we knew.

George Santayana (Spanish author and aphorist, 1863-1952) said, "Whoever it was who searched the heavens with a telescope and found no God would not have found the human mind if he had searched the brain with a microscope." That's the truth. When Sir Arthur Stanley Eddington (English astrophysicist, 1882-1944) spoke about the nature of electrons, he said: "Something unknown is doing we don't know what." Just like God is doing.

Science and the arts, such as literature, both have a need for new ideas and new understandings about the universe. Their new ideas all need to be organized and communicated. Both seek explanations for what we don't understand, and their explanations are stored and shared by using words or numbers. Therefore, we find ideas from Albert Einstein (or science) crossing over into the arts. Each discipline, hoping to be more precise, is becoming more specialized. And as each discipline rises, they converge, as predicted by the French philosopher priest Pierre Teilhard de Chardin, S.J., (1881-1955).

Art using science is shown by the following examples. In literature, various characters, without leaving the present moment, go through transitions, And various characters, like rays of light, start at different points in space and time to converge. Modern movies flashback in time suddenly, or move forward in time suddenly, or show time as flashes of a sequence that looks like a flashing strobe light illuminating a fight scene. In science fiction, there's light-speed and warp-drive. And in painting, we have images in art which are like phrases in literature, which are used in various combinations, with time shaped by multiple relationships and influences so that it doesn't seem to flow linearly. In addition, artistic tradition is bypassed to deform objects in their size, shape and scale, with time and space not the same for everybody. And perspective is rejected in favor of multiple views at once. Different images are used by cutting, pasting, and assembling fragments into a single collage, with all senses, not just the visual, used to capture the scene.

Because art tends to match the ideas of Albert Einstein, when Einstein observes that the subjective observer is important in objective science, the artists then show the importance of the subjective in their objective art. All of these modern ideas are considered to be "an act of liberation," that is, a "freedom" from the conventional notions of painting or of past art. It is all, of course, applauded by secular humanistic materialists and confusing to those trying to find the spiritual, because secular, humanistic, and materialistic new-age thinkers and like-minded artists are avoiding the spiritual path to understanding. They are choosing, instead, to follow the path of the scientists.

Confused ideas and muddy ponds appear deep.
—*Nicolas Gomez Davila, Columbian aphorist, 1913-1994*

Science can't explain why things exist and what their purpose is. Scientism is the view that science can explain everything, and science gives itself the privilege of explaining everything. But science can't tell you where the laws of physics came from. There are some deeply mysterious unknowns at the root of the universe. As the French philosopher priest, Pierre Teilhard de Chardin, S.J., pointed out in his 1966 book *The Phenomenon of Man*, God made a universe that has in it a participation of creativity, because God made it evolutionary and not static. And humans are biologic organisms and persons having spiritual worth. Because they are not the science model of an assembly of parts and elements that can be cut and pasted. Science purges religion of superstition, and religion helps science stay within the boundary of its discipline, which is needed, because science can't explain love, friendships, values, virtues, ideals, and principles. The truth is that science uses the metaphor of a machine to explain the universe, but it's more mysterious than that. Violence is not at the core of life, love is. There is a ghost in the machine, the ghost of a human soul and spirit. Life is winding up while non-living things seem to be winding down.

Science points out that matter cannot be destroyed, it just changes form. Religion points out that love, grief, and sorrow are also forces that change form and do not get destroyed. We pass from the deep pain of the loss of a beloved to a deeper sympathy, a deeper love and a deeper insight.

The Hindu philosopher, I.K.Taimni, in his 1970 book, *A Way to Self Discovery*, says, "In the infinite variety of forms and their constant destruction, nature is seen to have a definite, intelligible purpose, which is even now denied to her by science. Modern science is like a deaf man studying musical instruments of great variety and increasing delicacy. He studies the instruments with great care but refuses to believe that there is such a thing as music." Many secular scientists refuse to believe in God. However, you cannot reach new oceans until you are willing to let go of your view of the shore.

> Scientific study of the Bible is necessary and important, but in the end it is only an exercise of chopping kindling. It takes the Holy Spirit to set it on fire.
> —*George Montague, 2ⁿᵈ Earl of Halifax, 1716-1771*

Sometimes I wonder if science hasn't lost its way, being unable to recognize what is happening right before its eyes, namely, the material pointing to the spiritual. The essence of science is mystery and that is exciting; however, science pursues what it doesn't know by taking leaps of imagination and following hunches and by getting lucky breaks through accidents (God-incidences), such as the idea for the microwave that came when a microwave signal melted a chocolate bar in the pocket of the scientist Percy LeBaron Spencer, who worked for Raytheon Company. And the lucky break for science in finding that aspirin relieves pain by a mechanism that is still unknown. And the lucky break when the Scottish bacteriologist, Alexander Fleming, returning to St. Mary's Hospital in London from a holiday on September 3, 1928, found mold growing on one of his *Staphylococcus* cultures. He noted that no *Staphylococci* grew near the mold. Fleming investigated. He named the "mould juice" *penicillin* for the penicillium mold that produces it. Fleming, who died in 1955 at the age of 73, published his discovery in 1929, but it was a decade after that when Oxford scientists Howard Florey and Ernst Boris Chain isolated and purified penicillin for use as an antibiotic. While doing all that, science thinks it is authoritative and objective. The messy consequences of such so-called "authoritative objectivity" of science is a contradiction that is evident on science's every page.

Science doesn't even know if there is one reason why animals age and die or if there are many, each applying to a different branch of life's tree. Science believes that in a human there is a built-in obsolescence, similar to what Vance Packard (American journalist and author, 1914-1996) said in his 1960 book, *The Waste Makers,* about obsolescence built into cars and other products by manufacturing in order to sell more products. Science tells us that a cell has just so many cell divisions before it cannot divide anymore. But why are dog years different from human years? Science has recorded three humans so far who are able to remember every single thing that happened to them every day for decades. No one knows how they can remember that well. There seems to be a lot that science cannot explain. Because science lives and works with mystery in the universe, and God is mystery, why can't they work with God? There is a classic old story about the children of atheists. The children are always asking: "Daddy, do you think that God knows that we don't believe in Him?"

The mind seeks truth, the heart seeks love and the spirit seeks goodness and God.

This can be seen in the following chart that shows what makes us human:

1. Mind	2. Heart (Body)	3. Spirit
Rational	Emotional	Spiritual
Mental	Physical	Moral
Truth	Love	Goodness
Meaning/ Purpose	Intimacy	Virtue
Thinking	Feeling	"Seeing"
Pathos	Eros	Logos
Professor	Physician	Priest
Rational	Sensual	Sacred
Randomness/ Chance	Fertility	Moral and Natural Laws
Respect of Self	Respect for Others	Responsibility for Your Actions

Chart 2. List of Three Qualities That Make Us Human

The scientific principle called *Occham's razor* (sometimes spelled "Ockham's" razor) says that we should not multiply entities beyond what is necessary to explain the effect. In other words, all other things being equal, the simplest solution is the best, or if you are confronted with two explanations for something, choose the simpler one, as it is more likely to be correct. More and more science is being put into the position that the simplest explanation is the existence of God. "Occam's razor" is a principle attributed to the 14th century English logician and Franciscan friar, William of Ockham.

Science is bringing out many new reasons for the existence of God. One of these is that Earth is the only place in the solar system where a solar eclipse is seen, due to the sun being 400 times larger than the moon, and 400 times farther from the earth, making the two bodies appear the exact same size in the sky. Just before full eclipse dazzling beads called a "rosary" or "Baily's beads" appear where the sunlight shines through valleys on the moon. The last bead is largest and creates the impression of a diamond ring in the sky. At this awe filled moment some members of an eclipse-viewing expedition have been known to take advantage of it by proposing marriage. Earth is unique in terms of human habitability as well as human capacity for measurability. A perfect solar eclipse in 1919 helped astronomers to confirm the fact that gravity bends light as predicted by Einstein's general theory of relativity.

Another scientific proof for the existence of God is the Cambrian explosion or the "Biological Big Bang," which is distinct from the astronomer's "Big Bang." During the Cambrian period in geologic time, there arose the sudden appearance of most of the major animal phyla that are still alive today, as well as some that are now extinct. The Cambrian explosion has uprooted Darwin's tree, because the major groups of animals, instead of coming last at the top of the tree as Darwin expected, come first, representing 35 of the 40 major phyla (Charles Robert Darwin was an English naturalist and geologist, 1809-1882).

The statistical probability of the numerous random-chance coincidences that science needs to eventuate in conscious human beings is so high that it would take more time to accomplish than the age of the cosmos. It is likened to the chances of an explosion in a junkyard producing a passenger plane.

The idea that the universe was made just for us is known as the "anthropic principle." Brandon Carter (Australian theoretical physicist and Cambridge astrophysicist, born 1942) proposed this in 1973, when he pointed out at a conference in Poland that a purely random assortment of laws would have left the universe dead and dark. And that life seems to be what limits the values that physical constants can have, because the laws of physics themselves seem biased toward life. Everything about the physical state of the universe seems tailor made for life. Some researchers call this revelation the "Goldilocks principle," because the cosmos is not "too this" or "too that" but rather "just right" for life. When we start our search, we must find the right conditions for life in our universe, because if such life did not exist then we would not be here to find those conditions.

John wheeler (American theoretical physicist, 1911-2008) described a reverse theory of a participatory anthropic principle that holds that the universe is created by life and not the other way around. This is known as "biocentrism," which allows the observer into the equation for new approaches to solve problems associated with quantum physics and the "Big Bang." Life as a principle seems present in the very first atoms after the "Big Bang." Nevertheless, according to biocentrism, time does not exist independently of the life that notices it. Space and time become modes of interpretation and understanding as forms of animal sense perception (that is, as something biological, rather than as external physical objects).

> Rain reminds me again and again that the whole world runs by rhythms I have not learned to recognize, rhythms that are not those of the engineers.
> —*Thomas Merton, French author and Trappist monk, 1915-1968*

> Would it not be strange if a universe without purpose accidentally created humans who are so obsessed with purpose?
> —*Sir John Templeton, English Rhodes scholar, 1912–July 8, 2008*

> The purpose of life is a life of purpose.
> —*Robert Byrne, chess master, newspaper chess columnist and philosophy professor, born 1928*

Galileo's old aphorism (Galileo was a physicist and astronomer, 1564-1642) is, "Science tells you how the heavens go, and the Bible tells you how to go to heaven." In the Bible, God shows up where you least expect to find Him, for example, on a Cross. He is surrounded by miracles, because in the presence of love miracles occur and everything is healed, and God is Love. Modern people don't expect to find God in <u>poverty, chastity and obedience,</u> but that is precisely where the counterculture of religion is in relation to the American culture of <u>money, sex, and power</u>.

Science can optically explain rainbows, but seeing a rainbow and feeling the awe and wonder of it is something science doesn't study. If you are only open to what will accord with what you think that you already know, you may as well stay shut. A bird has feathers and wings and things, and we cannot know all about a bird simply by listening to the song it sings. This means that you can't know all about humans by studying just rational and emotional, because you also need to study spiritual.

The next chapter will explore more fully what science tends to leave out from its study of the qualities that make us human.

Chapter 5.

Truth, Love and Goodness

The mind seeks *truth*, the heart seeks *love*, and the spirit
seeks *goodness*.
—*Author unknown*

Once you think you know, fall in love, and you'll
immediately know more.
—*Author unknown*

It's time for us to steer by the stars and not by any bright
light that just passes by.
—*U.S. Army General Omar Bradley, at the end of
World War II*

The brightest star is spirituality with its truth, love, and goodness,
not any bright leader or secular atheistic scientist who may be shining our way.

Dirt glitters when the sun happens to shine.
—*Johann Wolfgang Von Goethe, German scientist poet,
1749-1832*

We turn from the light to see.
—*Don Paterson, Scottish poet, born 1963*

What is more thrilling than the prospect of **truth** (mind), or **love**
(heart), or **goodness** (spirit) that you do not yet know? For everyone,
there is literally a vast ocean of truth, love, and goodness (mind,
heart and spirit) lying undiscovered. "To myself I am only a child
playing on the beach, while vast oceans of truth lie undiscovered
before me" (Isaac Newton, British mathematician and physicist,

1643-1727). Because he was a scientist, he neglected to mention the vast oceans of love and goodness that also were undiscovered before him. This chapter explores these three qualities that we all have as human beings.

I call it a *duality* (dual, duo, two, binary) when two of the three terms from truth, love, and goodness (mind, heart, and spirit) are coupled together, such as *truth* (mind) and *love* (heart), or *knowledge* (mind) and *love* (heart).

The most common duality is contrasting polar opposites, such as joy and sorrow or consolation and desolation, as we have seen. Duality is clarified further in the next chapter.

Like the short parables in the Bible, which are masterpieces of literature, I find in wise sayings something of the same quality of masterpiece. I also find them to be truisms and somewhat like Greek sculpture, in which the ideal becomes tangible and loveable. Knowledge and love are two terms of a duality, and the two terms are like two mirrors facing each other, because the two words are reflecting something to each other of each other. Like two positives. The two terms are not strictly opposite or polar contrasts; they just seem randomly chosen, but there is some relationship to each other, and that relationship is shown below.

Knowledge and *love* are related into a duality of mind (knowledge) and heart (love). They are both taken from mind, heart, and spirit, which are the three qualities that make up a human being.

We see this relationship of knowledge and love below.

Truisms:

- Once you think you know, fall in love and you'll immediately know more.
  —Author unknown

- You can't love what you don't know.

- You only truly know what you have fallen in love with.
  —*Author unknown*

- Love is the way that mystery tells us messages. The most mysterious thing in the world is love. God is love.

- Things human must be known to be loved; things divine must be loved to be known.
  —*Blaise Pascal, French mathematician, physicist and philosopher, 1623-1662*

Truth is related in a duality to **1.)** love, and in a duality to **2.)** beauty, and in a duality to **3.)** goodness. We can see their relationships in their truisms below, which follow each duality.

  1.) There is a relationship between *truth* and *love*, a duality of mind (truth), and heart (love).

Truisms:

- Love increases by means of truth, and love draws near by means of truth.
  —*Pope John Paul II, Polish priest, 1920-2005*

- To feel beauty is to know the truth, and to know the truth is to be in love.

- Feeling is God's own truth.
  —*Irish proverb*

- Love is whispered truth. The message never gets louder, only clearer.

- Love is an expression of truth, and truth is an expression of love.

Truth and love are also put together in a duality, because it takes a lot of love to tell the truth, and often, what is said of love, we find to be true from our own experiences. Additionally, truth and love are the attributes of God, and when you have truth or love, or both, you are close to God. Patients in the 12-step programs get to a belief in a higher power and they get close to God, whenever they believe the truths told them in rehab, and they see the love of rehab staff and the love of their families, all of whom have love enough to tell them the truth.

2.) There exists a relationship between *truth* and *beauty*, a duality of mind (truth), and heart (beauty).

Truisms:

- For beauty is never without truth, nor truth without beauty. —*St. Francis de Sales, Bishop of Geneva, 1567-1622*

- Albert Einstein felt that a theory didn't have to be correct as long as it was beautiful in its simplicity, because later, the theory is likely to be found to be true.

- If you equate beauty with the visible body, or with the invisible feeling of knowing beauty when you see it, because you just feel it as known, then to feel beauty is to know the truth and to know the truth is to be in love.

3.) There is a relationship between *truth* and *goodness*, a duality of mind (truth) and spirit (goodness).

Truisms:

- Some things seem too good to be true.

- The opposite of truth is lies, which is classified as a badness. So the opposite of the duality of lies and badness is the duality of truth and goodness. Both dualities being opposite, in this case, makes for a duality of dualities.

- When I was in college, I was told that the purpose of education is to expose us to all that has been discovered so far about *truth, beauty, and goodness* (mind, heart, and spirit) so that we can graduate and go out into the world and be able to recognize and find more of truth, beauty and goodness for ourselves. Add *love* (more heart) to that.

The insight of **truth** is the spark, and **love** is the fire, and **goodness** is the refined golden result. Insight is the spark and is in your mind, but love is the fire and is in your heart, while goodness is in your spirit or soul.

The beautiful invisible positive extreme of the *mind* is *truth*;

The beautiful invisible positive extreme of the *heart* is *love*; and

The beautiful invisible positive extreme of the *spirit* is *goodness*.

(The opposite, invisible, negative extremes are lies, hate, and evil, which represent ugliness.)

Americans know that freedom is better than slavery, tolerance better than bigotry, love better than hate, and kindness better than cruelty. But in a world of lies, hate, and evil, we must defend all of our spiritual values in a world that does not universally embrace them. There are times when we do not find much of truth, love, or goodness in the world.

Beauty consists of truth, love, and goodness, which are the positive extremes of the mind, heart, and spirit.

Beauty lives in the positive extremes of truth, love, and goodness (mind, heart, and spirit).

Truisms:

- Wherever the imagination finds beauty there must also be truth. (Beauty reveals truth)
  —*John Keats, poet, 1795-1821*

- To really see anything, you must first see the beauty in it.
  —*Oscar Wilde, Irish author, 1854-1900*

- Beauty is the love we devote to an object.
  —*Paul Serusier, French painter, 1864-1927*

- We must put our heart into it.

- To love something, first see the beauty in it.

- Nothing, except God, is beautiful from every point of view.

- Where there is love, there is always truth, beauty, and goodness.

- God is love, and God's attributes are truth, beauty, and goodness.

- The way to love anything is to realize that it might be lost.
  —*Gilbert Keith Chesterton, English author 1874-1936*

- We may love beauty because we realize beauty can be lost.

- What makes cheery blossoms so beautiful to the oriental mind is partly due to the short existence of its beautiful bloom.

The truth is that "The best proof of love is trust" (Dr. Joyce, Brothers, psychologist, born 1925). I have lived long enough to see that in marriages, whenever there is loss of trust, there is also loss of love in the marriage. Dare I suggest that if you don't trust God, then you don't love God or even believe in God? And if you don't believe in God, then you'll make yourself your god. True abundance is to trust that God is big enough to solve all your problems and knowing that everything you need will be supplied. The opposite of that is lack of trust, with its worry that God is not big enough so you have to do it yourself, even solving what you don't control.

Trust begins with taking a risk, such as sharing your weakness, as happens with recovering alcoholics. When there are no guarantees, we always risk. Guarantees cancel out faith. Trust, belief, and faith in a higher power for alcoholics and drug addicts comes with no guarantee of recovery, which is good, because guarantees cancel out faith, and recovery requires faith in a higher power as well as the trust to step out in risk with no guarantees. Prayer is trusting to ask to be changed in ways you can't even imagine, and not just asking for what you think you want.

There is a classic story of a man taking a wheelbarrow full of bricks across a tightrope over Niagara Falls. He asks the crowd, "Do you think I can do this?" They all answer, "Yes!" He does it, and on coming back, he asks the crowd if they think he can do it again. They say, "Yes!" Then, the man empties out the bricks and says, "If you really believe that I can, then get in the wheelbarrow!" It's one thing to say that you believe in God, and another to trust Him, to take a risk on God. In the Bible in the Book of Acts, Chapter 16, Paul and Silas, who are believers in Jesus, have been severely beaten by being whipped, and they are in chains and leg stocks in prison at about midnight. (Today in America, it's getting close to symbolic midnight. And most of us feel pretty beaten up by life.) Paul and Silas have been arrested for preaching about Jesus, for speaking truth with love, but despite the severe beating and the injustice to them as Roman citizens, they are singing and praising God while all of the other prisoners are listening. To be able to sing in such circumstances is to have been transformed by love. For many of us in our current lives, there may be a lot of tape-recorded singing going on but precious little praising of God. Suddenly, there is a violent earthquake, which shakes the prison to its foundations. All of their chains fall off and all the doors open. The jailor, seeing the prison doors open, draws his sword to kill himself, as he believes the prisoners have all escaped. But Paul shouts at the top of his voice, "Don't harm yourself! We are all here!" which to me symbolically represents all of the true believers who belong to the Church. We are symbolically shouting at the tops of our voices, "We are all here!" And that's the truth. We can all be compared to **w**aiting, **w**akeful, **w**atching, **w**orking **w**atchmen. And we are calling out to others, "Don't harm yourselves by not believing, by not trusting, and by not having faith in truth, love, and goodness." Life really is all about the life and the death of our body, mind, and spirit. There are forces trying to kill truth, love, and goodness.

Here is an example of living with life and death. My brother, Don, and I grew up at a time when you could send away in the mail for almost anything, as long as you could pay for it. We sent away for pure sodium metal, which came in a can that was within a can to keep the sodium away from water. And the piece of sodium was the size of a standard flashlight's handle. After opening both cans, there seemed to be a white wax-like coating on the pure sodium metal. I cut carefully through it and saw the pure silvery-pink metal of the element sodium, that could be cut with a knife. I don't think there are too many people who have seen the silvery-pink color of sodium. It is a beautiful sight that is mesmerizing. I felt quite excited. Anything new is marvelous, and it was new to me. It was then that I realized that the coating wasn't wax but a crust of sodium hydroxide or sodium oxide that formed a coating. I never touched this crust or the sodium with my fingers but used metal forceps. From the safety of being around the corner from a washtub, I threw a small piece of the sodium into water that was in the bottom of a washtub. As soon as the sodium touched the water, there was an explosion of sparks that shot up to the ceiling. That reaction was so violent it was scary. I was grateful not to have that experiment blow up in my face. I was also grateful that I didn't make the error of touching the sodium with my fingers.

There's another color that few people have seen. I haven't seen it. I've been told that when the sun is almost gone below the horizon, when you look out to sea, there is a very brief green flash of color due to the angle and the refraction of the sun's rays. It is an emerald green that is said to be a marvelous thing to see. So many things interfere with seeing it, such as timing, clouds, weather, fog, etc. that I have never met anyone who has seen it, but I have read about some people who have seen it.

Another possible life and death situation of mine was when I bought a piece of pure phosphorus, about the size of your thumb, which had to be kept under water or else it could burst into flame. This is the opposite of sodium, which has to be kept away from water. It pays to know your opposites, contrasts or dualities. You could take the phosphorus out of the water and look at it by holding the phosphorus with forceps, and as soon as it was out of the water, the phosphorus glowed a beautiful light-green luminescent color, which is called *phosphorescent* after the word *phosphorus*. Looking at that color is mesmerizing. One day, while I was enjoying its lovely greenish glow by holding it out of water with a forceps, I accidentally dropped the phosphorus onto a scrap piece of linoleum that was used as the floor covering in the area where I had my chemistry set, which was basically a long table with a shelf above it to hold a row of chemicals and a Bunsen burner on the table. The phosphorus slid in a line across the linoleum, and wherever it had touched the linoleum, it instantly burst into flame, as a long line of fire. I shouted to my mother who came in quickly and she smothered the flames with a towel, while I attempted to retrieve the phosphorus with my forceps. It really is a miracle to grow up unscathed. This is true even after we're all grown. Life at its essence is really all about life and death, not only physical death, but also the death of our mental, emotional, and spiritual lives, and therefore the death of our truth, love, and goodness.

On another occasion, my brother and I bought a roll of magnesium metal, which comes in the form of a tape about the width of a paper match. If you cut off an inch of the thin metal tape, hold it with a forceps and light the end, it suddenly catches fire with a brilliant blue-white glow and copious white smoke. This is very impressive (and best done outdoors). The Franklin Institute in Philadelphia had a similar display where you touched a button and a small strip of magnesium tape protrudes, and it is ignited by a flame for a brief show of bright light and smoke under glass. This is the first exhibit Don and I would head for when we returned on a few occasions to this museum. One day, there was a sign saying "Out of Order," to our disappointment. Life always changes. At least we knew that we didn't break it. The truth is that since all we do is not without some fault, or error, or fallibility, which we call humanness, we are saved by forgiveness. We are saved by love.

Being the adult child of an alcoholic (ACoA) makes it difficult for me to put in this book any examples from my childhood life of love. I'm sure that the presence of a Bunsen burner at my chemistry set was an act of love that was unrecognized by me as love. I'm sure that my parents loved me in their own way, but there was not all that hugging, and telling you how special you are, and how much they love you, and how happy they are that you are their child, which everyone needs. But I can insert some love references involving my wife and children.

Here is an example of when the child's action says, "I love you!" In a family, you can often notice acts like this that are miracles of love. When Margaret had chemotherapy after the surgery to remove her left lung by pneumonectomy for a malignant tumor, our son, John, shaved his head in solidarity, because the chemotherapy made Margaret lose her hair. To all of us, that creative act was a moment of truth in which our son's love for his mother was vividly expressed in action.

The highest expression of love is creativity. Certainly the creation of a child is the highest expression of the parents' love for each other. The motivation for all creative work should be love. You should not go into any career unless you love it.

The joy is in the creating and not in the maintaining. This has to be true, because creating has what doing things for the first time has, namely a revelation of sudden, unexpected joy and insight, opposite from the mundane in our everyday lives.

Truisms:

- Love is not love until it is given away.

- There is no love so great that it can thrive without incarnation. Lover and beloved need to get together.

- The Bible tells us that "God loved the world so much that He gave his only Son".
  —*John 3:16 GNB*

- You cannot love alone.

- We can only give what we have been given

- You cannot teach another unless you have been taught by another.

- You cannot love another unless you have been loved by another.

- Existence is an expression of love.

- The love of a man and women results in the creation of children.

- Creation is an expression of God's love.

I can give you an example of the opposite of love. I went to a medical convention at Atlantic City, were the Convention Center opens onto the boardwalk itself. During a break in talks at the medical convention, I went onto the boardwalk and toward a shop that advertised magic for sale. It looked as if there were people on the boardwalk scattered around. When I got to the shop, I found that it was closed for the season. I was looking over what was in the window, when I noticed that there was no scattering of people on the boardwalk anymore, only a circle of youths coming toward me that I could see reflected in the window glass. I felt that I was about to be mugged; therefore, I went to the side of the glass window by an alley, as if still looking at the shop's goods. And then I ran down the alley as fast as I could run and as long as I could run, for about a city block, and then I turned around to see that the youths were just seeing that I had escaped from them. I quickly turned and ran some more, but I soon realized that the alley goes in about two city blocks from the boardwalk in Atlantic City, and I didn't know what was at the end. It ended at the back freight entrance to the Convention Center. I worked my way into the building to my hotel room and then collapsed in relief that I was now safe. I suspected these youths were part of the drug culture out to get money by roaming in gangs or packs at the shore, particularly around a medical convention.

In addition to only truly knowing that which we have fallen in love with, we also only truly know that which we have experienced.

And since we all have experienced the truth of our own emotions, something from our hearts, such as love or its opposite, fear or hate, then we all truly know something of love's fire.

Truisms:

- The truth is that love awakens something in our hearts that is beyond knowledge.

- Love gives us privileged moments of insight that are meant for us alone.

- The world never gives you permission to shine, only love does that.

- And if you have love, you are no longer at the mercy of all the powerful forces in the world that are beyond your control, but you become the most powerful force in the world.

- There is nothing that will not reveal itself if you love it enough.
  —*George Washington Carver, Hall of Fame agricultural researcher, 1864-1943*

- A loving heart is the truest wisdom.
  —*Charles Dickens, English novelist, 1812-1870*

- Your heart will always make itself known through your words and your deeds.

- The more you judge, the less you love.
  —*Honore de Balzac, French novelist, 1799-1850*

There are times when Margaret and I are in a doctor's waiting room and someone sees how solicitous we are toward each other; they sense our love and they smile at us. We are asked, "How many years has your husband been opening the door for you or holding your coat to help you put it on?" What they really are asking is, "How many years does it take to get bonded together in love?" It is said that you are truly married when you understand every word that your wife is not saying.

I was asked "the secret" once, and the only answer I could give was that when we started out, we both were committed to our marriage, our relationship. There was a song in vogue at that time with the words, "When I fall in love it will be forever, or I'll never fall in love" ("When I Fall in Love," words and music by songwriters Edward Heyman [1907-1981] and Victor Young [1900-1956]). And that's how we felt then and still do.

Pleasure grasped is no pleasure, because a proper relationship of love is open nerves and not clutching muscles. A proper relationship of love is giving and not getting. Love cannot be forced, because that would be seeking the future before it arrives, thereby cutting off the experience itself. It would be like forcing yourself to sleep, which only serves to keep you awake. So, too, hearing is not improved by straining, and neither is anything else, such as love.

71

Walt Whitman (American writer, 1817-1885) pointed out; "As in the flint the fire, as in the seed the tree, as in the cocoon (or shroud) the butterfly, so is God's love hidden in everything I see. To me everything is a miracle." Surrender to God means surrender to love. The truth is that the purpose of your life is to give birth to the best that is within you. The best that is within you is love.

I hope to transmit the truth of the existence of values with this book to a world obsessed by politically correct speech, double-talk (suggestive innuendo or double entendre or double meanings), attack ads, spin masters, spin doctors, propaganda machines, partisanship, old and new prejudices, false photos, embellished and posed pictures by reporters, and a cheating culture caused by permissiveness and lack of enforcement.

There is still truth and honesty everywhere if you look. It is found in bus drivers, pilots, doctors, nurses, bank workers, post-office workers, police, firemen, average persons, and most Christians. People do not do what you expect; they do what you inspect, so all the inspectors everywhere are keeping us honest. Honesty is still the best policy.

There is truth, love, and goodness everywhere you look. You need proper eyes to see. Sherlock Holmes told Dr. Watson: "We see, but we do not observe."

The truth is that at the current time, the world tries to downgrade love and marriage and family by saying that the woman in the home is like a bird in a cage, a trapped prisoner. But Gilbert Keith Chesterton (English author, 1874-1936) said that she is really a bird on a nest, which represents true freedom and not captivity. The attack on marriage and family is becoming an attack on the children, and that is evidenced by embryonic research that kills embryos and by abortions. Christians, particularly Catholics, are being asked to adjust to a world with divorce, abortion, morning-after pills, the destruction of embryos for stem cells, human cloning, homosexual marriage, and homosexual adoption, etc. The Church's teachings won't change, and for the near future, it's not likely the world will change, either. Life will continue to be about the choices we make, and I hope they will always be based upon the highest of values, virtues, ideals, and principles. Gospel values are not the world's values; Gospel values are higher.

We need to think new thoughts and see through the propaganda of spin masters and the dead-end stalemate duality of partisanship. There is a third way. The truth is that the world will not be saved by another great novel, another great movie, or another great business venture. It will only be saved by the appearance of great people of character, integrity, and values. And what will make them great is love. When love reaches a critical mass, the world will experience a radical shift.

There is only one drama going on in life: our walk away from love and our walk back. "The only place outside of Heaven where you can be perfectly safe from all the dangers...of love is Hell" (Clive Staples Lewis, Irish author, 1898-1963). "We don't need another seminar, another degree, another lifetime, or anyone's approval for love to have the will of God be done on earth as it is in Heaven. Not later, but now. Not elsewhere, but here. Not through pain, but through peace; through love" (Marianne Williamson, contemporary author, activist, and founder of the Peace Alliance, born 1952). A loving person is like an evolutionary mutation, which, by putting love first, creates a context in which they have the only orientation that will support our own survival and our own evolutionary potential.

Growth is never anyone else's problem but our own. When I was growing up, my problem definitely seemed to be that I needed more growth, or I could have been blown away. My brother and I mixed charcoal and potassium nitrate together, and we put the mixture into copper tubing of about six inches in length and one inch diameter. To save money, we had learned to make charcoal for ourselves by heating wood scraps in a cast-iron container with a loose lid, which we would put, for a short time, into the coal furnace in the apartment house that was our home. We lived in a basement apartment, so we could get to the furnace area easily. By crimping the bottom end of the copper tubing in a vice and partially crimping the top so as to leave a hole, we could attach a fuse composed of paper that was soaked in potassium nitrate (saltpeter) and then dried. On lighting the fuse, it would ignite the mixture, which would cause sparks to shoot six feet into the air. The copper pipe was first partially driven upright into the ground. We did not put sulfur into the mixture, which was fortunate, because if we did, then we would have produced dynamite, and that would have created a pipe bomb. It sounds dangerous, but it was something we loved to do. It's a hard thing to grow up unscathed; we were "lucky," which is another way of saying, "We were blessed." Being safe was a God-incidence. Looking back on it, I would say it was a miracle of God's love.

Margaret, because of cancer and inactivity from chemotherapy, is prone to get blood clots. Sure enough, she had blood clots develop and go to her remaining lung and its pulmonary artery, causing shortness of breath that required hospitalization, oxygen, and anticoagulation medicine to "thin" her blood and keep it from clotting. This is a critical time where everything is in delicate balance physically. I stood by, all the while, expressing my love and concern, and with the help of prayer, she was discharged home on low-dose maintenance coumadin medication to prevent any new clots. She developed high blood pressure and so-called "cotton wool" exudates on the retinas of her eyes, which impaired her vision. With medication, her blood pressure is now controlled, and these exudates are clearing, but her vision is about the same. She also has mild cataracts. Cataracts reportedly change the correction on your glasses to make you more near-sighted, and she has had prescriptions for new lenses for her glasses. As you get older, it seems that it's one thing after another that needs attention. It helps to have a loving spouse. It is a cross they both have to bear. I now read to her, and she has to read by using a bright light and by using some magnification. She is able to watch TV but can't read the captions fast enough in the time it takes for her to make out the letters.

In the presence of love, everything is beautifully healed, changed, transformed.

> The best way to know God is to love many things.
> —*Vincent Van Gogh, Dutch artist, 1853-1890*

Like in the children's stories of "Sleeping Beauty" and "Snow White," it takes Love to awaken love. The wicked can try to kill beauty (love), or put beauty (love) to sleep, but Love (God) always comes to awaken love. When a frog becomes a prince after being kissed by a princess, it shows how our highest potential naturally blossoms in the presence of love.

> If the heart be right, it matters not which way the head lies.
> —*Sir Walter Raleigh, British explorer, historian and poet,*
> *c. 1554-1618*

Looking back over the years, it seems like my love was for many things beginning with the letter "M." First of all there is "M" for Margaret, and after that, "M" for **m**y family, **m**edicine, **m**useums, **m**usic, **m**inerals, **m**ovies, **m**agic, **m**ystery (Christianity, Church, chemistry), **m**otion (skates, bikes, cars), **m**ental, **m**oney (coin collection), **m**iracles, and **m**ud and **m**ire (gardening, to which Margaret introduced me).

Now, you might say, "Why not the letter 'S' for interest in **s**cience, **s**ex, **s**ports (basketball and baseball as a child), **s**tamps (stamp collection), etc.?" Let's not forget "F" for **f**riends, "C" for **c**onventions attended, and "T" for **t**win, etc. It's said that you should mind your "P's and Q's", but it seems you should mind the whole alphabet.

Going to the movies made me "street smart," from seeing *The Dead End Kids*, gangster movies, and action flicks. When I was in the Boy Scouts, we put on a skit or little play in which we did imitations of movie stars and acted like Groucho Marx, the comedian. Groucho would say, "Walk this way, please." with a funny walk, and everyone would follow him walking just as funny as he was walking. And Groucho would pretend to be a doctor and he would say to the patient, "I'm the doctor!" And the patient would say, "I'm dubious!" and Groucho would say "Well, hello Mr. Dubious." I did imitations. I imitated the movie actors Peter Lorre, Walter Brennan, James Cagney and Edward G. Robinson. I sensed the love flowing up from the audience in sympathy with us on the stage as the audience laughed at our jokes, and as they relaxed and smiled, and understood in camaraderie that we were just amateurs trying our best to entertain them.

Love is the greatest gift and the greatest wonder.

> The world will never starve for want of wonders, only for (the) want of wonder.
> —*Gilbert Keith Chesterton, English writer, 1874-1936*

Breathless moments occur whenever the sight of invisible things such as truth, love and goodness by the eyes of our heart strikes us, giving us memorable beautiful impacts.

As a surgeon, I didn't mind the blood and gore, but what is challenging to a surgeon is getting up at 2:00 or 3:00 A.M. to be in the morgue alone, cutting out the eyes of a deceased eye donor to send to the eye bank.

Speaking of time, don't wait for retirement to do things. Work things in while you are still working at your career, because health issues may prevent you from doing all that you thought you would or could do in retirement.

Donation of your body parts after death is an act of love. Corneas available for transplant are in the ratio of one available to every one hundred needed. So that you only get one cornea at present if two are available, because the need is so great.

There is a balance in life. Doctors are leaving the practice of obstetrics due to the lawsuits, and they are leaving other fields, too.

Doctors are retiring early as paperwork increases and litigious risks increase. The doctors say, "It's no fun anymore." Additionally, if it takes from January to April to pay for taxes, doctors have to work extra to pay for malpractice insurance premiums that may be as high as $120,000 or more a year. There comes a point where it's not worth the time, effort, and risk to work, particularly if there is much overwork caused by staffing shortages from doctors leaving so that there is the feeling of being constantly on call. I used to work every other night and every other weekend, and then my schedule later in life was every third night and every third weekend. The first schedule felt like constantly working, and the later schedule felt more like having a little time off. But both are grueling. You can't go to work feeling tired all the time. Surgery in the morning and overfull clinics in the afternoon and covering emergencies at night is too much to expect of anyone.

The best things in life are not visible things. The best thing in life is love, and love is not a visible thing. God's best gifts are not visible gifts but rather, invisible opportunities. All of the values, virtues, ideals, and principles are invisible things, which are also included in the best things in life.

Love's truisms:

- Prayer is the overflow of inner love.

- You can only live your life for love.

- Love turns the other cheek to our slaps.

- True love is willing to suffer. Love is the Cross.

- That is what love is, what love does, and what love receives, suffering.

- Love can change an end into a beginning.

St. Teresa of Avila (Carmelite nun, Spanish visionary mystic, 1515-1582) said that from heaven, the most miserable earthly life will look like one bad night in an inconvenient hotel!

The next three chapters move us from a lower level to a higher level of understanding of what transformation is, and the relationship of transformation to duality and trinity.

Chapter 6.

Duality (Polarity and More)

There are two kinds of people in this world, those who divide the world into two kinds of people, and those who don't.
—*Robert Benchley, American humorist and newspaper columnist, 1889-1945*

The greatest good you can do for another is not just share your riches, but to reveal to him his own.
—*Benjamin Disraeli, British Prime minister and novelist, 1804-1881*

A *duality* is defined as twofold, double, dual, duo, binary, two parts, a pair, bi-polar, a couple, a duad, a twin, dualistic or a dualism.

A duality is any thinking in terms of two or any categorizing in terms of two—in other words, any coupling of two terms. Duality is a world view, a way of seeing, but there is always more than two. Coupling comes out of the way that we speak, because we always use such terms as: them/us, either/or, but/also, the opposite is, both, then/now, in contrast, by comparison, two out of three, twins, twinning, etc.. We also, are always being confronted with the truth striking us in the back of the head and in the dark, which means the sudden unexpected truth, which is opposite or new to what we are thinking. All of that makes us think that two is all that there is to life. And life to us becomes a twofold philosophy or *a point of view of two*.

You will find duality everywhere because it is ubiquitous, prevalent, and all pervasive. This chapter will prove that point. A clear picture of duality is needed in order to contrast it with Trinity, which is the next chapter. Trinity is an elevation from duality, which will bring us closer to our understanding of transformation, which is the chapter after trinity.

Duality comes not only out of the way that we speak and the way that truth strikes us, but also, from the choices that we have. For example: In medicine there are many horns-of-a-dilemma in which there exists a delicate balance between the therapeutic dose and the side effects of medication, or between the choice of surgery and/or radiotherapy, as in prostate cancer, for example.

Additionally, duality is pervasive in the way secular science avoids spirit or spirituality, which is the third part of being human. There are three parts to being human: first, our mind seeks truth; second, our heart seeks love and third, our spirit seeks goodness and God. The spirit that a person has is more than personality, or their mood, or the amount of energy that they have, or the level of their emotional state, or their demeanor. It is something more, something beyond, which we call their soul, and which relates to character, morality, immortality, spirituality, goodness, and God.

Life seen from the point of view of only two is shown in the following examples of duality:

hot–cold	day–night
left–right	front–back
top–bottom	before–after
parietal–visceral	inside–outside
secular–sacred	letter of law–spirit of law
divine–human	whole–broken
conservative–liberal	traditional–modern
judgment–mercy	beautiful–ugly
old–new	success–failure
organic–inorganic	order–chaos
linear–cyclical	visible–invisible
seen–unseen	reality–illusion
truth–lies	cooperation–competition
yes-no	happy–sad

Chart 3. Examples of Duality

Here are two examples of how we think and speak in duality:

1.) People don't do what you expect, they do what you inspect.

2.) John Foster Dulles (Secretary of State of the United States, 1888-1959) said, "The measure of success is not whether you have a tough problem to deal with, but whether it is the same problem you had last year." Notice the duality thinking relating to problems: old/new, last year/this year, then/now, same/not same, success/failure. But above the duality of the problems is a third way of thinking, namely, measuring success, and finding what constitutes real success. In this example, if your point of view about life is only the duality of problems, then you will miss seeing the measuring of success as a third way out of the duality of problems. This may be clarified by the next paragraph below.

I explained in the Introduction that my wife and I were able to get into the garden of transformation with our son by experiencing the love and concerns of a vast group of medical personnel, family and friends, and many others who were struggling with their own similar medical situations. Also, prayer and having faith helped a lot. We moved into the garden with the help of faith, hope and love. We needed that help to get out of the duality of joy and sorrow or consolation and desolation. We needed that "more," that third way, namely, spirituality and all of its values, virtues, ideals, and principles, including truth, love, and goodness. The word "spirituality" can be substituted for the word "transformation." When we are transformed, we are more spiritual; we gain more spirituality, we go from consolation and desolation to "spiritualization" (transformation).

Simone Weil (French author, 1909-1943) pointed out that every separation is a link. She pointed this out when she said: "Two prisoners whose cells adjoin communicate with each other by knocking on the wall. The wall is the thing that separates them but it is also their means of communication." It is the same with God (spirituality) and us. Every separation is simply a possible way to link us and God (spirituality).

Every time we experience the separation of opposite contrasts of consolation and desolation, joy and sorrow, like two mirrors facing away from each other, we should stay aware of the existence of a link, which is a third way. Transformation is our link with love and with God, who is love, and with all of the values, virtues, ideals and principles (spirituality).

Normally, consolation and desolation seem so widely separated and opposite that they are like seeing two sides of a coin, and we just notice the impressions or illusions of heads or tails and miss seeing the link of precious metal of which the coin itself is made. Or we just see both separated ends of a stick (duality, bi-polarity), which are just the limits of the whole stick and we fail to notice the whole stick by being distracted by the separated duality of two contrasting opposite ends. There is always a third way, the precious metal of the coin itself or the solid stick itself, both representing, symbolically, love, which is the link of all links and a kind of common denominator.

A third way, in addition to love, includes any of the other values as well, such as truth, goodness, beauty, humor, worship, etc., which constitutes our transformation into higher levels of thinking and living. Duality reminds us that every time you are stuck on the horns-of-a-dilemma or are confronted with paradox, look up from that duality for the third way as your way out, because any separation can be a link.

Dr. M. Scott Peck (psychiatrist and author, 1936-2005) said, "Until you value yourself, you won't value your time. Until you value your time, you will not do anything with it." The two values of yourself and your time are a duality. The third way out is doing something of value.

You immediately know there is more when you consider the pessimistic aphorism: "The world is divided into two categories: failures and unknowns." There is at least another category of celebrity successes, which adds some optimism.

Visible and invisible are a duality. We have our visible government in Washington, and we have nature's laws, which are the invisible government of the earth. The third way out of this duality is spirituality and God's moral laws, in distinction from Government's laws and nature's laws. There is always more than just duality. A life of secular or scientific duality (mind and heart) is living a life that is diminished when it avoids spirituality.

A world without God is diminished in love, because God is love. Secular philosophies containing a life without God are illustrated in the chart below:

Man is god =	Humanism, Eastern esotericism
Life without God =	Secularism, Scientism, Atheism
Life without the spiritual =	Materialism, Indifferentism, Modernism, Consumerism

Chart 4. Secular Philosophies Containing a Life without God

The coupling of two terms into a duality is done in three ways:

1.) A contrasting opposite polarity (bi-polar);

2.) Two out of three related terms; and

3.) Any coupling of two related terms.

1.) A contrasting opposite polarity (bi-polar).

Symbolically, the two terms are like two mirrors facing away from each other. Those who divide everything into a duality, such as: positive and negative, happy and sad, mind and heart, day and night, front and back, organic and inorganic, do so because everything has its polar opposite. The "rational thinking" of the mind has its opposite "irrational emotion" of the heart. This goes along with the old oriental expression: ***"The very instant that beauty was discovered, ugliness was born."*** The two opposites seem solidly interrelated, like the act of selling is related with the act of buying, or the act of giving is related with the act of receiving.

Another example: Some people are so heavenly minded that they are no earthly good, and vice-versa, some people are so earthly minded that they are no good to heaven.

2.) Two out of three related terms.

They are not just randomly chosen, but there is some relationship to each other, and that relationship is not strictly opposite, as polar opposites are. For example: Truth and love are related as a duality in the expression, "Love increases by means of truth, and love draws near by means of truth" (Pope John Paul II, Polish Pope, 1920-2005).

Truth and love are two out of three terms that are themselves all related: truth (mind), love (heart), and goodness (spirit). We find that these three qualities are all related to being human, because the mind seeks truth, the heart seeks love, and the spirit seeks goodness and God.

3.) Any coupling of two related terms.

The two terms may seem to be random, but they are related in some way, such as "to be useful and happy." Notice in the following list that there is some relationship in the following terms that seem, at first, to be random.

Each two represent a duality.

You are meant:

- Not just to look but to laugh.

- Not just to learn, but to live.

- Not just to live, but to love.

- Not just to teach, but to touch, move, transform, open, enkindle, inflame, fire-up and emblazon.

- Not just to know, but to be known.

- Not just to point the way, but to follow it.

- Not just to proclaim, but to plant.

- Not just to touch base, but to get home.

Dualities always suggest something more, something higher. And I explain that more fully in the next Chapter 7, entitled "Trinity" and Chapter 8, entitled "Transformation."

Because I'm a twin, I notice anything that's double more than another person might. And so I simplify by calling any combination of two a "duality," just to recognize the fact that there is always more than two, because there is trinity or three. This knowing that there is more beyond becomes important when we realize that in our secular society, we have a modern horns-of-a-dilemma paradox of duality in the fact that people kill in order to preserve life and that they sometimes violate their values in order to maintain those values.

This is seemingly in violation of three ethical principles that have always been found to be true, namely:

1. Might does not make right.

Just because you can take candy from a baby doesn't make it right. And just because you have a large army doesn't make it right to take over any nearby weaker country. The reverse is true, that right makes might. Abraham Lincoln (16th President of the United States, 1809-1865) said, "Let us have faith that right makes might and in that faith, let us, to the end, dare to do our duty as we understand it. Be sure to put your feet in the right place, then stand firm."

2. **The end doesn't justify the means.**

You cannot kill someone just because you think that doing so will make the world better or safer. Doing so makes you judge, jury and executioner.

3. **Always choose the lesser of two evils.**

If you have a choice between punching a teacher who is going to flunk you or flunking, choose flunking.

Of two evils, we must always choose the least.

As I mentioned in Chapter 2, as a child, I felt isolated, as though I were living in a parallel world, because I felt way behind everyone else. And as a twin, I felt different from everyone else who was not a twin. And the older I got, the more I felt caught in the middle balancing the duality of science and religion. Living a third way, I was precariously balanced at the fulcrum of a see-saw. I was balanced between flood-light and spotlight, between holistic religion and reductionist science, between seeing the big picture and seeing only a part. I was between the philosophies of the East (Orient) and the West (Occident).

Holistic deals with the big picture, leading to such expressions as: "You cannot disturb the weakest flower without disturbing a star." It's the classic "butterfly effect" of the small perturbations of a but-terfly's wings flapping in China giving rise to rain in America. It emphasizes the interconnectedness of everything.

So, out of the feelings in my own life, I was always keenly aware of duality (two, double, paired, coupled, duo, dual, binary, bi-polarity). When I met my wife to be, Margaret, I became keenly aware of trinity (three, tri, triple, triangle, trinity). Although I was happy as a twin, I was even happier with Margaret. Twins are the same, but Margaret is different. The greatest happiness is love. I love Don as a brother, but Margaret I love as my beloved spouse. She is like a different country to me that is mysterious and changeable. A spouse you savor and appreciate without attempting to understand or predict in any way.

> Love is the only gold.
> —*Alfred Lord Tennyson, British Poet Laureate, 1809-1892*

There are two types of people in the world: those who come into the room and say, "Well, here I am!" and those who come into the room and say, "Ah, there you are!" And in surgery, there are two kinds of people, yourself and those who look at your work and say, "That's what you did, but I would have done it differently." I recall using a flexible scope to inspect both large-bowel channels of a colostomy to see if the bowel could be safely repaired, when another surgeon came in, remarking that he would have repaired the bowel at the first operation without making a colostomy in order to save the patient a second operation. I said, "You should have been there at the original operation to see the condition of the bowel to realize that the safer course at that time was a colostomy." There is no argument against experience and actually being there at the time of decisions.

There is a lot of duality in the world. In psychology, the distinction is between physical and mental. The two are combined into the word "psychosomatic." In theology, the distinction is between good and evil, the Creator and the creature, and mankind having two basic natures, physical (natural) and spiritual.

And many aphorisms and truisms are worded as a duality. Poets, writers, and aphorists keep pointing out duality; for example:

1. There are two kinds of light—the glow that illuminates and

the glare that obscures.
—*James Thurber, American humorist and cartoonist, 1894-1961*

2. I will love the light for it shows me the way, yet I will endure the darkness because it shows me the stars.
   —*Og Mandino, American essayist and psychologist, 1923-1996*

3. The fire which enlightens is the same fire which consumes.
   —*Henri Frederic Amiel, Swiss author, 1821- 1881*

4. Only by losing sight of the land can you find the stars.

5. The ocean contains all rivers (trinity is found in: "but not all lakes").

6. Things may come to those who wait, but only the things left by those who hustle.
   —*Abraham Lincoln, 16th President of the United States, 1809-1865*

7. Don't ask God to guide your footsteps if you're not willing to move your feet.

8. Living is a thing you do. Now or never—which do you?
   —*Piet Hein, Danish author, poet and inventor, 1905-1996*

Growing up with a twin brother is a blessing, because you always have someone your own age to compete equally in games. However, another person, even a twin, doesn't have exactly the same interests as you do. I went into Surgery and Don went into Internal Medicine. By being a twin, I could always feel the duality of contrast between cooperation and competition. I also felt the duality of comparison, with people always comparing me with my brother. I believe that helped me to see other dualities more easily.

I could envision the duality of visible/invisible, organic/inorganic, linear/cyclical, etc.

Additionally, what may have helped me understand duality was being interested in magic and having a chemistry set as a child. With magic, the contrast of reality and illusion is obvious, and with chemistry the contrast or duality of what is seen and what is acting unseen is demonstrated in every chemical reaction.

When my wife, Margaret and I went to see Blackstone the magician on one of our early dates, we were in the first row, and the magician asked for volunteers to come up on the stage to verify what he was doing. He pointed to me to come up on the stage with several others. He had a card that he showed the audience, and then, at some point in the trick, we were to verify later that this was the card that was found. But the magician whispered to us all to go along and say, "That's the card," when it wasn't. Especially with magic, there is that age old lesson of the duality of truth and lies. At this point, you may be feeling that I am belaboring this point about duality, but I want you to feel just how prevalent it is in our lives. And I want you to get a clear understanding of duality so that you can see the difference between it and trinity, which is the next chapter.

Competing for grades in school is a duality balancing act between cooperation and competition. This was shown clearly to me in college when I took Analytic Chemistry. We were all given an unknown to analyze. The first substance I had to identify was a piece of native sulfur. Since my brother, Don, and I grew up with a chemistry set, I could recognize sulfur just by looking at it, and so when I went through the analytic steps, I knew what I was analyzing and what I was expecting it to be.

Having had a chemistry set at home, I was comfortable with bending my own glass tubing and working with reagents. You clean your glassware and put pure reagents together to use in the analytic testing. Sure enough, after going through the steps of analysis, I found sulfur. One jealous, competitive classmate asked to borrow my reagents and deliberately contaminated them; therefore, I got the next analysis wrong. I knew right away that there was something wrong with the reagents. It was a chore to clean my glassware and to get more of the pure reagents together again, but the professor and I were now keenly aware of how competitive the pre-med classroom was becoming.

I always keep my eyes open for competition versus cooperation, because it is keenly felt by twins. When I was in the Air Force, I saw competition in other airmen as they tried to get a good price when buying something. A flight surgeon would come back from Spain with a footstool that looked like an odd saddle-shape, made of leather, and he would tell other doctors of the bargain price that he paid for it. And, sure enough, others would pay him to get them a footstool at a bargain price, whenever he was back in Spain on a flight. Then they would brag about how inexpensive it was to others. But frankly, I wouldn't want the footstool, because it just didn't look good and it wasn't that functional. One of our doctors on the base had a reputation for never buying anything retail unless he could have the price lowered, even just a little bit, and he did this by talking to the manager. It was like a hobby of his to go into the nearby town and try to buy something on which the price was lowered.

We humans seem afflicted with the duality of competition versus cooperation. We also have the duality of sensitive awareness versus indifference.

When we are young, we are incredibly sensitive. Let me give you my prime example. My brother and I used to go onto the roof of the apartment house where we lived and where my dad worked. The roof was a place to go and to get away as a child. One time, I threw a light bulb off the roof to hear it smash down below in the alley between our building and the next building. It didn't sound at all like a gun shot, which is what I was expecting it to sound like. Then I wanted to see if I could toss a bulb all across the divide between our building and the next building to the other roof. I tossed it hard, but the light bulb was too light (not a pun) and, as a child, my arm was too weak, and the light bulb fell in a descending arc right into the middle of a large picture window of a bank, which was in the other building. The light bulb failed to go over to the other roof, and as it kept dropping lower, I could see it heading for disaster. I high-tailed it out of there to hide under my bed. As I ran, I could hear the bulb as it smashed into the window, and I could picture a cracked window as the very minimum of damage. Our best friend from school was visiting us just then, and he came into my room and asked why I was hiding. I explained, and he said that the bank's picture window smashed and the police are there and it's quite a scene. I was horrified and terrified with alarm. Then he laughed and said that nothing really happened except that the bulb broke and not the window. I was so relieved and sad at the same time, as I thought how insensitive he was to me, knowing that I was so sensitive about the whole situation and so scared. I promised myself that I would never be that insensitive to anyone else.

In Villanova College, now a university, I was required to take a semester of Public Speaking in the pre-med curriculum. I remember how each of us had to stand up in class, which was difficult at my stage of growth. How hard and embarrassing it was on that first day of class for me just to stand and say my name, which was expected from everyone else in my class. How sensitive I was to the idea of making a mistake. I believe that was part of my dysfunctional childhood. Adult Children of Alcoholics (ACoA's) feel that they are a mistake. And they are afraid to make a mistake (God doesn't make mistakes.). That was how the course in Public Speaking started on the very first day of class, but we all grew more by the end of that class. One thing I've always remembered from our textbook on public speaking is that "Poise is to pause and pose." The presence of two things in a duality implies that there is more, a third thing. Pausing and posing suggests something more, poise.

Nevertheless, when we are young we are all incredibly sensitive. Hillary Clinton tells a story about the time she came home with a report card that was all "A's," and her father, instead of complimenting her, said, "Well, I guess your school is too easy!" She felt very badly, and you could tell she still does, and I'm sure her dad was just making a joke with her.

To a sensitive child, telling them the wrong thing can be psychologically toxic.

In addition to toxic situations and/or people in your life, there can be physical toxins in your life, as well.
When I think back on my life, because of my scientific interests, I had opportunities to be exposed to numerous toxins. I'd break long fluorescent lights and scrape the beryllium powder, which then coated the inner walls, off the glass tube. I would put the powder into a small, glass container as part of a fluorescent display exhibit. However, I was careful and I tried to avoid breathing in the toxic beryllium dust, because breathing beryllium dust causes a fibrotic lung disease called berylliosis.

In school, we coated silver dimes with mercury to see the bright slippery shiny amalgam appearance that occurred. I tried to pay a bus fare with one of the dimes and the driver threw the dime on the counter of the bus while muttering something, which probably included the word "counterfeit." My clever joke was not appreciated.

I melted my lead soldiers. I was exposed to coal dust and cigarette smoke. I grew up with years of pesticides, insecticides, herbicides, vehicle exhaust fumes, fluoridation of drinking water and toothpaste, lack of sunscreen, the use of a sunlamp to treat acne, and other environmental hazards such as lead paint. And I received, for a short time, female hormone therapy for acne that resulted in feminization of my bones. That became a blessing in disguise, as my small hands and arms were an asset in surgery. There is an old expression in surgery: "A surgeon must have the heart of a lion, the eye of an eagle, and the hands of a woman."

And to top it all off, when I was growing up, we didn't wear any bike helmets! I recall one childhood incident when my sled hit the rear wheel of a parked car on the street that I was sledding down. I felt so relieved that I didn't accidentally go under the car.

The truth is that living is a matter of life and death, and it is hard to grow up unscathed. Protect yourself physically, mentally, emotionally, and morally.

Because of my involvement with science all my life, and because of religion in my life from my parents and from my own faith and practices, and because of my feelings of being caught in the middle, I have been balancing most of my life on a seesaw between nature controlled by science's human thought and human thought controlled by love in religion. I have lived between the floodlight of holistic religion and the spotlights of science, where science breaks everything into parts to study. Breaking anything into parts takes away some of its meaning. A sensitive person going through life feels precariously balanced between many divisions. Being caught in the middle only serves to make you feel that there's a third way. I know that's true, because I've been there and felt that. I'm sure you have, too.

Duality confronts us everywhere, and it's important that you get a feel of how prevalent it is. Please bear with me as I give you some further examples of duality from my life:

When I was in grammar school (the first eight grades), there was a bully in one of my classes. My twin brother, who loves me, tried to tip me off that this bully always backs down if you stand up to him, and that this backing down is guaranteed. And Don said that the bully would be coming up to me shortly and that I should just stand up to him. Sure enough, the bully came up loud-mouthed; I stood up to him and verbally snapped back at him, and he backed down. What helped was my brother standing there and whispering in my ear: "Not to worry, just stand up to him, it always works, and he will back down." My inability to stand up for myself as a child at that time of life may have been a reflection of the low self-esteem that is part of being a child of an alcoholic. I was amazed at how it all played out and I wondered how my brother knew the bully was coming for me. Don, himself, must have been tipped off. Duality or division is illustrated here in the balance between peace/conflict, knowledge/ignorance, fear/courage, isolation/unity and self-esteem/ lack of esteem.

My brother, Don, and I wanted to go to Jefferson Medical College (now called a university), but we were first accepted by all three of the other medical schools in our Philadelphia area (Hahnemann, Drexel and University of Pennsylvania). Since the other three schools wanted to know soon about our acceptance or not, we used our acceptance at the other three to get an answer from Jefferson, which made their selections later than these other medical schools. I remember one of the interview questions to get into Jefferson was, "Why do you want to go to medical school?" Everyone knew that the wrong answer is, "I lived near a hospital, and so I always wanted to go there." That's the equivalent of saying: "I'm in a garage, so that should make me a car." We honestly could say that we were interested in helping people, and we were always interested in science, and we named the science museums we visited in the Philadelphia area, including the Mutter Museum of pathologic medical specimens. Being accepted at other medical schools but wanting to be accepted at Jefferson medical school was the duality that we were living at the time.

Life is not just a duality of consolation, with its comforts, and desolation, with its suffering. Life is not just mountains and valleys, or even just two parallel rails like a railroad track, where good and bad are going on at the same time. We all, eventually, begin to ask if duality is all that there is. It's then that we discover that *there is always more*, there is always a third way, something higher than two. We discover that third way out of consolation and desolation, leading to transformation by finding higher levels of thinking and living. We often overlook love, the highest thing possible, that is always present, which is the transformation from out of our consolation and/ or desolation. Love is the reason why male and female transforms into a child, and love is the reason why any dualism can creatively progress into something higher.

Katherine Mansfield (New Zealand author, 1888-1923) said, "Everything in life that we accept undergoes a change, so suffering must become love, that is the mystery." However, to undergo a change, we must truly accept our suffering, and that means we must willingly carry our cross. Only love can help you carry a cross. Love is the way to transformation. God is love. God is the way to transformation. In addition to physical and mental, there is also spiritual. Humans are a trinity of body, mind *and* spirit. The spirit, or spiritual, deals with Love and with Other (God, who is love) and with all of the accompanying values, virtues, ideals, and principles, the possession of which is transforming.

Some words to a song are: "Since love is Lord of heaven and earth, how can I stop from singing." In the same way that we are not designed to love alone, we are not designed to celebrate or suffer alone. And since love is above all things, and love is such a joy, we can't help but to sing out with rejoicing. We are not alone; we have God who is love. And you can't love alone.

Duality is found in the works of many songwriters, writers, authors and poets. They know all about duality, and most of them also know all about something further beyond, called spirituality, which includes love.

> "We are all in the mud, but some of us are looking at the stars."
> — *Oscar Wilde, Irish author and poet, 1854-1900*

> Two men looked out from prison bars; one saw mud, the other stars.
> —*Martin D. Buxbaum. Virginian Poet, born 1912*

Edward Rowland Sill (American Poet, 1841-1887) wrote a poem that resonates with me, which is called "The Fool's Prayer." It shows duality by contrasting a king and his jester, and it contrasts other things that I'll point out at the end of the poem. But it also shows transformation. (I've changed the poem's wording slightly to read more like modern English.)

> The royal feast was done; the King
> Sought some new sport to banish care,
> And to his jester cried: Sir Fool,
> Kneel now, and make for us a prayer.
>
> The jester took off his cap and bells,
> And stood before the mocking court;
> They couldn't see the bitter smile
> Behind the painted grin he wore
>
> He bowed his head, and bent his knee
> Upon the monarch's silken stool;
> His pleading voice arose: "O Lord,
> Be merciful to me a fool.
>
> It's not pity, Lord, that changes the heart
> From red with wrong to white as wool;
> Punishment must heal the sin: but You O Lord,
> Be merciful to me a fool!
>
> It's by guilt alone that we stop the
> Onward march of truth and right, O Lord;
> It's also by our follies that we hold so long
> Heaven away from earth.
>
> These clumsy feet, still in the mud and mire
> Go crushing blossoms endlessly.
> These hard, well-meaning hands we thrust
> Among the heartstrings of a friend.
>
> The truths that we spoke so ill-timed
> Who knows how badly those words hurt?
> The words we didn't have sense to say
> Who knows how grandly they might have rung out?

We shouldn't ask any tenderness for our faults
Whippings must cleanse them all.
But for our blunders in shame
Before the eyes of heaven we fall.

Earth has no comfort for mistakes.
Men crown the knave and whip the tool
That only does his will. But You, O Lord,
Be merciful to me a fool!

The room was hushed; in silence rose
The King, and sought his gardens cool,
And he walked apart, and murmured low,
"O Lord, be merciful to me a fool!"

The duality in this poem is shown not only in the contrast of king and jester, advantaged versus disadvantaged, but in the contrast between words that could have been spoken or not, and in the jester praying for the king, on the one hand, and insulting the king, on the other hand, in referring to the fact that men crown the knave (the king) and whip the tool (the jester) who only does the king's will, which will was for the jester to say a prayer. And there is a duality in the king insulting the jester by asking for the prayer and the jester insulting the king in the prayer. And there is duality in the court mocking the jester who with a bitter smile says a mocking prayer. The jester is asking for God's mercy, when it should be the king who is asking for God's mercy, because of the king's arrogance and lack of humility and lack of compassion. The king is missing these values in the beginning of the poem when he is with the crowd at court, but the king finds these values at the end of the poem when he is alone in his garden.

Transformation is shown by the values, virtues, ideals, and principles, which make up the spirit and soul. The virtue of mercy is shown by the fact that the king is merciful to the fool in letting the jester's insult to the king pass. God is merciful to the fool just as the fool's prayer requests God to be. The king seeing his folly is an answer to prayer. And the loving God is merciful to both the king and the jester in that they both are able to see invisible values enough for them both to become sincere as they pray to God for His mercy. Mercy, like love, is all-encompassing and encompasses all in the poem.

Additionally, the king's humility and recognition of his being arrogantly overbearing is the beginning of true greatness and transformation for the king. Bishop Fulton J. Sheen (Roman Catholic Bishop, author, 1895-1979) symbolically pointed to humility when he pointed out that the branch that hangs the lowest has the most fruit. And the building that has the deepest foundation rises the tallest.

Another poem illustrating duality is "The Measure of a Man" by an unknown author:

> Not—"How did he die?" But—"How did he live?"
> Not—"What did he gain?" But—"What did he give?"
> These are the units to measure the worth
> Of a man as a man, regardless of birth.
> Not—"What was his station?" But—"Had he a heart?"
> And—"How did he play his God-given part?"
> Was he ever ready with a word of good cheer,
> To bring back a smile, to banish a tear?"
> Not—"What was his church?" Not—"What was his creed?"
> But—"Had he befriended those really in need?"
> Not—"What did the sketch in the newspaper say?"
> But—"How many cried when he passed away?"

Duality is found in the contrasts of opposites, such as die/live, gain/give, and not what the man seemed to be but who he really was, measured on a scale of this or that. Transformation arches above the duality of contrasts (bi-polarity) to trump them by all encompassing love, which is shown by those crying over their lost loved one, who was loving to others in his lifetime doing his God-given part.

A surgeon gets to see a lot of "man's inhumanity to man" in knife stabbings and slashings and gunshot wounds. It's the opposite of love. It's part of a pattern of defenses called fight, fright, flight, fun, and falsity which I'll elaborate on in Chapter 13, entitled "Defenses." People wonder how a doctor, particularly a surgeon, gets used to seeing all that blood and guts. It's a gradual apprenticeship of moving from one phase to another. In any career, it takes doing whatever you're doing again and again to get good at anything. You get used to it. There are literally hundreds of knots that have to be tied in any major surgical operation. And it's possible to tell just by how fast a knot is being tied what is the level of someone's surgical experience. And it's not just the speed but also the care in seeing that the knot is properly tied and set. An apprentice surgeon working up the ranks from internship to residency, to assistant surgeon, to surgeon with attending-doctor oversight, to your own practice, requires years of a constant series of practice and training with evaluations by others before you are officially certified as a surgeon. It requires many written tests and practical tests. You live the duality of: you can do it, or you can't; you will make it, or you won't.

The tensions of a duality creates new activity, new thinking, and dialogue in an attempt to bring out the best, to bring about some balance—a third way of thinking. It generally is accompanied by compromises so that no one gets exactly all that they want, but they do get more than they had in just the duality.

The partisanship of politics, which recently is so often a stalemate, needs to learn the lesson of compromise, which follows discussion and dialogue. Both sides, who are opposite (duality), need to know that there is always a third way (trinity) out of stalemate, and the way out is based on higher values, virtues, ideals, and principles—namely, spirituality.

Life is not supposed to be a process of having and getting, but a process of being and becoming, of giving and not getting. You can't take it with you. The only thing that you can take to heaven is love.

Nevertheless, I have a hobby of mineral collecting, and I am ashamed to say, collecting seems so much like having and getting. Maybe it's part of being a twin and finally having something of my very own, for myself. It does have its share of giving in that my wife and I teach about rocks and minerals, and we give each student a grab-bag full of labeled mineral and crystal specimens. It also has its share of being, because it seems to be who I am and who I'm being. I'm a rock hound, and I'm not alone. There are others like me, but I still have that sense of isolation, or being out of the mainstream, because my hobby seems to be the one hobby in which the general public seems generally uninterested.

Can you call this hobby a conspicuous conscious compulsion of consumption, an obsession, or a helpful hoarding instinct? Am I that compulsive and/or neurotic? I like to rationalize it as an interest in both science and art, because nature artistically develops crystal shapes into things of aesthetic beauty. And art is the dualistic opposite of science. Perhaps it relates to my father working in the Shenandoah, Pennsylvania, coalmines when I was very young, and my being a rock hound is my attempt to get closer to my dad vicariously. Or maybe it's the fact that when my twin brother, Don, and I made our visits to the museums in downtown Philadelphia, we saw one of the world's best mineral collections, which sadly was sold in 2006 by the Philadelphia Academy of Natural sciences. And maybe it's my attempt to get closer to my childhood, vicariously, by my taking a sentimental journey of mineral nostalgia.

In any event, my interest in minerals allowed our children to go "rock hounding" into quarries with me, and they won science fairs. Children, by the way, are not called rock hounds but *pebble pups*.

This chapter on duality has by now convinced you, even over convinced you, of the pervasive, prevalent and ubiquitous (everywhere) nature of the philosophy of two. So now it's time to move up to the philosophy of three, trinity, which is the next chapter, as we progress in our understanding of transformation and its relationship to duality and trinity.

Chapter 7.

Trinity

What lies behind us and what lies before us are tiny matters compared to what lies within us.
—*Oliver Wendell Holmes, Associate Justice of the United States Supreme Court, 1841-1935*

As each specialty or discipline rises it will converge.
—*Pierre Teilhard de Chardin, S.J., philosopher, author, Jesuit priest, 1881-1955*

In the same way that some people divide everything into two, as we've seen in the last chapter, there are some people who divide everything into three. Those who divide everything into two use such categories as: living and non-living, organic and inorganic and terrestrial and extra-terrestrial. Those who divide everything into three use such categories as: things found, which are animal, vegetable (plants), or mineral; things found, which are in the sea, on land, or in the air; and things found, which are in our solar system, in our galaxy, or in our intergalactic system.

We've already considered the division into three of city, desert, garden or consolation, desolation, transformation. Trinity is also found in: Creator, creature, and creation.

Trinity is defined as a third way (three, trio, triple) beyond the two of duality. Trinity leads to transformation.

Transformation:

Trinity is not transformation. But trinity can lead to thinking about, and living with, high levels of values, virtues, ideals, and principles, the possession of which constitutes transformation. I'll cover trans-formation in the next chapter. In this chapter I want to give you a clear picture of trinity, so that you will not confuse trinity with trans-formation. Some examples below, will help to clarify that.

For example: There is a trinity in waves of light, or in any wave, be-cause there are three parts to a wave. These three parts are frequency (wavelength), phase (relative position of crests and troughs), and amplitude (wave magnitude). Science breaks everything down into parts, which tends to take away the meaning of the whole.

Waves of light in a sunset can be scientifically broken down into that trinity, but transformation is the higher experience beyond trinity of enjoying the sunset and what it does to a human being's mind, heart, and spirit or what it does thoughtfully, emotionally, and spiritually. Science rationally thinks about waves in terms of three or trinity, but human beings go beyond that trinity to feel emotionally lifted to a higher level of thinking and living as they are reminded by sunsets of love, spirituality, and God. Transformation is further explored in the next chapter entitled "Transformation."

Another example is in the attractiveness of flowers to insects. It has been shown that color and scent influence a flower's attractiveness to insect pollinators—but a third way, beyond that duality to make a trinity, is the slimness of the flower's stem. The ability of a flower to sway in the breeze beckons pollinators, as suggested by a study from Wales' Aberystwyth University. Sea campion plants with slim stems attracted the most insects, as they fluttered more than flowers with average size stems. The average stemmed plants, however, set the most seed, because pollinators visited more stable flowers for longer. The study is the first evidence that a trinity of waviness, color, and scent are influences of a flower's attractiveness to insect pollinators. But human beings go beyond that trinity to feel lifted into a higher level of living as they are reminded by flowers of love, spirituality, and God. A woman given flowers feels loved and special.

Humans, in their natural tendency to categorize and condense, choose three over a duality, partly because trinity includes all three qualities that make us human. A human being is not just mind (truth), and heart (love), but is also a third quality, namely, spirit (goodness), which leads to spirituality, soul, and God, from which we receive our transformation. Secular science wants to ignore and not deal with this third spiritual quality of being human and so tries to concern itself with just rational and emotional (mind and heart). But by being able to see all of the three aspects of what makes us human, we can make statements that are more complete, such as: "You should not let compliments go to your head, or criticisms go to your heart, or compromises go to your spirit." Charlotte Bronte (English novelist, poet, 1816-1855) said, "I try to avoid looking forward or backward and try to keep looking upward."

Humans summarized into three is shown in the following chart:

1	2	3
Body (Heart)	Mind	Spirit
Emotional	Rational	Spiritual
Physical	Mental	Moral
Sensual	Rational	Sacred
Feeling	Thinking	"Seeing"
Physician	Professor	Priest
Love	Truth	Goodness
Eros	Pathos	Logos

Chart 5. Humans Summarized into Three Qualities
(Note that this is similar to Chart 2 in Chapter 4, page 55)

The difference between *trinity*, which is a categorizing or division into three, and *transformation*, which is a higher third way, is that transformation is a higher level of thinking and living that is beyond both duality and trinity, which are both just category divisions. Transformation is a spiritual trumping of them both.

Poets, writers, and aphorists keep pointing out trinity, but not all of them point to transformation beyond trinity.

Here are some examples of just trinity being pointed out:

1. All mankind is divided into three classes: those that are immovable, those that are movable, and those that move.
   —*Benjamin Franklin, Founding Father of the United States, 1706-1790*

2. There are three kinds of people in the world: those who learn by reading, those who learn by observation, and those who have to touch the fire to see if it's hot so they can learn by experience.

3. Humans are capable of three things: think, speak, and do.

4. The universe is not hostile, nor yet is it friendly. It is simply indifferent.
   —*John Henry Holmes, author, 20ᵗʰ century*

Here are some examples of trinity referring to transformation beyond trinity. Transformation is where love conquers all and where you possess truth, love, goodness, and all of the values, virtues, ideals, and principles.

1. There is a land of the living and a land of the dead, and the bridge is love.
   —*Thornton Wilder (American author and playwright, 1897-1975)*

2. Some men succeed by what they *know*; some by what they *do*; and a few by what they *are*.
   —*Elbert Hubbard, American author and artist, 1856-1915*

3. Life is like a flower of consolation of beautiful appearance and fragrance but with the desolation of thorns, briars, and dewy tears all around it. But despite the tears and the thorns and the briars, transformation is the growing, blossoming, and blooming above everything else, just like all encompassing love.

4. I slept and dreamt that life was joy. I awoke and saw that life was service. I acted and behold, service was joy.
   —*Rabindranath Tagore, Indian poet, 1861-1941*

Remember, trinity is important because it is part of our awareness that there is always something more (transformation) beyond the categories of both duality and trinity. The duality of mind and heart is not all that there is to being human. There is a third quality that makes us human, and it is this third quality of spirit or spirituality, which brings us to all of the higher values, virtues, ideals, and principles, which like love, are above everything else.

To illustrate the importance of three (trio, triple, trinity) that can lead us to transformation in our analysis of life, some common trinities are listed in the chart below.

Body—Mind—Spirit	Money—Sex—Power
Faith—Hope—Charity	Anatomy—Physiology—Psychology
Dating—Engaged—Married	Poverty—Chastity—Obedience
Eyes—Heart—Brain	Sea—Land—Sky
Mother—Father—Child	Petting—Foreplay—Coitus
Father—Son—Holy Spirit	1st degree—-2nd degree—-3rd degree
Artist—Professor—Priest	Sun—Moon—Stars
Beauty—Truth—Goodness	Possible—Probable—Improbable
Eros—Logos—Agape	Time—Talent—Treasure
Light—Color—Sound	Grow—Bloom—Blossom
Past—Present—Future	Good—Better—Best
Positive—Negative—Neutral	Surgery—Medicine—Psychiatry
Time—Mass—Space	Giving—Loving—Forgiving
Awe—Wonder—Worship	Living—Loving—Laughing
Love—Beauty—Happiness	Physical—Aesthetic—Metaphysical
Big—Medium—Little	Birth—Life—Death
Rational—Imaginative— Inventive	Unseeable—Untouchable—Unknowable

Chart 6. Common Trinities

In the 2005 book, *Blink*, by Malcolm Gladwell (British-born Canadian journalist and author, born 1963), he points out that you can learn as much, or more, from one glance at a private space, sizing things up, than you can learn from hours of exposure to a public face. For example, what does one look at your bedroom, or your whole house, tell about you? We drink things in and then we get a hunch of a first impression. Brilliant generals are said to possess "Coup d'oeil," which is translated from the French to mean, "power of the glance." We can sometimes learn more in the blink of an eye than we can from long rational scientific analysis. There is a difference between a fast blink and a slow think, between instinctive and logical, between intuitive hunch and deliberate rational thinking, and between aesthetic judgment and scientific analysis. You know what you like and what you don't like, and you know it when you see it. Malcolm Gladwell in his book, *Blink*, tends to divide everything into two. It's possible to know, without knowing why we know. And it's also possible to know, even though you can never know everything. But there are *three qualities* that make us human. And because there are three, we can complete the three ways in which we can know quickly:

1.) Your *mind* can give you a snap judgment from just a quick slice of information, because your judgment is a logical choice based on your previous experiences. Your rapid cerebral cognition is like being on autopilot, adapting almost unconsciously to what you need. It's possible to make decisive, rapid-fire decisions under conditions of high pressure and with limited information. You can edit through vast quantities of information and find patterns that give understanding and not just informational knowledge, so that you can jump to a conclusion that turns out to be more often right than wrong.

2.) Your *heart* can give you an instinctive gut feeling as an emotional first-impression type of reaction of intuition that isn't entirely rational. You just know it, because it feels right or not.

3.) Your *spirit* can give you a sudden impact from serendipity, and its fortunate discovery, which seems to be more than coincidence, because it is a God-incidence. Within life's spontaneity and benevolence you find something beyond just thinking in rational words and pictures of the mind. It is, also, beyond just feelings of emotions in the heart. That something is beyond words and emotions. It is too fluid and amorphous. It is too non-verbal and too invisible. It is felt in the soul, like suddenly being in love. It is indescribable, indefinable and ineffable, because it is too overpoweringly lofty and sacred. Something can suddenly be learned by being in awe, wonder, and worship.

Engineers who design cars for Nissan/Ford Motor Co. use what is called a "third suit" to help modify car designs for older, aging drivers. Instead of using the term "old-age suit" they say, "third suit." Because older, more mature drivers may not like to be called by a "politically incorrect" term that makes them sound old. The suit approximates the effects of aging for purposes of designing a car, so that older persons can get in and out of the newly designed car, and drive it. Do you think they have first and second suits for youth and middle age, because of the trinity of youth, middle age, and old age?

The world always sees bullies uniting against the good. Bad guys get together into a gang, or a mafia, or a nation, or a group of nations. They come after you with a knife, and you get a gun. They come after you with a gun, and you get a machine gun, until finally you have to get an atom bomb. The good are asked by intimidating evil to pay "protection" fees. But all the crooks, bandits, pirates, thieves, and evildoers meet up against the high principles of decency and honor and goodness to their eventual defeat. It may take a long time, but light is stronger than darkness. Transformation is stronger than consolation and desolation. Love is stronger than hate or fear. Freedom is better than slavery. Tolerance and unity are better than bigotry. And kindness is better than cruelty. What adds more to one side over the other is spirituality (goodness), the third quality that makes us human besides truth (mind), and heart (love). We should never underestimate the blessing of goodness, as it brings us to something more and to something beyond.

I am blessed to have all five of my children graduate from college. Three went into science and two into art. One son became an electrical engineer, another a mechanical engineer with, later, a Masters in Business Administration (MBA), and a daughter became an Obstetrician and Gynecologist. One son almost obtained his master's degree in Communication, except that his cancer diagnosis cut the time for the defense of his dissertation too short. One daughter spent time training in Architecture, and she then went into Art. She teaches art in addition to accomplishing beautiful works of art. She recently won a First Place award for a clock that she designed that resembles Fenway Park in Boston, the home of the Boston Red Socks baseball team. It's a beautiful, one-of-a-kind grandfather clock with even a secret compartment to store signed baseballs. She is a single mom, raising her daughter alone, because her husband fell and struck his head, causing his death.

There is always more. A king once had a ring with the words: *"This too shall pass"* to remind him to be humble. It may also be useful to have a ring that says: *"There is always more."* One ring's saying is in the past, and the other ring's saying is in the future. It may be useful, also, to have a third ring for the present that says, *"Virtue is in the middle."*

Trinity's three, without the transformation, may be compared to a kind of spectrum. For example:

- Life is not all black and white, but many shades of gray.

- It is not just day and night, but twilight, and later it is dusk (the darker stage of twilight).

- It is not just hot and cold, but warm and lukewarm (mildly warm; tepid).

There are times when we can't see a trinity because there appears to be no "more" or no larger ground to contain a duality, or even no middle ground between duality's two contrasting ends. It is at these times that we should keep on looking for a bigger context that contains everything. This bigger context is like a common denominator in mathematics. Sunrise and sunset is a duality that disappears when you get a bigger floodlight picture by being out in space looking down on the earth and the sun, instead of being on the earth with a smaller spotlight picture on looking up.

There are two ways to communicate: verbal and non-verbal or audible and non-audible. Communication is the bigger context that includes all ways to communicate, including the visual and non-visual ways to communicate. Consider the buggy whip business. Before it went out of business, it considered itself to be only in the buggy whip business and not in the transportation business.

There are times when there appears to be no "more" and no larger-ground, and even no middle ground, but *only just one pole* of the polarity—for example, the illusion of advertising that there can be better and better without worse and worse. Also, there is the misconception that we can arrange everything to the desires of our mind without everything becoming undesirable. To advertising, it seems there is only one pole, but there really are two. Advertising, if truthful and with values, can transform the lives of its viewers. Henri Nouwen (Dutch priest and author, 1932-1996) said: "Somewhere we know that without silence, words lose their meaning, that without listening, speaking no longer heals, that without distance closeness cannot cure." Even though there might appear to be no larger ground and no middle ground and only one pole, you will find that there is always a duality from which an elevation to trinity, and then a further elevation to transformation can occur, to give you all of the values, virtues, ideals and principles that are in transformation.

The stock market is a classic example of being fooled into thinking that there is only one pole. There are times when the stock market seems to be going up and up, and no one thinks it will ever go down.

It always does, and usually in a dramatic way for each generation. And the usual fluctuations up and down, both undergo gradual rise in tandem with the price of oil. What will happen to the stock market when the world runs out of oil is to be seen. Hopefully, alternate fuels may be able to substitute for oil and stabilize our economy. As a child, I used to be able to go to the movies for ten cents and buy penny candy. It's a lot more expensive now. And I expect that to continue.

The Principle of Triangulation:

There is an old principle of *triangulation* that allows you to establish the precise position of something by observing it from two different points of view.

I'm triangulating the truth of the existence of a third way by observing it from two points of view, namely, the duality of both the visible and invisible points of view, or the verbal and non-verbal, or the speakable and unspeakable, or the Western and Eastern philosophies.

Someone once noted that truth is in the middle, and we are all in a circle around it and viewing the truth from our own perspective. On sharing our point of view, we may help all of us to see truth in its full entirety. Or to put it another way, *no one of us knows more than all of us*. The floodlight of transformation will always see more than the spotlights of duality and trinity. Truth and high moral values must, and will, trump all. "It is the province of knowledge to speak and it is the privilege of wisdom to listen" (Oliver Wendell Holmes, Associate Justice of the United States Supreme Court, 1841-1935).

> There is no stick hard enough to drive me away from a man from whom I can learn something.
> —*Diogenes, 404 B.C.-323 B.C.*

In the symbolism of India, there is a duality of the right-hand path (male way) that seeks liberation by detachment from the world into the spirit, and the left-hand path (female way) that seeks liberation by total acceptance of the world with the world symbolizing nature and woman. The left-hand way (cyclic) and the right-hand way (linear) are like the two halves of a circle that may seem to be each going in opposite or separate directions, but they curve back to complete the circle, just as the *yin* and the *yang* of the Chinese is the complete uniting of the male and the female to create a new wholeness. This new wholeness being more than the sum of its parts is symbolic of a balanced third way of transformed completeness.

Some people look upon the six-pointed Star of David as another form of yin and yang symbol of transformed completeness. Because a triangle with it's peak pointing up is considered a male symbol, and a triangle with its peak pointing down is considered a female symbol. And when you superimpose both triangles you get a six-pointed Star of David. The triangle pointing down is a "V"-shape or a cup or a receptacle in shape, as well as the shape, roughly, of a uterus. What is more impressively triangular is the cavity of a uterus.

The difference between the right–hand way and the left-hand way is shown in the chart below:

Right-Hand Way	Left-Hand Way
Masculine	Feminine
Linear (divided, categorized)	Cyclic (organic, simultaneous)
Add on from the outside	Growth from the inside
Spirit	Nature (plus woman)
Active, isolated	Passive, related
Grasping, exploiting	Receptive, Open
Clutching muscles, technique	Open nerves, spontaneous
Hard, penetrating	Soft, absorbing
Ego, lust, I, no restraint	Abandonment, intimacy, passion
Taking, moving, forcing	Receiving, waiting, watching
Makes happen	Happens to, receives

Chart 7. The Right-Hand Way and the Left-Hand Way

> Hypotheses are scaffolding erected in front of a building
> and then dismantled when the building is finished. They are
> indispensable for the workman, but you mustn't mistake the
> scaffolding for the building.
> —*Johann Wolfgang Von Goethe, German scientist poet,
> 1749-1832*

One day, I was looking out of the window at night in the post-operative intensive care unit of the Berthold S. Pollak Hospital of Chest Diseases in Jersey City, New Jersey. The window looks out across the river to the lights of New York, but all I saw was blackness. I wondered if there was fog or something. I asked the nurses if they had seen any lights earlier. They were surprised, too, as they thought that they had. It was the night that the lights had gone out in New York due to a power-grid failure.

When something strange happens, you can't believe your eyes and you wonder if there is something wrong somewhere, maybe with yourself, and you reach out for help.

During my Surgical Residency, I lived in New Jersey with my family in a rented apartment across the street from the hospital. There was a race riot in Jersey City at that time, and we could hear gunshots coming from down the street about two blocks away. Life has a way of teaching you to be alert for the unexpected and that life is all about life and death—if not physical death, then possible mental, emotional, or spiritual death. We also learn that life is not just one way or the other, not just this or that, but that there is more, there is a third way. There is always the unexpected.

Pierre Teilhard de Chardin, S.J. (French Jesuit priest, author, philosopher and geologist, 1881-1955) pointed out that as each specialty or discipline rises, it will converge like going up the sides of a cone or pyramid with God at the top. So as engineering's technology and biology/medicine come together, we should expect heart-lung machines. And as religion, psychology, psychiatry, theology and philosophy all rise and get closer together, we should expect to get something similarly life-supporting in the spiritual plane. We expect more for the future.

No discipline and no religion can go higher than truth, love, and goodness (mind, heart, spirit).

Suffering makes philosophers of us all; therefore, the older you get, the more you'll think philosophically because of the increasing amount of sadness with which you'll be living. When you begin to think philosophically, you'll see beyond duality to a state of something greater or higher, like love, which encompasses all. There is always more than a duality; there's a third way, trinity, with transformation above and beyond that.

The thing to remember is that there's always more than two, there's three: Those who remember the **past** are enriched by the ages; those who prepare for the **future** are enriched by their foresight. But those who enjoy the **present** moment, fleeting though it is, are able to see that life is a gift and, therefore, all are gifted. (The past is history, the future is mystery and the present is a gift, that's why they call it the "present.")

Because everything has its opposite, you can always get a duality. And because any two can be combined to make something that is a whole greater than the sum of its parts, you can always get three. This three is not just a mixture but a true combination, a common denominator, an inclusive whole, or a link. However, it takes elevation into values, virtues, ideals and principles to get transformation, which is beyond just a simple category of trinity. Additionally, the balancing of two is a third way. For example, experiments, published in 2007 by Stanley Tan, M.D., Ph.D. from Loma Linda University, have suggested that everything is not what it seems, because there is a balance in life that involves laughter. Dr, Tan had two groups of diabetic heart-attack patients. One group watched something funny on TV for half an hour every day, and the other group didn't. 7% of the group, which incorporated humor in their lives, had a subsequent heart attack, compared to 42% of the control group that did not watch the humorous shows. The group that laughed had fewer arrhythmias, had less need for nitroglycerin and had lower blood pressure. Patients who did not laugh enough got heart attacks and died, suggesting the capability of nature to kill us if we're not as happily balanced in life as another group might be. There is a balance in nature.

William Blake (English poet and visionary artist, 1757-1827) said, "We are put on earth for a little space, that we may learn to bear the beams of love," because *to love is to suffer*. And we have seen that suffering love or self-sacrifice is transforming. What is important is the way out of the dualism into the nuanced third way, because life is not just joy or sorrow, happy or sad, consolation or desolation. There is always more beyond.

Our rational thinking mind, which is seeking truth, can be closed or open.
Our emotional feeling heart, which is seeking love, can be hard or soft.
Our restless searching spirit, which is seeking goodness and God, can be temporal or eternal, in other words, living in time or in eternity.
All of this tends to match the parable in the Bible of the Sower of the Seed (Luke 8:4-15 GNB), where seed was sown along the path, where it was stepped on, and the birds ate it up. Some of it fell on rocky ground, and when the plants sprouted, they dried up because the soil had no moisture. Some of the seed fell among thorn bushes, which grew up with the plants and choked them. And some seeds fell in good soil and bore grain, one hundred grains each.
Being closed-minded is like the seed being choked out.
Being hard-hearted is like the seed being on rocky ground.
Being temporal-minded spiritually is like living on the common, social, hazardous, beaten path instead of being with the eternal. Transformation is beyond that trinity and is like the highly productive seed in good soil.

The next chapter will explore that transformation.

Chapter 8.

Transformation

It's unreasonable to think that a person who can *think* would be put into a crazy, empty world in which there is nothing to *think*.

It's unreasonable to think that a person who can *love* would be put into a crazy, empty world in which there is nothing to *love*.

This chapter gives you a clearer picture of transformation, which becomes clearer still with each upcoming chapter (Chapter 10, Chains, and Chapter 11, Cycles).

In the movie about the life of Mahatma Gandhi (spiritual leader in India, 1869-1948), a man approaches Gandhi and asks what he can do to stay out of hell, since he feels such guilt over randomly killing out of hatred someone of an opposite sect and of an opposite religion. Gandhi says to the man that there is a way to get out of hell by adopting an orphan of an opposite sect and raising the child in the religion of that sect, even though the religion is not the same as that of the man asking for help.

The way out of duality is trinity, and the way out of trinity is transformation, which involves spirituality that is above and beyond duality and trinity. Spirituality as a solution entails a higher unity of brotherhood and forgiveness, and a higher generosity of holding hands together in peace. The solution involves lofty values, virtues, ideals, and principles, and that is exactly what constitutes transformation. "To be changed is conversion. To be transformed is Holiness" (Mother M. Angelica, Franciscan nun, contemporary author and founder of Eternal Word Television Network, born 1923).

The way to move out of the trinity of past, present and future into transformation is to avoid looking backward or forward or even just living in the present, but to look upward.

Life is like a thrown baseball that is always coming at us day by day. It can come as a duality in a fastball of consolation or a curveball of desolation, but there is a third way, or trinity, that is like the baseball bat that can send this ball of life into orbit and lead us into the high level of transformation where there is truth, love, goodness and all of the values, virtues, ideals, and principles.

In the history of medicine, we are indebted to those researchers who put themselves at risk to help others. Some researchers infected themselves in order to test their own designed inoculations, antibodies, or treatments. In modern times, surgeons, including me, have risked being exposed to x-rays while injecting dye into bile ducts to test patients for residual gallstones and during fluoroscopy to pass wires into the heart for pacemakers to control heart rhythms. It is part of the gain and loss decisions of life and death, the duality of which is always trumped by all encompassing love. That trumping by love is transformation. And transformation is where such doctors are living.

> I submit to you that if a man has not discovered something that he will die for, he isn't fit to live"
> —*Martin Luther King, Jr. American clergyman, civil-rights activist, and 1964 Nobel Peace Prize winner, 1929-1968*

Transformation that is more than trinity is illustrated by putting *life* at one end of a stick and *light* (enlightenment, wisdom) at the other end of the stick with *love* in between representing the whole of the stick. Life may be desolation and light may be consolation, but transformation is the whole stick of love, with love conquering all.

Transformation that is more than trinity may also be illustrated by a symphony, and not just a simple jingle of up-and-down notes, which starts and quickly stops.

Another classic example is the caterpillar and the butterfly. In our lives, we are like caterpillars—earthbound, eating, sleeping, and gathering experiences out of the dirt that we push around. But we have an inner sense of something missing. We begin weaving a web of reflection and self-examination until there may be a total desolation of darkness that we feel cocooned within. In this painful transformation process we no longer focus on sad self-pity or happy self-indulgence, but we begin to alter our nature by wanting to fly into the sunlight of love, compassion and goodness to sip the nectar of truth in our transformation. We emerge from our focus on self-protection and self–interest to grow beyond our accustomed boundaries; then we can fly away from just survival. We flutter our wings with our ever-increasing mobility, plus maybe we even use the Internet, to be able to influence the other side of the world, similar to chaos theory with its sensitive dependence upon initial conditions, and where small initial changes can lead to large results later.

> The man who views the world at fifty the same as he did at twenty has wasted thirty years of his life.
> *—Muhammad Ali, United States heavyweight boxing champion, born 1942*

Transformation is like the precious metal of a whole coin with added numismatic value, and not just a duality of heads and tails stamped as an illusion into the metal.

Transformation is like an extensive journey and not just a beginning and an ending of a short and fast trip to a destination, where the journey was not savored.

> Every part of the journey is of importance to the whole.
> *—St. Teresa of Avila, Spanish mystic, 1515-1582*

The journey of every person's life shows how every part is important to the whole. When I was in my chest-surgery residency, we operated on a number of cases of advanced tuberculosis that had complications, such as abscesses, requiring surgery. Newer medications have helped diminish the need for such surgery for tuberculosis. I recall encountering one elderly, retired surgeon, who was hospitalized for other reasons. He was bemoaning the fact that he had performed in his time so many operations to cut the phrenic nerve in the neck to paralyze the diaphragm and put the lung at rest as an attempted cure of tuberculosis by such rest. He was feeling, in retrospect, that it did no good. I had never met the patient before, so I didn't know if he had the rambling fixation of a senile mind. I tried to assuage his feelings of guilt by telling him that what he did was one of the very few things available at that time and that his patients may have had the benefit, in any event, of the placebo of hope. Certainly, rest cures are still used today to treat lung infections.

A trinity in medicine is that treatments are either active, reactive, or proactive.

If you will permit me a little play on words here:

Trinity is beyond the duality of *formed* and *reformed*, and into a third way of *informed*. But there is more beyond that as a higher way, namely, *transformed*. To be transformed is to possess values, virtues, ideals, and principles.

Here are some other examples of transformation:

1. To fall in love is a transformation. The moment you start to think about what you are experiencing, you are analyzing and interpreting. It's at this point that you are no longer in the experience but into the *words* about the experience. You are no longer looking at the experience but *avoiding* looking at the experience, because now you are in a haze of words.

    It is not the time, while you are experiencing something, for thinking, brooding, analyzing, interpreting or philosophizing. Doing any of that would be similar to someone asking you if you are having any fun yet, which takes away all the fun.

When lovers are together they hold hands in silence. Something
is conveyed; the message is given. It is a wordless message.
Silence is the language of love. It is a transforming silence.

> Love's worth is love's cost.
> —*Karol Bunsch, novelist, 1898-1987*

2. When people kill in order to preserve life, they do it as part
of their service against evil in a just war or in a sanctioned
police action. And people sometimes seem to violate their
values in order to maintain those values, as they choose the
lesser of two evils. But honor, decency, and high values
are the guiding keys opening to a third way, away from the
duality of paradox or the horns-of-a-dilemma.

3. You are transformed by what you already know intuitively,
instinctively and automatically, such as the existence
of truth because you can ask questions, and such as the
existence of all of the values, virtues, ideals, and principles,
because you find them in yourself. We may substitute
the words "getting spirituality" for the words "being
transformed."

   When you recognize what it is that you already know
   intuitively, some people call it waking up, being awakened,
   or being enlightened, enlightenment, seeing the invisible with
   the inner eye, etc.. What you already know is instinctively in
   you as part of being human. Secular science doesn't want to
   deal with transformation or spirituality and all that it entails
   in terms of values, virtues, ideals, and principles.

4. Transformation is being able to recognize intuitively or
internally that some things are sacred in your unwillingness
and hesitation to cut or harm the human body.

5. Transformation is knowing intrinsically the right thing to
do, and also knowing that the hard part is in doing it.

6. Transformation is being able to recognize the existence of all of the values, virtues, ideals, and principles because you can put them into the following sentence as a substitute for the word "*think*": It is unreasonable to think that a person who can "*think*" would be put into a crazy empty world in which there is nothing to "*think*."

7. Transformation is being able to recognize invisible things that are being pointed to by their material symbol. It is seeing beyond the material to the invisible spiritual.

8. Transformation is being able to recognize that the mind searches for truth and the heart searches for love and the spirit searches for goodness and God; and that there is that third part of being human that is spiritual.

9. Transformation is knowing, in the same intuitive way that you know that truth exists and all the values exist, that your bonded love for your spouse after your many years of marriage will also be eternal, when he or she dies. Your love is part of a greater eternal love, and you both just know this intuitively in your heart.

10. Transformation is knowing that there is something more than duality and trinity, and that humans are more than body and mind, because humans are also spirit.

11. Transformation is knowing that as high as you may be spiritually, that there is always more, because the closer you get to the light (God) the clearer you can see your own darkness, and that darkness needs further work by you for its elimination.

12. Transformation is getting into the garden by means of the love of medical personnel, family, friends and others, and moving away from the city of joy and the desert of sorrow.

13. Transformation can be found whenever you're attuned
    to looking above and beyond your present circumstances
    towards love, and finding it. When you perceive this love
    directly, and you try to indicate what you *see or feel*, rather
    than what you *think or say*, the best that you will be able
    to do is a wordless recognition, "That's it! There it is!"
    Not even wise words or sayings can express inexpressible
    unspeakable all-encompassing transforming love any better
    than that.

14. Transformation is more than the passion of the heart or
    the pride of the mind, but is the journeying, side-by-side
    commitment of love out of the soul that occurs between
    soul mates. Transformation does not depend on the good
    times or the bad times, the breezes or the gale, but on the
    steady set of the sail.

15. Transformation is the ball of life floating to the heavens,
    instead of just being earthbound in joy and sorrow as the
    ball is either bouncing your way or at other times being
    deflated by someone or something.

16. Transformation is being grateful that the human body is
    so wisely designed, that you can neither pat yourself on
    the back in joy nor kick yourself in the butt in sorrow.
    The body is designed for something more noble and
    transforming than that.

17. Transformation is reaching by the grace of God the third
    step of a 12-step program, where you make a decision to
    turn your will and your life over to the care of God as you
    understand God to be. "It is a waste of time to try to destroy
    old things. If you are truly able to become new, the old
    has already been destroyed" (Toson Shimazaki, Japanese
    author, 1872-1943).

18. Transformation is inspiration by the grace of God from out of your own life. For example: Bill Wilson, founder of Alcoholics Anonymous, in a talk he gave at the National Clergy Conference on Alcoholism in 1960, said that he wrote the 12 steps in about 20 minutes in the 1930s.

19. Transformation is in the realm of the Promised Land as shown by the Virginian author, Matt Bondurant, Ph.D., in his 2004 book, *The Third Translation*, wherein he points out that the Egyptian understanding of the "two lands" refers to the divided kingdoms of the upper and lower Nile valley, which every king had a goal to unite. This union would create a "Third Land" as a metaphor for a kind of promised land that would integrate the two into a more perfect way—similar to the way we might wish we could unite any duality, such as, life and death, ancient and modern, male and female, organic and inorganic. This ancient Egyptian concept symbolizes taking Western philosophy of progress and trying to reconcile it with Eastern philosophy of organic unity, similar to the way yin and yang strives to seek oneness or wholeness as a new completeness. The *third way* is the balance, the middle path, the perfect solution. The Third way is the dream of reconciling by combining dualities, whatever they are. Not as a mixture, but as a true combination. The third way is the whole being greater than the sum of its parts. It is like the explosive element sodium and the erosive element Chlorine combining to become the life sustaining salt of the earth.

There is an old Latin expression: *In medio stat virtus*; in the middle stands virtue. Moderation is the key. You can be too thin, too fat, or just right. The miser is at one end, the spendthrift at the other end and the wise spender in the middle. Your meal may be too cold or too hot or just right. Out of two comes three as the "more" from the middle ground. Out of good and better comes best.

20. Transformation is an upgrade:
    Leonard Q. Ross (a pseudonym of the humorist and
    journalist Leo Calvin Rosten, 1908-1997), he united
    "happiness" and "usefulness" into a duality when he said,
    "I cannot believe that the purpose of life is to be "happy. I
    think the purpose of life is to be useful, to be responsible,
    to be honorable, to be compassionate. It is, after all, to
    matter, to count, to stand for something, to have made some
    difference that you lived at all." And when you do all those
    things you are happy. You are even more, you are a third
    way, you are a blessing. What is needed is for the Phoenix
    to rise from the ashes of the dualities. The rising Phoenix
    is the whole that is greater than the sum of its parts. The
    Phoenix of spirituality gives an upgrade to everything.

21. Transformation is when spirituality is born:
    Human nature is like a stable inhabited by the ox of passion
    (the uncontrollable emotions of the **heart**) and the donkey
    of prejudice (the misinformed thinking of the **mind**). These
    animals, which most of us feed quietly on the side, take
    up a lot of room. And it is there between them, pushing
    them out, where Spirituality must be born. And *in their
    very manger* it must be found—and these animals will be
    the first to fall on their knees. Sometimes Christians seem
    far nearer to these animals than to simple poverty and self-
    abandonment to God (modified from Evelyn Underhill, in
    Watch for the Light: Readings for Advent and Christmas,
    Plough. She was an English Anglo-Catholic writer and
    pacifist, 1875-1941).

22. Transformation is being reunited with love.
    Harvard Professor George Eman Vaillant, M.D. (American
    psychiatrist, born 1934) believed that the deep joy of
    spirituality is not the same as happiness or excitement but
    more like the emotional joy of being reunited with someone
    you truly love. I find that to be true in my love for Jesus.
    Finding spirituality releases us to believe in the un-seeable,

to touch the untouchable, to know the unknowable and to see the un-seeable, and to have nothing ever to be the same again.

23. It has been my experience that when neighbors help neighbors, and even when strangers help strangers, both those who help and those who are helped are transformed.
    —*Darryl K. Lester, Founding partner HindSight Consulting, Inc. Community Investment Network in Raleigh, N.C.*

Truisms:

- Things start to get real when you discover love.

- The universe is embraced by what is at its heart—love—and this love is always embracing you.

- Violence is not at the heart of the universe; love is.

- The world is full of beauty when your heart is full of love. And this love lies at the very heart of the creative process.

- There is a Maori proverb: "Turn your face to the sun (truth, love, goodness, God) and the shadows (everything else) fall behind you."

- Emily Dickinson, (poet, 1830-1888), said, "Truth must dazzle gradually or we all should be blind." Love doesn't mind if it dazzles.

Love is a commitment that encompasses the good and bad times. In sickness and in health, until death us do part. Margaret and I love each other, and we can laugh, as well as cry, together. You know you love someone if you know what makes him or her cry. We can remember how our eyes were full of light as we danced on our wedding day. And we can remember the many times we have cleaned, rocked, consoled, fed and bandaged our children. And we have seen the many changes occurring in everyone growing up, including ourselves.

And we are delighted and happy in each others' company, which is endlessly stimulating and, at times, so heartrending that we go pray and walk and recall that "I'm no gleaming glittering prize either." We remember everything and we smile and laugh in love.

Laughter is like the springs on a wagon, which eases the rough journey for the wagons of our lives. A bond of love is easy to find in an environment of joy. When we laugh together, we speak a universal language, and we feel closer to one another. I have loved the stars too fondly to be fearful of the night. I have loved too fondly the memories of our consolations and our transformations ever to be fearful of our desolations.

A married couple is like two unmovable pebbles on the ocean's moveable shore. They experience the push and pull of life's waves, the ebb and flow of life's good times and bad times, being transformed into shiny gems reflecting their glow of love for each other onto each others' faces to light up the world in transformation. "*Grow old along with me! The best is yet to be*" (Robert Browning, English poet, 1812-1889). There is something higher, something eternal.

Margaret had a chance to see an actual operation, once. She said it would help her to visualize what I was doing and where I was going when I left for work. Having that visualization would be a form of togetherness. Student nurses, residents, and others knew more than she did about the operating room (OR).

The opportunity for Margaret to see an operation happened one night when the Chief of Surgery asked his wife to see an operation for her first time. I asked if Margaret could come too, and it was approved. The case went well, but because it was a gunshot wound of the abdomen, there was a lot of blood and guts—more than in our usual elective-surgery day.

Both ladies didn't seem to mind. Student nurses are usually told that if they feel faint, to try to fall away from the operating table. I can recall one student nurse fainting in my lifetime. She just sort of crumpled at the knees to the ground. But both ladies stood up well. The fact that they wanted to be there was a sign of their love.

During an operation, when a surgeon puts out his (or her) hand toward the instrument nurse, it means that he (or she) wants a hemostat put into it. It is a wordless language that is smooth and timed just right, as the nurse is anticipating the doctor's need. Some surgeons have their own team that they hire. The nurse handing the instruments seems on the same wavelength of thinking with the surgeon. She seems to know and anticipate just what surgical instrument the surgeon will need or ask for next. Normally, surgery has a certain camaraderie or solidarity feeling to it, with an *esprit de corps*, but it seems even more so when everyone there is always on the same team. The hired team takes care to clean and sterilize everything afterwards and keep it separate for use the next time around, just for that one surgical team. This team approach avoids having personnel at various levels in training. It just has the experienced team members. I was assisting such a team once, and I was explaining something that I had read in a medical text that night about similar cases, when the loyalty of the team showed through. The first assistant to the surgeon said, "Dr. 'Blank' does not read books; he writes them!" Having loyalty, love, and values is living on higher ground.

George Spencer-Brown (English polymath, mathematician and author, born 1923) points out that all mathematics is basically a set of instructions, such as "describe a circle, drop a perpendicular." If you follow certain instructions, you will understand certain things that cannot be described. All mystical writing, really, is basically instructions. It is *not* an attempt to describe the universe, to describe God, or to describe ultimate reality. The very word *mysticism* comes from the Greek root "muin," which means "silence." Mum's the word, and then you will understand, because the instructions are to *listen and look*. Only don't *say*, because that will spoil it.

In the same way that a picture is worth a thousand words, what is unspeakable says far more than what is speakable in words, even though a small drop of ink may make millions think, when the ink is used to print words.

"When the oak is felled the whole forest echoes with its fall, but a hundred acorns are sown in silence by an unnoticed breeze" (Thomas Carlyle, Scottish historian and writer, 1795-1881). So, too, very often we learn in quiet, unobtrusive, inspired ways.

The shocking impact of truth quietly changes us. We feel something has happened in us, but we can't explain it, except perhaps by the word "growth" or a feeling of being transformed.

> Intelligent silence is the mother of prayer...a growth
> of knowledge, a hand to shape contemplation, hidden
> progress, the secret journey upward.
> —*St. John Climacus, Syrian Abbot, 6ᵗʰ century*

Robert Ellsberg (publisher, author, born 1955) said, "It is not enough simply to escape the noise of the world. There is still the matter of our own inner noise. Even when it is quiet outdoors, we are filled with internal voices and alarms, reminding us of what needs to be done, what we have done poorly, what has been done to us in the past. These voices incessantly distract us from the time and place—here and now—where we actually exist. They convince us that we will be happy in the future, if only we can meet the next deadline, earn the proper credential, land the perfect job, or settle old scores. Yet if we are constantly living in the past or preparing to live in the future, how can we be sure that we are ever truly alive?"

Ellsberg also pointed out that we like the agitation, because it takes our mind off thinking about our inner life; that is why *we prefer the hunt to the capture*. To sit quietly implies the cultivation of an inner life, rather than the surface life of anxious cravings, quick fixes, distraction, consumption, the latest tabloid sensation, or the next big thrill. Being physically quiet must be joined with being internally quiet.

> Man goes into the noisy crowd to drown his own clamor of silence"
> —*Rabindranath Tagore, Bangladesh author and poet, 1861-1941*

> Kids today are violent because they have no inner life; they have no inner life because they have no thoughts; they have no thoughts because they know no words; they know no words because they never speak; and they never speak because the music's too loud.
> —*Quentin Crisp, English writer, illustrator, and actor, 1908-1999*

My twin brother's daughter is deaf, but her child is able to hear. This hearing child has learned some signs to communicate with her deaf mom. Her hearing dad is fluent in sign language. And mom can read lips and understands her daughter. It's a beautiful relationship to see. What seems desolation or handicap to some is just the way things are to others. The deaf community is a culture of its own. I learned that some deaf folks refuse cochlear implants, which would cause them to hear, because that would be to them like saying deafness is an illness that needs to be healed. My niece understands this community, and she is a counselor trying to help them.

When Margaret and I lived on an airbase, we noticed the noise of the airplanes taking off and landing, but we soon got used to the noise. When I first reported to duty, I had to buy my uniform at the post-exchange store, or PX, on the airbase. I didn't get a chance to go through basic training and buy my uniform there, because there was a need to assign me to the airbase promptly as Chief Surgeon. The PX had the latest-style Air Force uniform for sale. When I reported for duty, those in the room with the Hospital Commander seemed more interested in my uniform than in me, because they inquired about where I had bought my uniform, and they were curious about the differences in my uniform as compared to their old uniform.

I was a surgeon at the airbase, and not what is known as a flight surgeon, because flight surgeons are doctors, but they don't do any surgery. They accompany airmen on their flights and oversee their health. A flight surgeon told me about a time when he went to Spain and put an aspirin on a restaurant table, because he had a headache, while he waited for the waitress to bring their order and drinks. She thought it was drugs of some kind; the police were called, and he had a lot of explaining to do. He told another story about a flight surgeon who was allowed to sit in the co-pilot's seat while the co-pilot went to do something else in the airplane. Shortly after the co-pilot left, the pilot signaled an emergency, and those who were sitting in seats were ejected to safety, including the lucky flight surgeon, as compared to the unlucky co-pilot. I asked him what the black boxes were on the flight line that seemed guarded by soldiers with rifles. He laughed and said, "You mean you didn't know that's where they keep the atom bombs?" It seemed unreal to be on a base with a lot of atom bombs. This was during the "Cold War" with Russia. When you are staring at bombs, you are not reminded of love.

I do remember one time when my parents showed that they loved me. My brother and I would go to a movie most Saturday afternoons, because there were four theaters within walking distance from where we lived. One was just across the street. We went to see *Gone with the Wind* one Sunday afternoon, but we didn't realize it was three hours long, instead of a usual two-hour show. Because we came in after the movie had started, we stayed to see the start of the next showing by staying in our seats, which was allowed at that time. By the time we got home, our parents were upset that we were so late, but we didn't realize it was a three-hour show, and we wondered what they were so upset about. It was a confusion of misunderstanding, but somehow the fact that our parents must love us was shown to us by their angry concern. What became evident to my eyes out of the duality of parent and child confusion was a higher view of the love that my parents had for me that was masked by their anger at me.

Those who are in love are dancing to the music of a different drummer. "Those who danced were thought to be quite insane, by those who could not hear the music (Angela Monet, wife of Claude Monet, the French Impressionist painter)." The *size* of your love, which is symbolized by a boat's sail, tells you where you are, and the *set* of your sail tells you where you're going. No wind is a good wind if you don't know to what port you're heading. It's the set of your sail and not the winds and the gale or the calm that makes all the difference. When love sets its sail, that is transformation beyond the joy and sorrow of calm or gale.

My wife, Margaret, and I have always set our sail to make our home a shelter and an oasis of hospitality: My twin brother's daughter stayed with us for a couple of years to finish her education and work part time. She met her future husband while she was under our care. Our daughter brought home, one day, a classmate who had been put out of her house by her mentally ill mother who had made the girl into the scapegoat of the family for no valid reason and the mother didn't want her anymore. She became our foster daughter. The love and caring atmosphere of our home was a beacon of hope. Our foster daughter has had a successful career in the Army. Margaret's brother, who was a diabetic, following his severe heart attack, lived with us until his death. He was of short stature and had received injections of pituitary gland extract to try to get him to grow taller as a child. I believe that he harbored in his body a virus (Creutzfeldt-Jakob) from those injections that eventually led to paralysis from the neck down shortly prior to his death due to this variation of present-day "mad cow" disease (MCD), which is also known as Bovine Spongiform Encephalopathy (BSE). He never married, which may have been because he may have felt that he would be a burden to a spouse with his diabetes. We hosted my son and his wife and her family when they had to flee a hurricane in their area, requiring all of them to evacuate to our safe area.

Margaret's mother died, in Margaret's early childhood, of Hodg-kin's lymphoma. Her dad remarried, and Margaret had a loving stepmother. Her dad died of a lymphosarcoma, and before he died, he asked me to take good care of Margaret. And I have always kept that deathbed promise. Because I love her, I would have done so even if he never asked. My parents retired near me, and we arranged a small nearby cottage for them, where one of my mom's sisters also stayed until my aunt's death by cancer.

Love (God) is our way out of the horns of any dilemma, paradox or duality. But we must accept spirituality. If you equate freedom to mean capitalism, you must be sure of what you mean. You must be sure that capitalism is not greedy capitalism of materialism and commercialism, where sex sells and is sold. We must be sure that our capitalism is not a capitalism devoid of spirituality, because that kind of capitalism has been weighed and found wanting; it has come up short, because it doesn't have what it takes. True freedom is something that unites under a banner of spirituality that includes truth, love, goodness, and all of the other values, virtues, ideals, and principles. It's what makes our justice system work. Its principles are those upon what our nation was founded. It's like the kite string that keeps the kite sailing and not floating free and crashing. Spiritu-ality is not restriction, but true freedom. "No man is free who is not master of himself" (Epictetus, Greek philosopher, c.55-c.135).

Before getting to Chapters 10 & 11, where transformation becomes clearer and clearer. I want you to consider the next brief chapter, which looks at life in terms of four (quadruple) instead of trinity (three), to convince you that it is easier and less complicated to use trinity (three) as you move beyond trinity to transformation

Chapter 9.

Quadruple (Four, Fourth, Fourfold)

The idea of a higher education is not to take an empty mind and fill it, but to take a closed mind and open it.
—*William Shelton, English Member of Parliament. 1929-2003*

A chain is no stronger than its weakest *link*, and a brain is no stronger than its weakest *think*.
—*Author unknown*

An increase in complexity occurs when you look at life as four instead of three. In the chart below follow the numbers each *vertically* or follow the numbers each *horizontally*.

1	2	3	4
Physical	**Mental**	**Emotional**	**Spiritual**
Do	**Think**	**Feel**	**Say**
Acting	Thinking	Feeling	Transcending
Body	Mind	Heart	Soul
Hands	Head	Heart	Spirit
1. Do	Industrious	Priest	Good
2. Think	Intelligent	Philosopher	True
3. Feel	Sensitive	Artist	Beautiful
4. Say	Wise	Prophet	Inspired

Chart 8. An Increase in Complexity of Life with Four

Once you begin to think in four, instead of in trinity, life becomes more complex. You find that the simplicity of resorting to trinity or duality makes it easier to understand.

In ancient times, people believed in four elements, namely, *earth, air, fire and water*.

So, fire boils off water into vapor in the air, and water quenches fire, leaving earthy ashes, which is an excellent simplification of a quadruple into a duality of earth and air, after the action of fire and water is over.

In the Bible, the action of fire and water is used to symbolize as a metaphor the action of the Holy Spirit as flames of fire (Acts 2:3) and living water (John 4:11 and 3:5). You are not meant to choose one or the other, but there is a reflection back and forth in resonance, giving a greater nuanced meaning as you use them both simultaneously. This is the whole becoming greater than the sum of its parts. The Bible also uses a metaphor of a mighty wind for the Holy Spirit (John 3:8, Acts 2:2), which simplifies the quadruple of earth, air, fire, and water into a unity of one (uno, mono). A mighty wind in the air will evaporate water, extinguish fire, and disperse or blow away the ashes of the earth.

- Some authors add "unconscious" to *id, ego, and superego* to make a quadruple.

- Some authors add "goddess" to *physician, professor, and priest* to make a quadruple.

- Some authors have a quadruple of: king, warrior, goddess (or queen) and magician (or shaman or trickster).

- The *king* represents rule and law.

- The *warrior* represents power and might.

- The *goddess* represents the feminine and sex, also pleasure, senses and nature.

- And the *shaman* represents the higher law of God, also priest, magician or trickster.

- The *id* represents instincts, the child, playfulness, euphoria of youth, and humor.

- The *ego* represents adult seriousness and mental life, such as professor.

- The *superego* represents law, conscience and the parent.

- And the *unconscious* represents myth and ancient types or symbols (such as king, warrior, goddess, shaman-magician-trickster or priest-God.)

Another quadruple is how we evaluate a poem: meter, metaphor, alliteration, and lineation. We also have the four seasons: spring, summer, autumn, and winter. And the four directions from out of which, to the ancients, the winds were supposed to come, namely, north, south, east, and west. And modern medical x-rays detect four densities in an image that correspond to fat, water, gas, and bone.

Someone once pointed out that we have put a web of words over the earth to try to explain everything, almost like longitude and latitude, and then we try to fill in the blank spaces between the lines. What we know is increasing steadily, and the web of words to explain every-thing is steadily becoming thicker or tighter, but as we approach that point, we are suddenly surprised to find that what is unknown is not a mere blank or empty space getting smaller all the time in the web of words, but an opening, which is not an opening onto ignorance, but onto wonder.

The open mind knows that the most minutely explored territories have not really been known at all but only simply named, marked and measured many times over. Johann Wolfgang von Goethe (author and poet, 1749-1832) said, "The highest to which mankind can attain is wonder." The end of all education is contemplation. All action should start from there. We have had our noses in the guidebook for most of our lives and have never looked at the view, much less, fully appreciated it.

Truisms:

- Don't let your learning lead to knowledge; let your learning lead to action.
  —Jim Rohn, American author, born 1930

- Destiny is not a matter of chance; it's a matter of choice. It's not a thing to be waited for; it's a thing to be achieved.
  —William Jennings Bryan, U.S. Secretary of State, 1860-1925

- You have removed most of the roadblocks to success when you have learned the difference between movement and direction.
  —Joel Griffith, contemporary Christian minister since 1988

- Don't just make a living, design a life.
  —Jim Rohn, American author, born 1930

- The poorest man is not he who is without a cent, but he who is without a dream.
  —Pennsylvania School Journal

- There is nothing better than a dream to create the future.
  —Victor Hugo, author and poet, 1802-1885

- Dreams don't work unless you do.
  —Peter J. Daniels, Australian author, born 1932

- Waste your money and you're only out of money, but waste your time and you've lost a part of your life.
  —Michael LeBoeuf, Ph.D., American author, born 1942

- The best preparation for good work tomorrow is to do good work today.
  —Elbert Hubbard, American author and artist, 1856-1915

If duality, trinity, and quadruple are too much for you, then you can simplify to a mono (one, uno)—because truth is one. "Facts are many, but the truth is one" (Rabindranath Tagore, Indian poet, 1861- 1941). "The flower that is single need not envy the thorns that are numerous" (Rabindranath Tagore, Indian poet, 1861-1941).

Mother Teresa of Calcutta (1910-1997) gives us a splendid mono (one, uno) in this reflection called "Life":

> Life is an opportunity, benefit from it.
> Life is beauty, admire it.
> Life is bliss, taste it.
> Life is a dream, realize it.
> Life is a challenge, meet it.
> Life is a duty, complete it.
> Life is a game, play it.
> Life is costly, care for it.
> Life is wealth, keep it.
> Life is love, enjoy it.
> Life is mystery, know it.
> Life is promise, fulfill it.
> Life is sorrow, overcome it.
> Life is a song, sing it.
> Life is a struggle, accept it.
> Life is tragedy, confront it.
> Life is an adventure, dare it.
> Life is luck, make it.
> Life is too precious, do not destroy it.
> Life is life, fight for it.

Notice that this is like a single command, "Do this!" There are no contrasts or opposites, as in a duality. But even so, a transformation is found in its spirituality. Spirituality, like love, encompasses all.

Spirituality reminds us that we are an integral part of the universe and that we should behave responsibly.

If you do not raise your eyes you will think that you are the highest point.

—*Antonio Porchia, Argentine aphorist born in Italy, 1886-1968*

We have seen so far that there is something more that is always beyond any duality, which is trinity, which can lead to transformation. I hope to make clearer in the next two chapters what that "more" is that is transformation.

Chapter 10.

Chains (Occidental, Progress, Linear, Sequential)

A chain is no stronger than its weakest link.
—*Old Latin Proverb*

One cannot step twice into the same river, for the water in which you first stepped has flowed on.
—*Heraclitus, Greek philosopher, c. 540 B.C.-c. 480 B.C.*

"Chains" in this chapter and "cycles" in the next chapter together constitute a duality in that they contrast the philosophies of our Occidental West and the Oriental East. Additionally, since the twenty-first century is dominated by dissatisfaction, as you will see below, then dissatisfaction with Western philosophy leads into Eastern philosophy. And there is something more that is always beyond any duality, which is trinity, which can lead us to transformation. I hope to make clearer in these next two chapters what that "more" is that is transformation.

Linear thinking, or progress as a philosophy of life, is considered to be characteristic of the Occident, or the West, which includes America, Europe, and the Western Hemisphere. Geographically, this is the part of the earth west of Asia and Asia Minor.

An example of linear thinking is:

There are no birds in last year's nests this year, because birds always make a new nest every year.

Linear thinking is involved with progress where everything is new. It's symbol is a straight line or arrow slanting upwards, and it is a symbol of male.

Another example of linear thinking is: 'Lightning doesn't strike the same place twice," because once lightning strikes a place, it is not the same place but drastically changed. Linear thinking in other words is: "What goes around is not coming around twice the same way." It is not like seasons or tides or like the pendulum swinging. What is going to come around is new or progress.

Trinity thinking is a linear approach of expecting more or expecting something beyond just usual duality thinking.

Many years ago, a priest author by the name of John Powell, S.J., noted that *everything starts with thinking.* He gave, as an example, the following: Mistakenly thinking that your garden hose is a snake causes you to be afraid; and that causes you to go into your house and to not take your significant-other out into the romantic garden moonlight. Your one-on-one relationship then suffers, and when that happens, your work, or your one-on-many relationships, suffers. Then you go to a psychiatrist and say: "I'm all messed up; I can't even work!" The psychiatrist has to go back up the *chain* and ask about your relationships and what you were feeling, and, when you were feeling that way, "What were you thinking?" *The chain goes from thinking to feeling to doing to relating to working.*

- Life consists of what a man is thinking all day.
  —*Ralph Waldo Emerson, American essayist, philosopher and poet, 1803-1882*

- Man can alter his life by altering his thinking.
  —*William James, author, philosopher and psychologist, 1842-1910*

- Sooner or later, false thinking brings wrong conduct.
  —*Julian Huxley, British evolutionary biologist, 1887-1875*

- You will never go higher than your thoughts.
  —*Benjamin Disraeli, British Prime Minister, 1804-1881*

- An invasion of armies can be resisted, but not an invasion of ideas.
  —*Victor Hugo, French author and poet, 1802-1885*

- Progress is often just a good idea away.
  —*John Maxwell, American author, born 1947*

- More gold has been mined from the thoughts of people than has ever been taken from the earth.
  —*Napoleon Hill, American author, 1883-1970*

- Is your desire to improve your life strong enough to prompt you to change your thinking?
  —*John C. Maxwell, American author, born 1947*

- Thinkers learn from their experiences, but they also learn from the experiences that they don't have.

- Be Columbus to whole new continents and worlds within you, opening new channels, not of trade, but of thought. If a man does not keep pace with his companions, perhaps it is because he hears a different drummer. Let him step to the music which he hears, however measured or far away.
  —*Henry David Thoreau, American naturalist, author, and conservationist, 1817-1862*

- Beware of all enterprises that require new clothes, and not rather a new wearer of clothes.
  —*Henry David Thoreau, American naturalist, author, and conservationist, 1817-1862*

In addition to the thinking chain, above, there are other *chains*. For example, the chain of what dominates us: The Austrian psychiatrist, Sigmund Freud (1856-1939), said that *pleasure* and our *parents* both dominate our lives. (He dealt with Oedipus and Electra complexes, infantile regression, anal retention, repressions, inhibitions, pleasure and sex.)

A pupil of Dr. Freud was the psychologist Dr. Mortimer J. Adler (1902-2001), who felt that Freud was wrong and that *power* dominates our lives. (We have to rule the roost, be top dog, and be king of the hill.)

The Swiss psychiatrist, Dr. Carl Jung (1875-1961), said that what is *unconscious* dominates our lives. (He dealt with ancient types or symbols, which he called *archetypes*.)

Another Austrian psychiatrist, Dr. Victor Emil Frankl (1905-1997), who survived a World War II German concentration camp, said that *meaning* should dominate our lives, as we all need to know if our lives have meaning before we die.

The American televangelist, Dr. Robert Harold Schuller (born 1926), wrote a book on *self-esteem*, which he felt should dominate our lives, as we have to "save face."

Now we find that many modern psychiatrists are saying that *dissatisfaction* is dominating our lives. Perhaps this stems from the Vietnam War, when a popular song by the Rolling Stones had the words: "I can't get no satisfaction." "Men, or mankind, is divided into two parts or sorts: the one seeks and does not find; another finds and is not contented" (Ali Ibn Abi Talib, Arabian author, 599-661). We are dissatisfied with our air (which is polluted), with our water (which is polluted), with our food (which is non-organic), with our jobs (the evidence for which is that we understand and like Dilbert cartoons), with our politicians (we feel they're crooked), with our lives, with our institutions, etc., etc.

Basically, we are dissatisfied with everything, but the three most important things with which we are dissatisfied are: science (because of the atom-bomb and the threat of bioterrorism), the philosophy of Western civilization that we have gotten used to, and ourselves, which we have not gotten used to. Hoping to find satisfaction, we turn from what is dissatisfying to its opposite.

And so we go into art instead of science; we go into the philosophy of Eastern civilizations instead of Western; and we turn from ourselves into empty, rootless, adrift, detached, and alienated searchers.

But Jesus Christ said that what should dominate our lives is *love, giving, and forgiving.*

The story of the Prodigal Son (prodigal in the sense of meaning wasteful) in the Bible (Luke 15:11) is a story about duality (two sons), and also about trinity, because the father makes three, and he shows the trinity of *love, giving, and forgiving.* It doesn't specify which son is prodigal, as they both waste something of value. One son represents material loss of his inheritance, and the other son represents relationship loss with his brother and father. It starts out by saying: "A certain man had two sons." That "certain man" is God, represented in the story by the father. God and Jesus in the Bible show love, giving, and forgiving, just as the father in the story does. Jesus instructs us in the Bible that we're also to show that trinity of *love, giving, and forgiving.* That trinity should *dominate* our lives. Some say that the story should be called the Prodigal Father (prodigal in the sense of meaning generous), as the father is giving and forgiving generously and overwhelmingly out of his immense love.

Pierre Teilhard de Chardin, S.J., (1881-1955), pointed out another *chain,* a step-up chain, in his book, *The Phenomenon of Man.* He was a creative visionary philosopher, Jesuit priest, and geologist/ paleontologist. He said that there is always a step-up coming. First, there is inorganic matter, then organic matter in the form of plants as a biosphere covering the earth, then a nervous system covering the earth in the form of animals that are mobile. Then intelligent minds cover the earth, in the form of humans who love and who have introspection and who think about thinking. He treated human consciousness as a special event in the evolutionary story. Then communication by electronic technology covers the earth. Then scientists join together in cooperation to invent something they can't do alone, such as the atom bomb. He expects another step-up soon;

maybe it will be when genetics allows science to take control of evolution. Since the beginning of time, he saw the weaving of the cosmic tapestry as a digital record, with emerging threads showing a personality of a global being with a mind capable of great creativity and a heart capable of great passion and a goodness seen in our benevolent and serendipitous world. His synthesis envisioned a great work of becoming occurring in the cosmos with One (God) pulling it all together.

He likened progress to a pyramid or cone, and since he was a Jesuit priest as well as a scientist, he put God at the top point, where secular scientists refuse to put God. Along the sides were all of mankind's specialties or disciplines. He said that as each discipline rises, it tends to converge with other rising disciplines. We see that convergence now, as our engineers help our biologists and our surgeons to invent artificial hearts.

It is expected, as pointed out previously, that religion, philosophy, psychology, and psychiatry will come together in some way in the foreseeable future. He also felt that mankind started out emphasizing the <u>body</u> or the physical as mankind tried to survive, but as humans progressed, they emphasized the <u>mind</u> with pop psychology and psychiatry, then the <u>heart</u> of compassion, where we are now, because many are tired of war, and finally, hopefully, the world will emphasize <u>love and the soul</u> as all disciplines or specialties rise closer to the top of the pyramid or cone where God is at the top. And what rises must converge.

I have lived during a period when a great *chain* of discoveries has happened, which has created <u>a chain of ages</u>. There were: the aviation age, the transportation age, the antibiotic age or miracle-drug age, the television age, the atomic age, the holographic age, the 3-D age, the telecommunications age, the computer age, the start of the virtual reality age, the plastic-surgery age, and the advertising age. Due to the difficulty in getting rid of nuclear waste, you could say that we are presently living in the garbage age or garbAge. This is due to our living on the height of an exponential curve. An exponential curve is a line that represents human history, which starts out moving horizontally in a slight gradual elevation for a long time, and then there is a sharp curve, bringing the line up vertically.

The world is currently in the midst of changes so overwhelming as to be barely understandable, much less manageable by even the smartest of us. The ground is shifting beneath us so rapidly that we tend to lose our balance and perspective. The amount of information in a newspaper over the course of one year now is said to be more than a person in the 18th century would come across in a lifetime. An exponential curve reminds me of what Ernest Hemingway (American novelist, short story writer and journalist, 1899-1961) said when someone asked him how he went into bankruptcy. He said, "Slowly at first and then suddenly."

Kenneth Earl Wilber (American author, born 1949) showed another *chain,* a quadrant chain, in his 1996 book, *A Brief History of Everything.* In this book, he divided everything into four quadrants by drawing a cross in the center of a blank piece of paper. The four quadrants were: individual mind, individual body, group culture (group mind), and group society (group body). Ken Wilber went on to show the evolution, over time, of each of the four quadrants. His main point was that all four quadrants have to rise to certain levels in order to achieve an advance. One quadrant alone cannot advance very far beyond all the others, as it has to wait until the other quadrants catch up to be able to advance. His analysis overlooked the trinity of *body, mind, and spirit (soul)* or *physical, mental, and spiritual* because of his emphasis only on individual or group mind or body.

In the universe, there is order from universal laws and there is chaos of random chance, but beyond that, there is a benevolent upgrading progress of advancement that seems intelligent, purposeful, and meaningful—so much so, that religious people speak of benevolent good luck, God-incidence, serendipity, and miracles, while scientists speak of favorable mutations, successful adaptations, survival of the fittest, sexual reproduction, genetics, heredity, and evolution.

Rev. George V. Coyne, S.J., Ph.D. (born 1933), an astronomer and former director of the Vatican Observatory Research Group in Tucson, Arizona, looks at the origins of the universe as "a ballet with three ballerinas: chance, necessity, and fertility."

Not only are there single and multiple *chains*, but there also seems to be <u>a chain of trends,</u> one trend after the other, in the world.

One generation is into alcoholism and infidelity, another generation is into sex and drugs, and another generation is into abortion and divorce, etc. Our current generation may be into depletion and depression.

I think my grandfather's generation was into alcohol and sedatives. My generation was into tranquilizers and amphetamines (speed). My children's generation is into marihuana and drugs. My children's children are in a generation of harder drugs, tattoos, body piercings, plastic surgery, and sex. They seem to be living in a time of *spiritual deficit disorder*.

I was reading, on page 35, in the July/August 2009 issue of Discover magazine, an article entitled "Out of the Past" by Kathleen McGowan. She noted that Harvard psychiatrist Roger Pittman was the first to try the drug propranolol to treat post-traumatic stress disorder. When you take the drug and relive your memories, your heart rate and muscle tension ease while the drug is in your body. This makes reliving your memories more like relating a narrative rather than describing something intensely right in front of you, now. Afterwards, for a time, flashbacks return with less intensity. This made me wonder if there are other drugs being widely used that may have yet unrecognized side-effects that could dampen the usual moral outrage of a citizenry and keep them tranquilized.

> A creator is not in advance of his generation, but he is the first of his contemporaries to be conscious of what is happening to his generation.
> —Gertrude Stein, American author and poet, 1874-1946

When it comes to trends, there is a lot that we seem to take for granted, such as drinking and smoking, as if they are normal.

We once lived in a world that took slavery for granted. We now live in a world that takes war for granted. Women have been called the other half of the human race and the other face of God. Both halves, women and men, are needed now.

Just because it's in the nature of some people (dare I say men) to make periodic wars, that doesn't mean that women should give up their innate nature to nurture and preserve life.

It's the one who believes in miracles who becomes a miracle to the rest of us, just like the first Jew who stepped into the parting waters of the Red Sea. That person was a miracle to the others by stepping out in a miracle of faith, trust, and solidarity.

We must link arms with those on the other side of whatever divides us, in the hope that, in this meeting, we can come safely through the turbulent waters of life together. What separates us may be a link that unites us, such as when a wall between two prisoners which separates them may be the very thing that unites them in communication, as they knock on the wall to communicate to each other. Separation and the contrast of being opposite constitutes a duality, which may be the very thing which brings about a situation for a link to transformation.

When I was a boy, I remember that I had the gift, or the curse, of being able to see images in patterns. For example, in looking at the pattern in a rug, I would see two round spots, which together looked like eyes, and the rest of the face would sometimes be there as an incomplete and sometimes greatly distorted pattern. I can do the same with clouds, where I see a projection that represents a nose on a side view of a face, and sometimes the rough profile of a head is there, too, incomplete and sometimes greatly distorted. I remember being disturbed by seeing this sort of thing in the patterns of wallpaper, the patterns in our linoleum, and the patterns in our old-fashioned rugs. As an adult, I learned that this is called "eidetic images." *Dorland's Illustrated Medical Dictionary*, 28th Edition, defines *eidetic* as coming from the Greek word *eidos* which means: "that which is seen; form or shape." So, someone with eidetic vision can see faces, forms, shapes, and pictures in such things as the grain of wood, patterns in marble, forms of clouds, shapes of debris, etc. They tend to see the order in the chaos of life's random designs. It was disturbing to me, because the images were somewhat distorted, and more ugly and incomplete than beautiful, and they seemed to be patterns living in another dimension. If I tried to show my mother a pattern that I saw of a horse, for example, in the random pattern of the linoleum floor, she couldn't see it herself, even though I tried to trace it out for her. That's like, some people can't see the hidden pictures in modern 3-D art hidden-image stereograms, (hidden-image stereograms http://www.vision3d.com/sghidden.html) while others can. I don't know if that ability has helped me to see the big picture and to spot chains and trends in life, but it certainly can't hurt. I consider it a gift. Life progresses in a line that may be full of dualities.

Let us consider the *chain* of duality to trinity to transformation:

Here is a story to help you see more than just the duality of life. The story is about a Samurai warrior appearing before an old nun and wanting to know the difference between heaven and hell. "You wouldn't know the difference if I told you. You are clearly only the shadow of a man," the nun said. The Samurai angrily swung out his sword and brought it down an inch from her neck. She looked up at him calmly and said, "That, sir, is the gate of hell," The Samurai, struck by that insight of truth, dropped his sword in front of her, folded his hands over his heart and bowed to her slowly and deeply all the way to the waist. "And that, sir" said the nun, "is the gate of heaven." In this story, duality is found in the following: life and death, young and old, strength and weakness, heaven and hell, warrior of war and nun of peace, anger and calm, and a real man and a shadow of a man. What is the "more" of transformation is the insight of truth and values, virtues, ideals, and principles, held by both the nun and the Samurai, as symbolized by his folded hands over his heart and his slow deep bow. Look to values as your way out of the hell of just living the duality of joy and sorrow in life. This can be illustrated by this other example:

Ebenezer Scrooge, a wealthy miser, becomes aware of his own un-happiness by a series of apparitions that review the emptiness of his life. He finally sees the wider web of life in which each person is embedded. And he sees his effects on the happiness of others. And he sees how his own rejection of love in the past has harmed his own life. He sees the suffering that he has failed to prevent and the opportunities for love that he has lost. Finally, he sees his fate, to die *alone*—wealthy, unloved, and unmourned. You cannot love alone, and to die alone and unloved implies that Scrooge is to die without love. And since God is love, then Scrooge will die with-out God. This will sentence Scrooge to the only place that is with-out God, which is hell. Convicted by his vision, Scrooge changes his life by living in the true spirit of Christmas, which is to love and to be loved. He can see, with his inner eye, invisible spiritual things such as truth, love, and goodness. It transforms his view of the world around him, and he feels fully alive. "He went to Church, and walked about the streets, and watched the people hurrying to and fro, and he patted children on the head, and questioned beg-gars, and looked down into the kitchens of houses, and up to the windows, and found that everything could yield him pleasure. He had never dreamed that any walk—that anything—could give him so much happiness." He found out that hell is a place for those who refuse to love. He also found out that love is about more than words and feelings. Whether it is in loving one's spouse, neighbor, or even one's enemy, *love reveals itself in action*. Love is not love until it is given away.

The way that Ebenezer Scrooge ends up reminds me of doctors who love what they are doing. Throughout the history of medicine, up to modern times, with volunteer doctors in Doctors Without Borders, we see love in action by doctors who not only love what they are doing, but who are showing and sharing their love for others.

However, many people, similar to the earlier unchanged Ebenezer Scrooge, live enclosed in their own selfish self-love—a prison defined by the limits of their comfort, possessions, or reputation. Even the commonplace and routine can help us to see the infinite, as they did for Ebenezer Scrooge. This occurs when we grow beyond ourselves to the point where *giving-love is the unlimited horizon and not the self-love boundary* of our life. The infinite and giving-love are the transforming "more," which is beyond the duality of self and others. One need not be a saint in order to love. But only someone who has loved can be a saint.

We need to look beyond contrasting dualities and related couplings toward the positive *third way* of looking at things, toward the light. Because the nearer that you get to the light, the more clearly you can see your own darkness, which may be uncomfortable at first, but you are grateful because you are closer to the light, which represents the positive, the truth, God, and His enlightenments and illuminations—in other words, truth, love, and goodness—plus all of the values, virtues, ideals, and principles.

We must always be open to when we might interfere with *life, love, and laughter*. Because to really live, like Scrooge on Christmas morning, and to love and to laugh, is to be transformed. It is to have acquired the ability to see and to possess all of the values, virtues, ideals, and principles which are transforming. This is the "more," the transformation beyond duality and trinity. Transformation involves the spirit and soul, which is beyond body and mind. Awe, wonder, and worship are key spiritual dimensions of human fulfillment or transformation that goes beyond mere physical satisfaction of the body or mental happiness of the mind.

- We are in awe of the thrill of *living* (being alive);

- We are in awe of the wonder of *loving*; and

- We are in awe of the joy of *laughing*.

> There is no exercise better for the heart than reaching down and lifting people up. It is well to remember that the entire universe, with one trifling exception, is composed of others.
> —*John Andrew Holmes, author, 20th century*

No one has it "all together." That's like tying to eat "once and for all." Everything that occurs in the outside world can come inside to affect your family and you. The darkness out there is the elephant in the room that everyone tries to forget or ignore, but which is always around every family. The elephant is too negative for you to want to notice or think about. "I have the feeling that I've seen everything, but failed to notice the elephants" (Anton Chekhov, Russian short-story writer and playwright, 1860-1904). The world will not change until you do. The more light within you, the more the world will shine. Light shining in you is transformation.

It's true that what you reap you sow, and that what goes around comes around, but my wife and I do not feel responsible for the elephant in the room of the outer world's infidelity, divorce, illegitimacy, miscarriages, abortions, alcoholism, abuse, attempted rapes, accidents, drugs, cancers and diseases, mental illnesses, deaths, losses of faith, wars, and doctrinal differences, etc.

On the other hand, good things in the outside world can affect your family too, such as the increasing quality of medical care and increasing longevity; better home construction; better variety of entertainment, better museums, and better culture, etc.

While I was going through medical school, I frequently thought that it would be wonderful if everyone could attend medical school. Of course, I know that to be impossible, because everyone doesn't have the same interests. However, there is so much about life and human nature that is learned from the study of diseases and mental illnesses. When we are children growing up, we are so unaware of any of the mental illnesses, such as depression, obsessive-compulsive disorder, autism, paranoid schizophrenia, mental deficiency, attention-deficit hyperactivity disorder (ADHD), juvenile delinquency, epilepsy, sexual deviation, pedophilia, etc. Medical school brings us to the truth that *life, at its essence, is really all about life or death*, not only physical death, but also the death of our mental, emotional, and spiritual lives; and the death of truth, love, and goodness.

"You need to learn to be your own best friend because you fall too easily into the trap of being your own worst enemy" (Robert Thorpe, Yorkshire priest, martyr, died 1595). Being your own worst enemy is equivalent to beating your head against the wall because it feels so good to stop. It's so much better to know enough not to start. As children growing up, we have no idea that what we are seeing in life is tobacco addiction, alcohol addiction, compulsive eating disorder, anorexia, drug addiction, brain damage from substance abuse, senile dementia, tranquilizer apathy and indifference, etc.

Joseph Addison (English essayist and poet, 1672-1719) pointed out that joy comes into your life when you have something to do, someone to love, and something to hope for. That is a significant trinity of three. I hope that whatever you do is that which you love; and that whoever you love, and do for, is the one whom you have always hoped for.

The next chapter will explore the other half of the duality of: chains and cycles, symbolized by straight line and circle, to bring us to a clearer understanding of what is "more" as it relates to our understanding of transformation.

Chapter 11.

Cycles
(Oriental, Nothing-New, Organic, Seasonal, Tidal)

What goes around comes around.
—*Old proverb*

Everything starts to die the second it's born, because health is the slowest way to die.
—*Author unknown*

Thinking in cycles as a philosophy of life is considered to be characteristic of the Oriental East. This thinking in cycles is organic, like the seasons or the tides. This is characteristic of nature and, therefore, Mother Earth, and so it is considered to be female. What goes out comes in again. There is nothing new under the sun. It's symbol is an arrow going in a circle or a circle. Also, because the symbol of female is the letter "O" or a "V" or a triangle with it's peak pointing down, cycles or recycling can be symbolized with arrows pointing in the same direction forming a triangle. Additionally, cycles are sometimes symbolized as an ascending spiral or a pendulum.

The past does not repeat itself, but it rhymes.
—*Mark Twain, American humorist, novelist and lecturer, 1835-1910*

Repeating cycles can be found in the following expressions:

- "What you sow you reap."

- "Do unto others as you would have them do unto you."

- "What the tide brings out, it can bring back in again."

153

These expressions show the Oriental Eastern approach to understanding life, which emphasizes that human nature doesn't change, with nothing new, as compared to the linear Occidental Western approach, which emphasizes progress and wants everything new. The Western approach follows the old Latin expression "*Omne ignotum pro magnifico est*," which means "Anything we haven't seen before is marvelous." But the Eastern approach is more like a pendulum of what goes around comes around. As an example of the pendulum, just follow a trend. A thousand years ago, the Oriental East was the world's most advanced civilization, with Europe recovering from the Middle Ages and North America not yet discovered. Over a thousand years, the pendulum swung to reverse things with America now the most dominant, and Europe still second. In our modern times, now, we sense the pendulum swinging back again, as China is becoming predominant. It raises the questions of: "Must the pendulum swing or can all rise to move forward together?" "Does the philosophy of East or West prove to be the dominant one, or can they both add something together that is a greater whole than the sum of the parts?" Like the yin and the yang, together symbolizing a new wholeness or completeness with all of its potential creativity, or the symbol of an arrow hitting the bull's-eye in the center of a circular target, as a win-win situation.

The cycles of life and death, cycling and recycling were brought home to me in Anatomy class. The cadaver that I had for dissection in the class on Anatomy in medical school was a muscular, young, black male whom I later realized was probably a prisoner who had been hanged—and that he had nobly donated his body to science. I realized this when, much later, we were dissecting the neck and head, which we found congested with blood in the tissues.

Five students were assigned to each cadaver. My brother, Don, was assigned to a different table. My table had a male, and Don's table had a female. When it came time to make the first incision, no one at our table but me wanted to make the first incision. I was anxious to do it, but when I approached the body with the knife, I hesitated. I didn't think I would hesitate, but I did. It is a momentous step and a milestone. You have the sense that you'll be violating something sacred. Cutting the human body gives a sense of doing something forbidden. While I hesitated, some of the others began to say, "If you don't want to do it, I'll do it." Prodded on, I said, "No. I'll do it," and I went ahead. The body was totally wrapped in cloth, with just the front of the chest exposed, and we were to make a "Y"-shaped incision, with the top of the "Y" at each shoulder. One of the lessons I learned that day, by experiencing it, is that there are certain innate truths about some things being sacred or forbidden that we all know intuitively. The cycle of learning from "others" was also evident that day. There is an old Buddhist proverb: "When the student is ready the teacher will appear." The teacher, in this case, was my cadaver.

Cycles can be illustrated by the story of Cinderella.

In the story of Cinderella, the Fairy Godmother is a symbol of God in the form of the benevolent, magical, spiritual influences that are always present with those who seek truth and illumination in their thinking through prayer, which is talking to God. Cinderella is so natural at prayer and so obviously comfortable in the presence of God (the Fairy Godmother) that she seems accustomed to talking with her. C.S. Lewis (Irish author and Oxford scholar 1898-1963) said, "As long as you have to count the steps, you are not yet dancing, but only learning to dance." Cinderella has learned the dance. She knows how to pray—so much so, that she seems to know that joy happens again and again, and will, as long as she lives. The experience of joy is cyclical to those who, like Cinderella, are open to it.

In medical school, as medical students, we were required to visit the homes of women who had recently delivered babies to check on the home conditions of the babies and their mothers. We saw the appalling poverty at that time in the ghettos of Philadelphia. Many of the mothers, in their poverty, reminded me of Cinderella, with their calm acceptance of life and their stoic demeanor despite the poverty of their lives.

Despite the dangerous ghetto neighborhoods that we were in, we were unharmed. But the visitation practice as part of the curriculum was stopped shortly after our class.

Once, a car came quickly down the street to where a few other medical students and I were crossing the street, and the car stopped a few feet from us, as we were walking back to the medical school. We were wearing white shoes. The driver leaned out the window and said, "Don't worry doc, I won't hurt you."

The invisible things of trust, faith, love, and forgiveness bring pure, magical enchantment to us as well as to Cinderella. You can't see a trend visibly, but you know instinctively the trend for the stepmother and stepsisters. They're going to be big losers. Their big feet will take them nowhere. The ability to live serenely in the outer world is increased by your mastering the art of living serenely in the inner one, which Cinderella has done for years. Cinderella is living in the realm of higher thinking and living called *transformation*. Cinderella has hope, because hope is not the feeling that something good is going to happen, but that everything makes sense. No one can whistle a symphony. It takes a team called an orchestra, and no one can succeed in life alone. Cinderella finds that she is not alone, and that she is not helpless and hopeless. Her refusal to surrender to negativity is what puts Cinderella in the positive presence of the Fairy Godmother and on the side of God and with God (the Godmother).

About 1988, a Bantam book, called *The Cinderella Syndrome: Discovering God's Plan When Your Dreams Don't Come True* by Lee Ezell (contemporary author and humor therapist), came out encouraging girls not to wait to be saved by a knight in shining armor, but to become whole persons unto themselves. When a whole man and a whole woman enter into a marriage, they each are a support to each other. They are a team and not partners living parasitically on each other.

Cinderella is in the presence of that supernatural "magic" we call faith, hope, and love. An invitation not offered in love is not an invitation at all. Cinderella's invitation to the ball is because of her Godmother's love.

The stepmother is the opposite of the Godmother. The stepmother represents the cold, cruel world and the stepsisters represent all the greedy and selfish, ego-focused people in it. *That is no match for love.* Hate can summon the powers of the world, but only love can summon the powers of God. It's possible to look at darkness while at the same time denying its power over you. Whatever punishment you wish upon another, you only subconsciously attract to yourself. Cinderella is not wishing punishment on others; she is just wishing that she could go to the ball. The most powerful life is one like Cinderella's, in which she lives all the time in God's presence, even though God is not always visible. Living there, you can always work miracles. Living outside of there, you will always be in need of them.

Our problem is not a lack of magic in the world but that we don't believe in magic. We don't show up fully for life, and therefore life is not showing up more fully for us. Life is more than material; there is the spiritual. Life is more than the visible; there is the invisible. There is no greater miracle than a person becoming all that he or she can be. It's never a case of what we're not getting but always a case of what we're not giving.

Notice that Cinderella is not afraid, as her heart is full of love, and love casts out fear. Jesus was always going around saying, "Don't be afraid," (John 6:20 and Luke 8:50), which is another way of saying: "Love," because love casts out all fear (1 John 4:18). Every situation, even Cinderella's, is an opportunity to have faith, hope, love, wisdom, and forgiveness. Because we are all fallible, we are saved by forgiveness and love.

As a matter of fact, when the Fairy Godmother waves her magic wand, so much light surrounds Cinderella that Cinderella is over-enlightened and has to stop crying. Cinderella finds God where she least expects to find Him, in the disguise of a frail but loving old woman, a Godmother.

Cinderella is seeking not greatness but only the truth of why things are as they are. She wants the hope that everything makes sense. Nevertheless, Cinderella's life has been one of service. And through her suffering and through her service, we just know that Cinderella is going to end up great.

> If you want to be great, all you have to do is serve.
> —*Martin Luther King, Jr., American clergyman, civil-rights activist, and 1964 Nobel Peace Prize winner, 1929-1968*

> A life of service is a life of significance.
> —*George Bush, 43rd President of the United States, born 1946*

> There is only one road to true human greatness: the road through suffering.
> —*Albert Einstein, German theoretical physicist and 1921 Nobel Physics Prize winner, 1879-1955*

No matter where you are or what you are doing, there is an opportunity to be happy. Cinderella is not sabotaging herself with fear, judgment and blame. You can have faith in a world of limitation, or you can have faith in a world of limitless good. No one else's good fortune diminishes your own. What does Cinderella do, when she's left alone by her cruel stepmother and her two greedy selfish sisters, as they go to the palace without Cinderella to enjoy all the **p**restige, **p**ower, **p**leasure, **p**ersonality, **p**rivilege, **p**eople and the **p**rince that are found at the **p**alace? Does she get angry and run after them, blaming them or plotting revenge against them? No! Does she shout curses and obscenities, or shake with fear, or judge them, or go through all of the **f**ight, **f**right, **f**light, **f**un and **f**alsity of psychological defenses? No! She is happy for them and sad for herself, and she simply sits down and cries in touch with the reality of her own emotions and her own situation.

Sadness has to be experienced in order to be transcended. No situation can be transformed until it is accepted as it is. Accepted suffering becomes love; that is the mystery. Psychic pain, like physical pain, is there for a reason. We don't heal a broken leg by numbing it, and neither can we heal a broken heart by numbing it. Numbing is just another name for denial, transference, fight, flight, fright, fun, falsity and any other term on our list of defenses that we use to escape from facing painful reality. We must put our heart where our pain is, because the language of the faithful, loving, and forgiving heart, like Cinderella's heart, is the language we all should be speaking.

Cinderella's heart is more in touch with spiritual levels of faith, hope and love than with secular and material levels of money, power, and prestige shown by her stepmother and stepsisters. They think that Cinderella is disadvantaged, but they are the ones who are disadvantaged. They think that Cinderella is poor, but she is spiritually rich. They think that Cinderella is deceived, but they are the ones who are deceived, because they are deceiving no one but themselves. If knowledge is power, then there is more for the deceiver and less for the deceived; therefore, there is less for the stepsisters, as they are deceiving themselves. But Cinderella is neither deceiver nor deceived, and her power is increased, because their power is decreased, adding to her already powerful spiritual knowledge.

Like Cinderella at the stroke of midnight, you can run to go back to the way you were, or you can choose to stay in the light of love in the palace of the King (God). God commanded us to love one another as a way to remove from our midst all that is not love.
Where there is no love, do as Cinderella did; put love there, and you will find love. You will move from self-centered ambition to love-centered service, from exploitation to ministration, from spiritual poverty to spiritual richness. New beginnings are possible anywhere, for God is everywhere. God, like Cinderella's Godmother, works with what's there. Miracles always change the world, though not always externally.

Many feel that it is getting close to symbolic midnight for America and the world. We must make a choice between living with ashes and all that implies, namely, living ruled by selfish others, or finding something fragile that fits our walk in life, symbolized by the glass slipper for Cinderella's foot. That fragile something consists of the invisible values, virtues, ideals, and principles of spirituality, which fit all who have the spirit, love, and selflessness that Cinderella has. Having that fragile something will put you into the realm of transformation, into the palace of the King (God).

The lesson of the marriage of Cinderella is that those whom God has joined together, as He has joined us all, cannot be put asunder. It is only our thinking that separates us. Unity is the key to our happiness. We live in our own prison—not a palace—when our hearts are not open to allow us the experiences of unity, camaraderie, universal brotherhood, solidarity, team spirit, neighborliness, esprit-de-corps, friendship and/or family.

> Some people see things as they are and ask, "Why?" I think of how they could be and I ask, "Why not?"
> —*George Bernard Shaw, Irish author and 1925 Nobel Prize winner in literature, 1856-1950*

Imagining ourselves to be separate waves, we are tiny and powerless, when in fact, we are integral to the immense power of the ocean (God).

The Fairy Godmother reminds Cinderella of whose child she is, namely, a child of God. We are either host to God or hostage to our ego and hostage to others' egos. We are all creatures of both fertile earth and endless sky, ash and palace. We are meant to embody them both, as we "render to Caesar the things that are Caesar's, and to God the things that are God's" (Matthew 22:21, Mark 12:17, Luke 20:25).

Before everything comes together in the concluding summary of Chapter 14, Ethics, Morality, Spirituality and the Postscript, you need to understand the next two chapters on defenses that are used to defend against trauma, stress, and loss.

Chapter 12.

Humor

Instead of working for the survival of the fittest, we should be working for the survival of the wittiest; then we can all die laughing.
—*Lily Tomlin, American comedienne and actor, born 1939*

A well-developed sense of humor is the pole that adds balance to your steps as you walk the tightrope of life.
—*William A. Ward, American author, 1921-1994*

We feel, so often, that we are balanced between one thing or another and between this or that, but humor, which is one of our defenses, allows us a third way out of our duality, or out of our paradox, or out of our horns-of-a-dilemma. You've heard it said that when the going gets tough, the tough get going. But Joel Goodman, (M. Ed., Ed. D., contemporary author, humorist) says, "When the going gets tough, the tough get…laughing."

We must learn to live off the happiness of each other and not off the misery of each other.
—*Charlie Chaplin, American comedic actor, 1889-1977*

We don't laugh because we're happy—we're happy because we laugh.
—*Dr. William James, often called the father of psychology, and a graduate of Harvard Medical School in 1869, 1842-1910*

Joy is not in things. It is in us.
—*Benjamin Franklin, one of the Founding Fathers of the United States, 1706-1790*

> To laugh often and much, to win the respect of intelligent
> people and the affection of children…to leave the world
> a bit better…to know even one life has breathed easier
> because you have lived, this is to have succeeded.
> —*Ralph Waldo Emerson, American author, 1803-1882*

My life has focused on crystallized truths and wisdom found in short wise sayings and brilliant ideas, which can be called *light* (enlightenment, illumination). Another term is **Aha!** for this insight of light. And my life has also focused on trying to remain upbeat with humor, which can also be called **Ha-Ha!,** like the *life* of the party! My life has also focused on the transformation by *love*, which can also be called transcendence or **Wow!** In other words, my life has been a trinity of *light, life, love* or **Aha!, Ha-Ha!, Wow**! I like to think of it as *faith, hope, and charity*, because where there's light or enlightenment, there's faith; and where there's life, there's hope. And charity is often used synonymously for love.

> Laughter in our home is its heart beating.
> —*Bob Talbert, in Michigan Journalism Hall of Fame, 1936-1999*

My father had a good sense of humor, and he always had a joke or two to tell. He had a sense of timing that brought out the punch line. And I believe I have inherited that same sense of humor and joke timing. In medicine, there can be some dark humor to relieve tension. I was reminded of this when I heard that there was a contest to find the world's funniest joke by presenting two jokes on a television show. People watching the show voted on which joke was funniest. Then the losing joke was replaced with another joke, and the contest was repeated on and on. They found that one of the world's funniest jokes is an example of some dark humor: "Other than that, Mr. Lincoln, how did you enjoy the play?"

Thomas Merton (Trappist Monk and author, 1915-1968) said: "A happiness that is sought for ourselves alone can never be found, because happiness that is diminished by being shared is not big enough to make us happy."

Love may be responsible for our suffering, but love is also responsible for our happiness. Love gives us a duality of happiness and suffering. Another duality is work and leisure. "We will never get work right unless we get leisure right" (Michael Naughton, contemporary American professor and author). "We sometimes need to take a break from work altogether. We'll never get our giving right unless we get our receiving right, and the heart of receiving is found in this idea of contemplation" (Michael Naughton, contemporary American professor and author).

William Blake, (1757-1827), the English poet and visionary artist said, "We are put on earth for a little space, that we may learn to bear the beams of love," because *to love is to suffer*. What is important is another way out of the dualism, the nuanced third way of higher thinking beyond, which always includes values, such as love, when there is transformation. Life is not just joy or sorrow, happy or sad, consolation or desolation.

Love also makes us happy. The most revolutionary thing that you can do is to be happy. Robert Louis Stevenson (Scottish novelist and poet, 1850-1894) said, "There is no duty so much underrated as the duty of being happy."

St. Francis of Assisi, (Roman Catholic saint, 1181 or 1182-1226), when he renounced everything to become a poor beggar ministering to outcasts, said that he did it because he wanted to be happy.

We are obliged to be happy because it makes us better people.

> Most people are in such a rush to enjoy themselves that they hurry right past it.
> —*Søren Kierkegaard, Danish philosopher and author, 1813-1855*

Plenty of people miss their share of happiness, not because they never found it, but because they didn't stop to enjoy it.
—*William Feather (American publisher and author, 1889-1981*

Love in your heart is to be in heaven, hate in your heart is to be in hell.
We are no longer happy as soon as we wish to be happier.
—*Walter Savage Landor, British author and poet, 1775-1864*

As children, we try to be happy as best we can. I remember one Halloween, when my brother and I put together some peeled grapes, that in the dark, would feel like eyeballs; and a wet, canvas glove filled with sand, that in the dark, would feel like a dead man's hand; and cooked spaghetti, that in the dark, would feel like worms. Our school chums squealed in disgust as they touched the objects, but they seemed smart enough to know what they were touching. As children, we live the duality of seeking attention or wanting to be left alone, and life is more than just that.

Truisms:

- The happiest people may not have the best of everything; they just make the best of everything.

- A good laugh is sunshine in a house.
  —*William Makepeace Thackeray, English Novelist, 1811-1863*

- Most folks are as happy as they make up their minds to be.
  —*Abraham Lincoln, 16th President of the United States, 1809-1865*

- If the sun's not shining on you, then, at least it's shining on someone else.

My twin brother and I tried to keep happy and engrossed in our schooling. What makes you happy is what makes you wise.

We had a model train, read comic books, read Tom Swift and Hardy Boys novels, went to the movies, went window shopping, had an early television set, took piano and violin lessons, had a chemistry set, and had a pet rabbit. And we also kept busy making model airplanes and celebrating birthdays and holidays, such as Easter, Christmas, Halloween, and Valentine's Day. Lincoln's Birthday meant for us a cake shaped like a log. All this was possible only because our parents loved us, but for me as a child, it seemed only like what I expected my parents to be doing. My parents knew more about love than I knew.

Our piano lessons were given by a nun at grammar school, and by the time we were in the eighth grade, the nun contacted the Philadelphia Academy of Music to arrange an interview, because she felt we could advance even more there. We went for an audition and were accepted. We would practice on the upright piano in our basement apartment. There was a beauty parlor that moved into the space above us on the first floor, and the lady who owned the beauty parlor said that the patrons enjoyed hearing us practice. So did the tenants of the apartment house, who came to use the washtubs in the nearby laundry section of the basement. Piano recitals were always an anxious time for me, perhaps as a reflection of my being a child in a dysfunctional family from my dad's alcoholism, where a child is afraid to make a mistake. Reinforced by the natural sensitivity of all children.

What really gave us hope as children, to get out of our parallel world and dysfunctional world, was the getting of roller skates and bikes. It gave us a real sense of mobility, and a sense of getting away. We didn't have a family car, but we could go for an occasional Sunday drive as passengers in our Uncle's car. It was a real treat to get cool in the summer with the windows open, especially if we ended at a local traveling fair. Back then, there was no such thing as the use of air conditioning generally, only electric fans. One movie theater advertised itself as air-cooled, which meant that they had fans in the front of the theater blowing at the audience. In the summers, before we became old enough to go to work, my brother and I had to sit, sweating in our underwear, because it was too hot in our apartment to wear full clothing. We would, at that time, try to read or practice learning how to type on our typewriter. It was too hot to do anything else. Once a year, on Washington's Birthday, a nearby store would offer typewriters for sale for just a few dollars on a first-come, first-served basis. We tried to be first in line, and we made it one year. The typewriter that we bought cheaply was old, but it worked. I figured that if I could play the piano, I could learn to type. And I easily did, with a little practice. My dad, on the other hand, had tried to learn typing at one time, but he seemed to give it up, which I attributed to his drinking.

There was such joy in being mobile. Roller-skating was my childhood heaven. It started in the basement of the Stonehurst Apartments, and then went onto the streets. Pleasure delayed is pleasure denied. We graduated in our mobility to riding bicycles and then to riding a bus to the end of the line and back again on Sunday afternoons. The bus ride was ten cents each way. Often, we ended in Germantown to visit a Church there and sometimes we bought some chemistry glassware in a local store there. Eventually, as teenagers we went downtown into Philadelphia to the museums by riding the elevated subway train called the "el" (for elevated). We rode that same "el" for four years to West Philadelphia Catholic High School for Boys, which is at 49th Street.

Our mother liked to dress us alike and all in white, even to the shoes, so that we stood out like little angels, with sky-blue ties. We now know that twins should not dress alike. A reporter at one time spotted us, and he took our picture in downtown Philadelphia on our way to the Franklin Institute. He posed us looking up into the sky, as an eclipse was due that day. We really weren't looking at the eclipse at the time of the photo; it was a posed picture for the purposes of the newspaperman. We at first tried to avoid this man, who was running across the street trying to get our attention, but he caught up with us for the picture, and as they say, "The rest is history," because our picture ended up in the newspaper.

I bring all these things up to you because I'm writing about happy times and love's fire. The love of God kept me going, as did the comradeship and brotherly love of twins, and the hope of eventual graduation. The next big event in growing up, as I remember it, that gave me hope for the future to get out of my parallel and dysfunctional world, was puberty, along with the good feelings of knowing that I wanted to eventually marry the girl of my dreams, which I eventually did.

When the right man meets the right girl at the right time, everything is right. I knew Margaret was the right girl for me the first time I met her. I prayed to God to give her to me in marriage. She is a beautiful intelligent woman with a kind and compassionate spirit who loves children, and me too, fortunately. We were introduced through a classmate friend who knew her brother. I had to suffer all of life's uncertainties with dating, and the dating scene, until she knew that I was the right man for her, as she was very popular with all of the boys who met her. One of our first dates was to a magic show in downtown Philadelphia. Blackstone the magician was the show, and we had first-row seats, because I took care to get the tickets early. She eventually gave me her picture, that I cherish, and I cherish her. When I was at Jefferson Medical College, we had a date at my fraternity that was semi-formal, and she wore a long, light-colored dress. It was held at my medical fraternity, Phi Alpha Sigma, which was two blocks from Jefferson Medical College (now a University) and Jefferson Hospital. The fraternity colors appropriate for a medical fraternity were black and blue. We danced in the living room of the fraternity house and I held her, warmly glowing, in my arms. It snowed that night, and we had to take a taxi all the way from 5th street to 69th street into an area called Upper Darby, in west Philadelphia, where I lived with my parents. 69th Street is the end of the line for the "el" in west Philadelphia. And the apartment house that I lived in was just a short walk from there. We were married just before I started my internship following my graduation from medical school.

In Bacteriology lab in medical school, I learned that bacteria (germs) were everywhere. Bacteria are ubiquitous (everywhere). If stool bacteria (*Escherichia coli*) were fluorescent, then an ultraviolet light would light up the world. In Bacteriology lab, and the operating room, you learn sterile technique. It's a difficult concept for some people to learn. It's vital that you keep your clean and sterile gloves from touching anything that is not sterile. Every medical student has black carbon put on their hands and then they are blindfolded in front of a surgical scrub sink and then told to wash their hands with soap and a scrub brush for about 10 minutes or until the person scrubbing thinks that their hands are clean. When the blindfold is removed, there is the shock of revelation about how much carbon still remains around the fingernails and between the fingers.

During surgery, there is often incidental talking and sometimes joke telling, as it helps to relax the team. A team doing surgery seems, at times, to be able to read each other's minds in anticipation of what bleeding blood vessel ("bleeder") to clamp next or what step to do next in order to complete the operation. I once told a joke on our Chief of Surgery at a dinner in his honor. I said that I was telling my Chief, while we were operating, that the latest fashion style is for people to wear clothes of the same color as their hair. If you have brown hair, brown clothes; black hair, black clothes, etc. I said that I could read his mind; he was thinking, "What do you wear if you're bald?"

Humans are the only animals that laugh, cry, and enjoy music, and we are also the only animals that need to. Music by itself can make us laugh, cry, and be inspired.

- We cannot really love anybody with whom we never laugh.
  —*Agnes Repplier, American Essayist, 1855-1950*

- You can't be sexy if you're not funny.
  —*Carol Burnett, American comedian, born 1933*

- Among those whom I like, I can find no common denominator; but among those whom I love, I can: all of them make me laugh.
  —*Wystan Hugh Auden, Anglo-American author and poet, 1907-1973*

- It is a curious thought, but it is only when you see people looking ridiculous that you realize just how much you love them.
  —Agatha Christie, English crime novelist, 1890-1976

- The smile is the universal symbol for accepting others.
  —Susan Isaacs, contemporary American author and screenwriter, born 1943

- Those who do not know how to weep do not know how to laugh either.
  —Golda Mier, Israeli prime minister, 1898-1978

- Of all days, the day on which one has not laughed is the one most surely wasted. The most wasted day of all is that during which we have not laughed. That of all days is most completely wasted in which one did not once laugh.
  —Nicolas-Sebastien Roch Chamfort, French author and aphorist, 1741-1794

- An optimist laughs to forget; a pessimist forgets to laugh.
  —Tom Nansbury, contemporary American author

In the book *The Brothers Karamazov*, by Fyodor Mikhailovich Dostoevsky (Russian novelist, 1821-1881), we read, "For we are made for happiness, and anyone who is completely happy has a right to say to himself, 'I am doing God's will on earth.' All the righteous, all the saints, all the holy martyrs were happy."

Every person longs for happiness.

What if happiness is not subjective, not a question of how we feel, or not a matter of chance, not something that simply happens, and it is more an objective condition, something analogous to bodily health? Aristotle (Greek philosopher and author, 384 B.C.-322 B.C.) took this view. The word he used for happiness, *eudaimonia*, is not a matter of feelings but is a way of being, a certain fullness of life. Happiness, for Aristotle, has to do with living in accordance with the rational and moral order of the universe. It is more like the flourishing of a healthy plant than like Freud's pleasure principle. Happiness is more like sharing in the life and spirit and the happiness of God, which is happiness immune to loss, pain, and changing circumstances.

> Happiness is not a station you arrive at, but a manner of traveling.
> —*Margaret Lee Runbeck, contemporary author, 1905-1956*

This is evident when you stand outside a room where a group of Alcoholics Anonymous is meeting, and you hear the laughter from people who have lived with imminent alcohol destruction for years and from which they are now free and unafraid. Their belief in a higher power (God) has them holding God's hand and feeling safe enough now to be able to be happy and to really laugh.

The happiest people we see are those whose love and courage and inner balance seem to set them apart as people who remind us of God. They have found their own personal destiny and they know what God wants them to be. There is a relationship between "the duty of delight," holiness and happiness. And there is a relationship between happiness and the exercise of patience, humility, forgiveness, self-sacrifice, generosity, and the final goal of all spiritual practice, namely, love. God is love.

St. Irenaeus, a second-century bishop and theologian, (died 202), put it this way: "*The glory of God is the human being fully alive.*" To be fully alive is a matter of living out of the deepest part of oneself. Call it living out of the heart and the soul. Sanctity is really a matter of being more fully human.

> A sad saint is a sad sort of saint."
> —*St. Francis de Sales, Roman Catholic Bishop of Geneva, 1567-1622*

On August 15th every year for a number of years, my family returned for a picnic at a local park near Shenandoah, Pennsylvania, where my grandparents lived. The ride to Shenandoah by car always made me car sick, as we had to travel about 100 miles. My dad would smoke as he drove along, and I wonder if breathing in that smoke, and thereby getting a certain dose of nicotine, added to my motion sickness. I now recognize an allergy to tobacco smoke, which rapidly makes my nose stuffy. For all of us, it was a form of family reunion. Once we got there we would ride in an old-fashioned, open truck that belonged to my grandfather to the picnic grounds. The open truck had a roof and padded-leather parallel benches on both sides. Canvas curtains could be rolled down if it were to rain. It was like a hay ride without the horses or the hay, except for us saying, "Hey-Hey!"

There was a swimming pool in the park, and my dad dove off the high board, which really impressed me, but of course, I also was scared that he could get hurt or die, especially as he had been drinking, as usual. We would stay at my grandfather's house (my dad's father) in Shenandoah or at a nearby farmhouse of my Uncle Jimmy (my mother's brother). He didn't smoke, like my father, but he chewed tobacco. If Uncle Jimmy was driving, he would spit out the window of his vehicle, leaving a nauseating brownish stain on his driver's side window. His teeth seemed just as stained. On his farm was a lake, but no swimming or boating was allowed because of snakes. I got my first bee-sting by that lake. My mother and my aunt, uncle Jimmy's wife, would both harvest fresh corn from the farm and cook it for dinner as a special treat. They would also pluck and cook a chicken after uncle Jimmy would chop the head off. That gave everyone the opportunity to see a chicken temporarily walking around by reflexes, with its head cut off.

Thomas Merton (Trappist monk and author, 1915-1968) said, "If all you needed to be happy was to grab everything and see everything and investigate every experience and then talk about it, I should have been a very happy person." *But he was not.* He found out that there is a deeper purpose to existence, which is to live with the soul's joy in a world that is charged with the presence and reality of God. Why not be totally changed into fire yourself?

> To be awake is to be alive.
> —*Henry David Thoreau, naturalist philosopher, 1817-1862*

> It has always surprised me how little attention philosophers have paid to humor since it is a more significant process of mind than reason. Reason can only sort out perceptions, but the humor process is involved in changing them.
> —*Dr. Edward de Bono, British physician and author, born 1933*

My relatives did not think it humorous for me to shoot targets out of a bedroom window. Uncle Jimmy had a 22-gauge rifle, which Don and I used for practice shooting. One day, I shot the rifle out of the bedroom window before everyone woke up. I was told to stop doing that. I'm sure it made everyone afraid to step out of the house. In high school, later, Don and I were in the school's rifle club. I got a ribbon for shooting in a high school competition. At school, you practiced shooting lying down, but the competition shooting took place standing up. The competitive rifles were very heavy, and some official standing next to you was urging you to hurry up and to not put the rifle down between shots, which you wanted to do to rest your arms. I remember my first shot vividly, when the gun's sight and the bull's eye were perfectly aligned together just as the gun fired. The heavy gun and its gun sight were weaving and wobbling as I was simultaneously aiming and squeezing the trigger. I couldn't duplicate that good shot, because my arms were tired, and I couldn't rest them between shots because of the hurry. I began to suspect that the officials were more interested in getting everything over with than in giving everyone a fair shot. I was surprised to get a medal later that day.

Truisms:

- A person without a sense of humor is like a wagon without springs—jolted by every pebble in the road.
  —*Henry Ward Beecher, Protestant Clergyman, 1813-1887*

- Humor is the oil that keeps the engine of society from getting overheated.
  —Mary McNorton, Scottish author, born 1978

- Do not take life too seriously; you will never get out of it alive.
  —Elbert Hubbard, American author and artist, 1856-1915

- In this world, a good time to laugh is any time you can.
  —Linda Ellerbee, journalist, born 1944

- Earth laughs in flowers.
  —Ralph Waldo Emerson, author, philosopher and poet, 1803-1882

- Humor is a serious thing. I like to think of it as one of our greatest and earliest national resources, which must be preserved at all costs.
  —James Thurber, American author, cartoonist and humorist, 1894-1961

Laughter is a defense.

I remember that in order to get a grade of "A" in Physics in college, I had to get a 99 on the final exam. Grades of "A's" and "B's" were very important in order to get into medical school. There was an ambiguous question of interpretation that I asked the professor about during the exam. He said he couldn't give me any help; I would have to just do my best. I got a 99! This particular professor used to be in the Navy, so when he would put a problem on the blackboard, he would always say, "Let's put a few problems up on the bulkhead."

- When a thing is funny, search it for a hidden truth.
  —George Bernard Shaw, Irish author, 1856-1950

- Amusement to an observing mind is study.
  —Benjamin Disraeli, British Prime Minister and novelist, 1804-1881

- We rarely succeed at anything unless we have fun doing it.
  —Rev. John Naus, S.J., a priest who teaches a course on philosophy of humor at Marquette University, born 1924

- In life, pain is inevitable, but suffering is optional.
  —Hedy Schleifer, contemporary marriage counselor, born 1944

- If you haven't got a sense of humor, you haven't got any sense at all.
  —Mary McDonald, contemporary actress, born 1953

- Common sense and a sense of humor are the same thing, moving at different speeds. A sense of humor is just common sense, dancing.
  —William James, author, philosopher and psychologist, 1842-1910

- Joys shared are doubled, sorrows shared are halved.
  —Author unknown

I had a system to help me memorize for college exams. We all know the numbers from one to twenty, and so you attach a mental picture to each of them. For example:

- Number one is an alarm clock, because the first thing you do on waking up is to shut off the alarm.

- Number two is a pair of trousers, because it has two legs.

- Number three is a three-legged stool.

- Number four is a four-legged table.

- Number five is a five-cent nickel.

- Number six is a car with three people in the front seat and three in the back.

- Number seven is a policeman with his hand out saying, "Stop."

- Number eight is a revolving door.

- Number nine is a mailbox on a post.

- Number 10 is a ten-cent newspaper.

- Number 11 is a railroad track, and so on.

You then attach in your mind, to each number, a picture of what you want to remember. For example, if you want to remember what to buy at the store, you picture something like: eggs breaking on the alarm clock, string-beans in the legs of the trousers, a head of lettuce on the stool, etc.

I used that system to get an "A" on a test in college that asked for the 20 reasons why the Japanese attacked Pearl Harbor. Of course I can't remember the 20 reasons now, but that's the defect of the system.

**Humor is truth. Humor is love. Humor is beautiful.
To truly live is to love and to laugh.**

- Humor is not a trick, not jokes. Humor is a presence in the world—like grace—and shines on everybody.
  —*Garrison Keillor, author, humorist, born 1942*

- Imagination was given to us to compensate for what we are not, a sense of humor was provided to console us for what we are.
  —*English Proverb*

- Many a true word is spoken in jest.
  —*English Proverb*

- Happy people are beautiful.
  —*Drew Blyth Barrymore, film actress, born 1975*

At the current time, there is a doom-and-gloom atmosphere in politics due to intense partisanship with lack of compromising. And each party is trying to make the other party look bad. And there is doom and gloom over the economy, over the length of the war against terrorism and its cost, over the rising cost of gas, and over inflation with rising prices on most products and services.

We all are in need of a good laugh, which can possibly happen at any time. Instead, people focus on their need for a good pay raise. But they shouldn't hold their breath while waiting for a pay raise.

After World War II, older students were in our college classes getting an education on the GI Bill. One good friend in our pre-med class from the military could do a handstand on a chair with his legs straight up into the air. I couldn't do it, as my upper-arm strength didn't match my body weight. He seemed amiable and in good spirits, but I don't recall his ever telling any jokes. He went into anesthesiology. Years later, I heard the news that he was found dead on an operating table with anesthesia gas running, an apparent suicide or accident. I couldn't believe it, because he always seemed in control, at peace and not depressed. I remember about him that he was in the lab at college the night a huge moth flew in the open widow. It was so large that it seemed at first to be a bird or a bat, and he swatted it down for inspection. We saved it for our professor to see the next day.

That story reminds me of what was told by the psychiatrist, Carl Jung, of a situation of serendipity. He had a patient who dreamed of a golden scarab, which is a representation of a scarab beetle. This beetle is a talisman in ancient Egypt and a symbol of the soul. While the patient was telling the story, Dr. Jung heard a tapping on the window. He opened it, and in flew a golden beetle that he presented to the patient, saying, "Here, madam is the golden scarab of your dream." He said that this serendipitous event led to a breakthrough from whatever was blocking the patient's recovery.

Serendipity may be a breakthrough, but so are humor and laughter.

> People crave laughter as if it were an essential amino acid.
> —*Dr. Patch Adams, contemporary physician and American author, born 1945*

> Laughter and crying are two of the best healers we have.
> —*Peter McWilliams, American author, 1949-2000*

Sharing fun times and celebrations bind us closer together. These are times of intimacy.

> Failing to pursue intimacy in life undermines abundance because it leads to estrangement, a sense of alienation from others that can lead to feelings of despair and isolation, especially in times of trial.
> —*Gregory K. Popcak, Ph.D., contemporary psychotherapist and author.*

In my lifetime, I can recall a few occasions in which I was laughing so hard at something that I couldn't get my breath, and I wished I could stop laughing in order to breathe. To have the peak of laughing enjoyment at such times seems in retrospect now to have been such a blessing and a miracle out of the ordinary.

The next chapter will explore the other defenses that we use in addition to humor.

Chapter 13.

Defenses

Creative minds have always been known to survive bad training.
—*Anna Freud, wife of Sigmund Freud, 1885-1982*

Courage is what it takes to stand up and speak; courage is also what it takes to sit down and listen.
—*Sir Winston Churchill, British Prime Minister, 1874-1965*

In medical school, we all received training in administering ether to a child during a tonsillectomy, because tonsillectomy was in vogue then, before the use of antibiotics caused a great decline in the need for tonsillectomy. We were told never to leave the patient for any reason while administering anesthesia, because the patient is defenseless, except for you. You had to call someone else to get whatever you might need, because you were the patient's only defense. This chapter is about a different form of defense, namely, the defense responses of humans to stress, trauma and loss. This chapter will help you to get a clearer picture of real transformation.

The human response to the desolation of *stress, trauma, or loss* is that the person goes into defenses, which are represented by the stages of shock, denial, anger, isolation, bargaining, depression, and finally, resolution.

A short way of saying this is **fight, fright, flight,** and **fun**.

- **Fight** = anger, (psychological projection),

- **Fright** = shock, (psychological displacement),

- **Flight** = denial, bargaining and isolation, (psychological dissociation),

- **Fun** = to get over depression, (joking can be a form of psychological reaction formation). We use self-indulgence, as well as self-pity, to run away from our feelings of powerlessness and isolation, but that only makes us feel worse about ourselves and our lives.

The whole world seems, at the current time, to be on the defense with fight, fright, flight, and fun. We can even add in another "f" of "**falsity**," which is the world's dishonesty and hypocrisy as they pretend everything is "fine."

Love is the antidote to all these defenses. And since God is love, what we need is God. And with God (Love), instead of defenses, we are given **faith, forgiveness, friendship, fellowship,** and **forever**.

> Modern man overheats too easily. He lacks too much of the oil of love.
> —*Christian Morgenstern, German author, poet and aphorist, 1871-1914*

> If things are tough, remember that every flower that ever bloomed had to go through a whole lot of dirt to get there.
> —*Barbara Johnson, American author, literary critic and translator, born 1947*

Transformation is beyond consolation and desolation; it is a deep spiritual transformation and not a superficial bodily transformation that occurs whenever your identity is superficially transformed through fashion, clothing, or change of appearance. Fashion, just like stories of the superhero, allows you to dream and escape into a world of unfettered imagination and to become signified or symbolized as a more powerful or sensational you. This superficial transformation is more in the realm of defenses called: *fight, fright, flight, and fun*, rather than in the realm of true deep spiritual transformation, which involves *love, giving, and forgiving.*

Here's a sentence that I just made up: "How can the world that is so defensive be so offensive?" Defense and offense are opposites—and a duality. The cure for what ails the world is love, which is beyond the duality as a third way, or trinity, leading to our transformation.

In the world at the current time, there is a lot of anger, because people are using anger as a defense against all of their stress, trauma, or loss. Being both angry and peaceful is like trying to have day and night at the same time.

In psychiatry, there is an old rule of thumb that says anything that angers, annoys, or upsets you is a reflection of something that you *lack* and/or something that you *wish* for yourself.

A short way of saying this is: *If you spot it, you've got it.*

Another way of expressing this is: *Your enemy's shoe fits your own foot.*

For example, if seeing a supermodel upsets you with anger, or envy, or annoyance that she is prettier than you are, then it is a sign that you feel the *lack* of some prettiness or you *wish* prettiness for yourself.

Another example: If you get angry with anyone who keeps you waiting or with anyone who comes in late, it's because you *lack* being punctual yourself or you *wish* you had punctuality yourself or you *wish* that you could have the right to be late yourself or you *wish* that the person coming in late would respect the schedules of others.

> To show resentment at a reproach is to acknowledge that one may have deserved it.
> —*Tacitus, Italian author, c.56-c.117*

In America, the secular are angry at those with faith and those who are spiritual. America's culture of anger, therefore, may be a reflection that America *lacks* faith in God, or it may reflect that America secretly *wishes* that it had faith. And our hypocrisy (feigning, falsity) may be that we pretend that we don't wish it. Anger makes us act like bees, who, upon stinging each other, cause their own death.

> Cold words freeze people, and hot words scorch them, and bitter words make them bitter, and wrathful words make them wrathful."
> —*Blaise Pascal, French mathematician, physicist and philosopher, 1623-1662*

Kind words also produce their image on men's and women's souls, and it's a beautiful image. Kind words smooth, and quiet, and comfort the hearer. We need more honest and loving words to soothe America's culture of anger.

> Some say, "When a word is said, then it is dead." I say, "When a word is said, it has just begun to live."
> —*Emily Dickinson, poet, 1830-1888*

Doctors know that anger is equivalent to swallowing poison and hoping that your enemy will die, because anger releases all sorts of bad chemicals into the body of the one who is angry. Disease is a form of *dis-ease*. Growling all day makes you dog tired. Oftentimes it's not a case of what you're eating but rather, what is eating you. The time that is spent in anger is time spent away from happiness. The cure for anger is to have some values.

A child who grows up feeling valuable grows up having values. Children do not seem to be considered very valuable at the present time in America; in fact, people act as if they are angry with children. Just look at the world's high rate of the following: abortion, child abuse, pedophilia, dumbed-down education to a low common denominator, school drop-outs, suicides, juvenile delinquency, etc.

To conquer a nation, you don't need to go to war. You only need to weaken its children physically, mentally, and/or morally.

Additionally when it comes to children, doctors know that you don't have to drink in order to suffer from alcoholism. Non-drinking children living in a home with an alcoholic suffer in that dysfunctional family due to the alcoholism. The dysfunctional system is a method of survival used by alcoholic families, and it's called a dance—a painful, dysfunctional dance of defense. An alcoholic family plays dysfunctional roles, just like a hanging mobile that is out of balance. Every family member interacts with each other, similar to each individual piece on a hanging mobile. If we remove one piece because it is damaged, the whole mobile becomes lopsided, unbalanced, and dysfunctional. If one member of a family develops alcoholism or chemical dependency, the whole family becomes dysfunctional.

> No one is an island unto themselves and whatever
> Diminishes me, diminishes you.
> —*John Donne, English poet and priest, 1572-1631*

Family dynamics, similar to those found in alcoholic families, can be found in any family in which there may be a relatively absent father or mother, or a powerful spouse dominating a weaker spouse.

> The best way to raise children is to set a good example.
> —*Albert Schweitzer, physician and German theologian, 1875-1965*

I consider myself to be an Adult Child of an Alcoholic (ACoA); therefore, I grew up in a dysfunctional family situation. Some evidence of it may be seen in the following story:

My medical fraternity house, a few blocks away from my medical school, had copies of some questions asked on the anatomy exam over the years. One of the questions was to name all the muscles that attach to the scapula, which is a bone at the back of the shoulder "floating in a sea" of seventeen muscles. I was able to answer that question better than everyone else, even a former anatomy researcher/anatomist who was in our class and who had decided to go to medical school. After the test, the grades were posted on the bulletin board and there was a star after my name. I thought that star might mean something bad, like "go see the principal," until one of my classmates said that the star is a good thing indicating that mine was the best test score. My not being able to see something about myself to praise is characteristic of ACoA's. It's hard for them to say something positive about themselves. As you might expect, at the end of the year, the prize in anatomy went to the anatomy researcher, because he had years of previous study of anatomy.

Jefferson was different from the other three Philadelphia area medical schools in that you not only dissected an adult cadaver, but you also dissected an infant cadaver in Anatomy class.

Because I am an adult child of an alcoholic (ACoA), I can see some dysfunction in me in the fact that I don't go around complimenting our family by telling others about two of my father's brothers, my uncles Charles ("Hank") and William ("Bill"), who were inducted into the baseball hall of fame. This induction was for their record of accomplishments in the Shenandoah Baseball League in Pennsylvania. This is quite an accomplishment and honor for any family, to have some members in a hall of fame. I am proud of them, as I am of all of the accomplishments in our family, but it is hard for me to put it into words. I remember, as a child, feeling proud of my grandfather, when I saw his name engraved on a brass plate that acknowledged his donation of a beautiful stained glass window to a Church in Shenandoah, Pennsylvania. As we go through life, we all leave some mark on the lives of others that shows that we either built or that we tore down. I don't remember my father ever playing ball with me. My Uncle Bill was the one who gave a baseball bat, gloves and a baseball to my twin brother and me. We then went outside and Uncle Bill threw the ball into my new glove. He was a pitcher and could throw a good fast ball that could sting the hand of a boy just getting used to a new baseball glove for the first time. I could tell he had the knack for throwing the ball, but little did I know that he was so great and famous at the time.

My father, who was talented in carpentry, wallpapering, and painting, moved us when I was about five years old from Shenandoah, Pennsylvania, where my twin brother and I were born, to 69th Street in west Philadelphia, where he was able to get a job during the Depression, as a janitor, furnace-fireman, wall paperer, painter, plumber and jack-of-all-trades in an apartment house where we lived in the basement apartment. He was also a consistent alcohol drinker and smoker. He only had a high-school education, which was the norm at that time. My brother and I wanted more, and so we were determined not to drink or smoke, and to get a higher education. I didn't want to be like my dad.

My brother and I loved to read, which may have been helped by the fact that television had not yet been invented during our early childhood. I recall that when I was about eight or ten years old, I would have read an encyclopedia from A to Z, because I wanted to learn everything there was to know. When we finally did get an encyclopedia, that feeling had passed, but my love for reading stayed.

Past our teens, while my brother, Don, and I were walking around downtown Philadelphia, after visiting some of its museums, we found a medical-book store near Rittenhouse Square. And the summer before entering medical school, we bought anatomy books to study ahead, because we knew that there would be a lot to learn. This was a big help, because after the first medical school lecture, which was on the anatomy of the posterior triangle of the neck, the whole class was in consternation as to where to find what the professor had just outlined. Fortunately, it was right out of the book *Grant's Method of Anatomy* that I read that summer. I was able to help my classmates by telling them what books to get and read.

One day halfway through the Anatomy semester, the Anatomy professor, out of the blue, asked me to stand up and describe to the class the course of the auditory nerve. Fortunately, I could answer that because I had just read about that in the *Grant's Method of Anatomy* book that night, and I had a mental picture of the course of the nerve from the illustration that was in the book. The rumor was that our anatomy professor was a former surgeon. He wrote a book on the normal anatomy of the bile ducts and the gall bladder and variations in anatomy and anomalies of the bile ducts and gall bladder. Knowing such details is a great help to a surgeon and a defense against operative error.

I have always considered myself to be a sensitive *introvert*, but years ago, on a Meyers-Briggs Personality Type test, I tested to be a sensitive *extrovert*. I thought there must be something wrong with the test.

The psychiatrist Carl Jung (Swiss, founder of analytical psychology, 1875-1961) didn't believe that people could be permanently put into one category of personality or another. "Every individual is an exception to the rule," he wrote.

One of the things medicine teaches is that the common things happen commonly. When you hear hoof beats, think of horses coming, and not zebras. But when it comes right down to it, every person has a unique *body* (physique), *mind* (psychology), and *spirit* (personality and morality/character). After a doctor gets a patient's chief complaint and their medical history, and after he (or she) completes a physical examination of the patient, he (or she) then records in the chart the possibilities of diagnosis. This is called a *differential diagnosis*. You include on the list all of the possible diseases that the patient may have so that you can order appropriate lab tests and other studies to rule in or out all of the various possibilities. You will never diagnose leprosy unless you think of the possibility of it being present, based on the patient's symptoms and signs, and you have it included on your list of differential diagnosis.

I was fortunate in my training to help at surgery some of the great surgeons of my time, such as Dr. John Gibbon who, with the help of his wife, invented the heart-lung machine. I had the example of men of character and I had the privilege to learn and work with them. If I didn't work directly with them, I heard them lecture at medical conventions. My wife, Margaret, sat in on the overcrowded lecture given by the surgeon, Dr. Christian Barnard, who did the first successful heart transplant in a patient. *Life* magazine, at the time, had a picture on its cover of the patient standing and holding his own heart that had been removed. The patient was able to hold his old heart, because he was living with a transplanted new heart.

> One machine can do the work of fifty ordinary men. No machine can do the work of one extraordinary man.
> —*Elbert Hubbard, American author and artist, 1856-1915*

> The older I get the more I feel that faithfulness and perseverance are the greatest virtues. The future doesn't just happen. You must make it happen. Let's pray for stronger backs and not lighter burdens.
> —*Dorothy Day, author, co-founder of the Catholic Worker Movement, 1897-1980*

After taking the four-day Family-Group course at Fellowship Hall in Greenville, North Carolina, designed for relatives of an alcoholic, and after attending Al-Anon meetings and after reading Al-Anon literature, I had a new view of myself and a new self-recognition, I saw myself, for the first time, as *dysfunctional* due to my dysfunctional upbringing with a father who I considered to be an alcoholic. Seeing your father drunk on a few occasions is not a good memory for any child to have. In retrospect, during the time of my growing up, it was expected that drinks were to be offered to someone coming into your home. It was also expected, and shown clearly in old movies, that alcohol was to be taken at the first sign of any stress. My father had a hard life as a janitor, maintenance man, and jack-of-all-trades. Additionally, he lived with cigarette addiction and emphysema and black lung from working in the Shenandoah coalmines in his youth.

He used to tell stories about how he was under a low-ceiling section of coal in an underground mine. He left the section shortly before it collapsed. His fellow worker in the mine was sad, because he had seen my dad at that site earlier and thought my dad had been killed in the collapse. He was overjoyed to see my dad alive. My dad told other stories about how he would drive fast and elude police who were trying to catch those transporting liquor, which he was doing, during Prohibition. When my dad died at age 80, from a heart attack in his sleep, he had a small, inoperable lung cancer seen on an earlier chest x-ray. It was inoperable due to his general health. He started as a paperhanger and painter in Shenandoah, Pennsylvania, until the Depression in the 1930's caused us to move from Shenandoah, Pennsylvania, to the suburbs of Philadelphia. A famous dance band called the Dorsey Brothers (Jimmy and Tommy) had their start in Shenandoah.

When my dad died, the news was sent to me as I was operating and repairing a patient's hernia. The news was brought near the end of the operation. My assistant doctor said that he would finish the case. I said, "Thank you, but I can finish it." Then I burst into tears, and said, "Okay, you go ahead and finish," and I left the operating room.

My father once seemed irritated and anxious and asked if this is all there is to life. He was retired and old; I quietly reminded him in his ear saying, "Dad, you've had two sons who are doctors." He calmed down. In addition to his alcoholism gene, he may have had a depression gene, like my mother.

Adult Children of Alcoholics (ACoA):

1. The most profound characteristic is that they guess at what is normal as all they had in growing up was dysfunctional. *The significance of this statement cannot be overestimated.*

2. They feel that they are different from other people, because

to some degree they are, because they never develop normal social skills having lived surrounded by their family dysfunction.

3. They have difficulty in following a project through from beginning to end, and they are the world's biggest procrastinators, because they have not been taught, or have not seen, organization, only the disorganization of dysfunctionalism.

4. Having been part of a system of lies, cover-up, and negativity, they perpetuate it. This is shown in their lying even to themselves by denial, and living as two-faced with an outer public life to be seen and an inner life that is not to be seen or shared. When they are asked how they are, they say, "fine." They really are: **f**earful, **i**nsecure, **n**eurotic and **e**motional, but they are unwilling to share that secret, because they have never learned that you are only as sick as your secrets.

5. They judge themselves without mercy. When complimented for a job well done, because they are used to a negative self-image, they answer, "It was nothing," with false humility. Accepting praise for being competent means changing the way they see themselves. They need to learn that it's okay to make a mistake, because they are not a mistake. God does not make mistakes. It's hard for them to say something positive about themselves.

6. They take themselves very seriously and have difficulty having fun or being silly. They have feelings of insecurity and fear abandonment. Adult children of alcoholics do not appear to have any more or any fewer sexual problems than the general population. Adult children of alcoholics are not able to sit down and discuss anything with their parents, so sex, then, becomes just like anything else, not well discussed.

7. They over-react to changes over which they have no control. Since the young child is not in control, he or she naturally tends to trust their environment, and as a result, when the child becomes an adult he or she seems controlling, rigid, and lacking in spontaneity. ACoA's are creatures of extremes. "Nothing worth doing is worth doing in moderation," is their motto.

8. They constantly seek approval and affirmation. Having missed out on feelings of constant unconditional love as children, they have a mood of "How can anyone like what I am?"

9. They are either super-responsible or super-irresponsible. They take it all on or they give it all up. Saying "no" is difficult as they don't have a good sense of their own limitations, until they finally burn out.

10. They are extremely loyal, even in the face of evidence that the loyalty is undeserved. No one walks away just because the going gets rough. The so-called "loyalty" is more the result of fear, insecurity and dependency than anything else.

11. No matter what others do or say, the child of an alcoholic rationalizes that somehow they are at fault. That they are a mistake. They also don't know what a good relationship is.

Because I had been living all my life in denial (not the river in Egypt), to my surprise I still needed more truth *to spot it* to know that *I got it*, namely, *dysfunctionalism*.
That truth was given to me late in my life in family rehab teachings about discovery.

My failure to trust and my perfectionism led to me to say at one time: "All my life I've expected more of others, and I've always been disappointed." I was damaged in my ability to tell, feel, and trust. What was a big help all those years was having a twin brother as an equal peer, and my Christian faith in a higher power (God), plus what I suspect to be a protective effect of my depression gene making me just tired when I drank alcohol, instead of firing up an alcoholism pleasure gene with the alcohol.

I may have been okay physically, intellectually, and spiritually, but I was dysfunctional emotionally and psychologically. I was feeling chronic love deprivation. Call it *love deprivation syndrome.*

There is no way that you can offer a child too much love. That doesn't mean that you should overcompensate and give in to their every whim, but you must tell a child that you love him or her, hold them, kiss them, and let them know how lucky you feel that they are yours. That is loving.

It's said that if you put alcohol into the mouths of everyone in the world, 10% of them will have the alcoholism gene so they can't and won't stop and they will become alcoholics. It's similar to "I'll bet you can't eat only one potato chip." When it comes to alcohol, 10% can't stop at one drink. They can't take it and leave it.

Therefore, on having their first drink, or when they first use a drug, they won't be able to stop. They become "alcoholics" and "pot-heads." There are sayings which illustrate this fact:

1. To an alcoholic one drink is too little, and a thousand drinks are not enough.

2. An alcoholic is one drink away from a drunk.

3. 90% of the population who don't have the alcoholism gene can "take it or leave it," but the alcoholic "takes it and never leaves it."

You can't <u>c</u>ause alcoholism,
you can't <u>c</u>ontrol alcoholism,
and you can't <u>c</u>ure alcoholism.

This is known as "The 3-Cs," and it gives some comfort to spouses and family members who are aware of it. Otherwise they go around with feelings of guilt.

If you have a drinking problem, it will only get worse. This cannot be emphasized too strongly.

If you think you can help yourself you are in denial.

Alcoholism can't be cured, so it is always an alcohol<u>ism</u> and not an "alcohol<u>wasm</u>". The alcoholic has to be willing to *come* to a rehabilitation center, *come to* by being detoxified, and *come to believe* in a higher power that will help him or her recover.

It's not about good or bad or right and wrong; it's about survival as a family. The alcoholic in the family is like a crying baby asking for help, because he or she is powerless to help himself or herself until they get sick and tired of feeling sick and tired, which is called *"hitting bottom."* Everything the chemical dependent alcoholic does is a cry to attend to them or they will die. With such a strong focus on the alcoholic, the other family members must adjust to a feeling of relative rejection as they all try to keep related. Blackouts occur in the alcoholic, and the alcoholic uses them as excuses when people take personally the fact that the alcoholic's promises are not kept.

Doctors consider alcoholism a disease because:

1. It is a dysfunction of our genes that causes our body to crave alcohol and its pleasurable effects, and the alcoholic is powerless over this;

2. It is progressive with a chain of signs and symptoms; and

3. Treatment and recovery are possible.

Addiction, such as alcoholism, is loss of control, with a dependence on a chemical substance. Marijuana affects the memory, so the addicts say, "Let's go out and get stupid." Treatment or rehabilitation centers have a slogan, "Despair knocked on the door, hope (rehab.) answered, and no one (pothead) was there."

There is a rather high 50 to 60% relapse to cocaine. The first sniffing of heroin powder into your nose will make you into a heroin addict, and you will eventually inject it into your veins. Heroin is made from poppy flowers grown in Afghanistan, which supplies 90% of the world's supply of heroin at the present time.

There is no chemical solution to everyday living and its problems. Our culture tells us, at every turn, that we should have a drink whenever we encounter any stress. This conditioning, plus various people, places, and things are what keep reminding the alcoholic to drink. Recovery requires the avoidance of these people, places, and things. Those who sell alcohol products keep trying to call our attention to alcohol, in the same way that the tobacco people do. Alcoholism can be compared to a natural disaster. When it comes to natural disasters, people have many weaknesses. Some are unprepared, others procrastinate, and others are full of fears. Robert Louis Stevenson (Scottish author, 1850-1894) said, "You cannot run away from a weakness; you must sometimes fight it out or perish. And if that be so, why not now, and where you stand?" To win, you must know a force greater than your weakness.

Alcoholism has been called a combination of *a potato chip, a television and a rubber ball.* Because you just can't have only one *potato chip*, you must have more. The alcoholic reacts the same way; he or she can't have just one drink; they must have more. Additionally, they are conditioned to drink to relax, just as the non-alcoholic is conditioned to use the distraction of *television* to relax. Additionally, alcoholism is filled with negative thinking on the way down and positive thinking on the way up, like a bouncing *rubber ball.* In order to bounce back up in recovery, the alcoholic requires a lot of only positive thinking to prevent relapse, which is the going down with negative thinking.

There is a formula: CD plus CD = CD, Which means that Chemical Dependency (CD) plus a Co-Dependent enabler spouse (CD) leads to Children Dysfunctional (CD).

The dysfunctional children ("dry drunks") of an alcoholic family in turn marry, and even though they may be non-alcoholic, they continue to act precisely as they have been formed, namely playing a predictable role. The children of children-of-alcoholics (Second generation "dry drunks"), in turn, develop predictable roles, as if they were brought up in an alcoholic home. Roles are defense mechanisms that are used for survival of the family.

Truisms:

- You are only as sick as your secrets.

- To wear a mask is to stay addicted. If you say you're fine, it usually means: fearful, insecure, neurotic and emotional, instead of really fine.

- If you can stay grateful you can stay sober.

Roles	Dysfunction	Defenses
Alcoholic	Addicted	Financial
Spouse	Co-dependent	Falsity (Hypocrisy)
First Child = Hero	Supporter	Fright
Second Child = Scapegoat	Angry Delinquent	Fight
Third Child = Lost Child	Loner	Flight
Fourth Child = Mascot	Comedian	Fun

Chart 9. Characteristics of the Roles of the Children in Alcoholic Families

The non-alcoholic, healthy family has:

Family

Faith
Forgiveness
Faithfulness
Future
Financial stewardship

The alcoholic: Is addicted and chemically dependent, and all the organs of the body are affected detrimentally by the alcohol.

We speak of the alcoholic as being "pickled." They "have to have it every day." They cannot say that they'll only drink just for today.

The spouse: The spouse is co-dependent. A co-dependent person (enabler) is one who has let another person's behavior affect him or her and who is obsessed with controlling that person's behavior. He or she can't yet see that the *cause, control, and cure* of the alcoholism in their beloved is beyond their control. The spouse feels unable to do anything right, and his or her repressed feelings lead to physical illness. Enablers become persecutors of the alcoholic. The enabler is addicted to the family drama and the control of the alcoholic.

Sharon Wegscheider Cruse wrote the book on the roles that people play with each other in the alcoholic's family in their "family of shame and secrets" and their co-dependency with enabling (*Another Chance: Hope and Health for the Alcoholic Family,* published by Science and Behavior books).

- *The hero*: The first child in a "chemical-hurting family" can't medicate their pain of living with alcohol like the alcoholic can, but they can do it by feeling over-responsible to elevate their low self-worth. They often go into the medical profession.

- *The scapegoat*: The second child, unable to be as advanced as the first child, gets its attention by being opposite of the good first child, by being bad, hostile, and defiant. When you don't feel good and you're hurting, you need someone to "Notice me!"

- *The lost child:* The third child feels safety in avoiding the whole ugly scene that is the dysfunctional family by getting away and avoiding people. All members of an alcoholic family are at risk of alcoholism themselves because of the alcoholic gene in the family, but this child has a particularly high risk.

- *The Mascot*: The fourth child: This child uses humor to discharge feelings of anxiety and dark feelings and may be hyper-kinetic and hyperactive. The child acts out simply to fit in and is also high risk for becoming a new alcoholic in the family.

The family motto is: *Don't talk. Don't trust. Don't feel.*

The addicted family doesn't talk, doesn't trust and doesn't feel.

They don't talk due to secrecy of protecting the alcoholic. They don't trust because nothing works so far to stop drinking, and the alcoholic doesn't keep his or her promises. They don't feel because they disconnect to avoid pain. It is always "I think," not "I feel." Or "I don't know how to feel."

My intent so far in this chapter isn't to be a "sage on the stage," but to show to you what you intuitively already know, namely, the truth. I have not been trying to feed you information so that you can regurgitate it back—but to empower you. I have been trying to save your life! In my family, and in some of the families that have given us our spouses, the genes of alcoholism and depression are carried, and that can give to each of us, and to each of our families, alcoholism and/or depression. Having these genes could also predispose us to other possible disorders. I know of alcoholic families that have, also, autism and multiple sclerosis. Perhaps these alcoholism/depression genes predispose us to multiple other conditions associated with brain dysfunction, such as the spectrum of autism on one end and manic depression (bipolar disorder) on the other end, with hyperactivity disorder (HD) and attention deficit disorder (ADD) and possibly epilepsy in between. Some people like to think about genes affecting our brain as a case of genetic "bad wiring" of the brain that is also passed on to our children genetically.

Alcohol treatment is really family treatment. Treatment starts with detoxification (detox) and discovery in a rehabilitation treatment center and it ends with daily recovery taking place, life-long, one day at a time.

An open letter to alcohol and alcoholism:

Dear alcohol and alcoholism:

You are a pain! You deprived me not only of material things, but also of non-dysfunctional things. You have robbed me of a better childhood and have seriously damaged my children. Your depiction in movies as glamorous and having a drink as necessary in any kind of stress has allowed me to know how it feels as a child to see my father drunk, staggering with slurred speech, giving verbal and sometimes physical abuse to my mother.

Do you know how you have shattered dreams of a better home situation? Do you know of your ability to remove ambition? Do you know what it's like to see all your relatives gathering at vacations and holidays drinking, with some family members, very obviously, "under the influence?" Do you know how much smoking and cursing accompanies you? You keep people from church, from sharing shopping and sharing lives together, not to mention the tight money situation. Yet you always have enough money to buy your pack of cigarettes and daily beers.

Must you drink and smoke every single day? Do you know that you have been such a bad example that to prevent being like you, students take a pledge to avoid alcohol until they are age 21? Personally, I think you stink! What a difference between those under your control and those who are not. You are so chronic, destructive, and pervasive that prohibition was started to stamp you out. Why did you survive and prohibition didn't? You are so powerful! But, fortunately, only about 10% of us who start with you continue in your presence. Ninety percent of us can see you and take it or leave it. What a waste of talent, time, and treasure for those in your grip. Put a cork in it!

Your days are numbered as science finds out more about you. The past makes me sad with all of its regrets and the future is unknown and therefore makes me anxious and fearful, and the present is one of craving appetites for so many. But we are able to look above all that to a higher power, a higher eternal presence. We can hear the loud roar that is on the other side of silence, of invisible spiritual things such as love, and of family support that is training and learning all about your tricks. You might hide in our genes and get support from the 10% of us who are susceptible, and from the liquor and tobacco industries, but science and medicine and spirituality and trained families and graduates of rehab and AA and Al-Anon and *Nar-Anon,* etc., etc. will win in the end.

We arrested cancer because it was wanted for murder. Now we arrest you in the name of all that is decent, loving, good, noble, true, beautiful, pure, and holy.

In case you haven't noticed, you have been conquered by love. God is love. You have been conquered by God.

Sincerely,

Me

If a foreign power wanted to subvert our nation, they could do it very easily by subverting our children into obese, addicted, inactive couch potatoes. On the other hand, we are our own worst enemy by poisoning ourselves with chemicals in plastics, pesticides, insecticides, and herbicides. We take in fluoride; lead; mercury; second-hand smoke; alcohol; drugs; food coloring; sugars; fats; additive agents; bus, car and truck exhausts; radioactivity, etc.

> Let us not be justices of peace, but angels of peace.
> —*St. Thérèse of Lisieux, 1873-1897*

We are a litigious society. Prisoners just have to sign a paper to sue someone. And there are advantages to doing so, in that they can get out of jail and into a courtroom, for a time. Therefore, so-called *nuisance lawsuits* bedevil not only doctors.

- What is the use of living if not to strive for noble causes and to make this muddled world a better place for those who will live in it after we are gone?
  —*Winston Churchill, British Prime Minister, 1874-1965*

- The world will not change until we do.
  —*Rev. Jim Wallis, writer and political activist, born 1948*

- When we find more light within ourselves the world will begin to shine.

- I can judge the world and list all that I condemn, but judgments help no one.

- "Be the change you wish to see in the world."
  —*Indira Gandhi, Prime Minister of India, 1917-1984*

- The love of neighbor is the only door out of the dungeon of self.
  —*George MacDonald, minister, poet, novelist, 1824-1905*

- Do you want to know how to get others to like you? Like them first.
  —*John C. Maxwell, contemporary author and speaker on leadership, born 1947*

- You cannot shake hands with a clenched fist.
  —*Indira Gandhi, Prime Minister of India, 1917-1984*

- We all have to decide whether we will walk in the light of creative altruism or the darkness of destructive selfishness. Life's most persistent and nagging question, he said, is

"What are you doing for others?"
—*Dr. Martin Luther King, Jr. (American clergyman, civil-rights activist, and 1964 Nobel Peace Prize winner, 1929-1968*

- You will find as you look back upon your life that the moments when you have really lived, are the moments when you have done things in the spirit of love.
  —*Henry Drummond, Scottish evangelical author, 1851-1897*

- Healing, on some level, seems to take place whenever there is contact with invisible things, such as: beauty, truth, goodness, love, wisdom, wonder, and humor.

- Creative minds have always been known to survive bad training.
  —*Anna Freud, a daughter of Dr. Sigmund Freud, 1895-1982*

- This generation, like every generation, needs to get over the defenses that they put up in response to all of their stress, trauma, and loss by getting in touch with the invisible, the spiritual.

- Seek always to do some good somewhere. Every man has to seek in his own way to realize his true worth. You must give some time to your fellow man. Even if it's a little thing, do something for those who need help, something for which you get no pay but the privilege of doing it. For remember, you don't lie in a world all your own, your brothers are here too.
  —*Albert Schweitzer German-French theologian, musician, philosopher, and physician, 1875–1965*

- The Church is not a Museum for saints, but a hospital for sinners.

—Morton Kelsey, Episcopal priest, professor emeritus of Notre Dame, 1917-2001

We can help our neighbor by sharing what it means to live a better life of values rather than a bitter life of defenses.

The next chapter is the concluding summary of the entwining two chains that have been rising throughout this book. The first chain being a series of aphorisms and truisms, and the second chain being incidents from my life and that of my family in illustration of the truths found in the first chain. Following that is a Postscript as an extension of the final chapter, Ethics, Morality, Spirituality. If you have understood what has been presented so far, then the remainder of the book will be transformational.

Chapter 14.

Ethics, Morality, Spirituality

> Whoever exalts himself will be humbled; but whoever humbles himself will be exalted.
> —*Matthew 23:13*

> Life is eternal, and love is immortal, and death is only a horizon; and a horizon is nothing save the limit of our sight.
> —*Rossiter Worthington Raymond, American mining engineer, author and novelist, 1840-1918*

Our view happens to be limited by ignorance and unconsciousness. We all have blind spots. What is unknown and even unknowable can still be connected to by analogy, similarity, allegory, symbolism, and prayer.

At the current time, there are many who do not have the sense of ethics and morals that they need for their survival or for their nation's survival. This chapter reminds you of what is needed if you are to escape from a life of just joy and sorrow to something more spiritual that is called transformation.

> Words can never adequately convey the incredible impact of our attitude toward life. The longer I live the more convinced I become that life is 10% what happens to us and 90% how we respond to it. I believe the single most significant decision I can make on a day-to-day basis is my choice of attitude...Attitude keeps me going or cripples my progress...When my attitudes are right, there's no barrier too high, no valley too deep, no dream too extreme, no challenge too great for me.
> —*Charles R. Swindoll, evangelical Christian pastor and author, born 1934.*

1. We know that truth exists; otherwise no one would ask any questions.

2. And we know that it is unreasonable to think that a person who can think would be put into a crazy, empty world in which there is nothing to think. And that it is unreasonable to think that a person who can love would be put into a crazy, empty world in which there is nothing to love.

3. And we know that you can put all of the values, virtues, ideals, and principles into the above sentence to show their existence.

4. And we also know that truth, love, goodness, and all of the values, virtues, ideals, and principles are invisible things. We also know that the material world is always pointing to something that is invisible. For example, to say, "When it rains, it pours" is not trying to say that when it rains there is a lot of water dropping. But is saying that the material rain is pointing to something invisible in the fact that when trouble comes, it often comes as a lot of trouble.

5. We also know that when we are children, we are always trying to figure out the world. And that adults stop trying because they think they know the world, when what they really know is just the names for all the things in the world. Adults are constantly confronted with questions of evil, death, and meaning that only spirituality can answer, and not science.

6. The mind seeks truth, the heart seeks love, and the spirit seeks God. We have a built-in appetite for God in the same way that we have a built-in appetite for food, water, knowledge and reproduction.

7. We also know that you don't need a doctor to tell you that today's world is spiritually sick and needs to be spiritually

healed. God needs to be put first so that we can decide for the good and fight the evil. We need to stop talking peace and start living lives of peace. We need our lives to be living signs.

8. We know that God can make penicillin out of mold, and, therefore, God can surely make something healing for the world out of our existence.

It isn't the mountains ahead to climb that wear you out, it's the pebble in your shoe.
—*Muhammad Ali, American boxer and philosopher, born 1941*

Service to others is the rent you pay for your room here on earth.
—*Muhammad Ali, American boxer and philosopher, born 1941*

John Stuart Mill (British philosopher and author, 1806-1873) said, "The person who has nothing for which he is willing to fight, nothing which is more important than his own personal safety, is a miserable creature and has no chance of being free unless made and kept so by the exertions of better men than himself." Ethics, morals, and spirituality make us better persons; in fact, we are transformed by them. And we need them for recovery in our sorrows.

You don't know everything there is to know until you think the unthinkable, ponder the imponderable, try to know the unknowable, and dream the "undreamable." You haven't done all there is to do until you expect a miracle and try to do the impossible. You haven't seen all there is to see until you see the invisible.

• What the mind of man can conceive and believe, it can achieve.
—*Napoleon Hill, author, 1883-1970*

- Man is so made that whenever anything fires his soul, impossibilities vanish.
  —*Jean de la Fontaine, French fabulist and poet, 1621-1695*

- Determine that the thing can and shall be done, and then we shall find the way.
  —*Abraham Lincoln, 16th President of the United States, 1809-1865*

- When faith makes all things possible, it is love that makes all things easy.
  —*Evan H. Hopkins, Christian author, 1837-1918*

- The greatest pleasure in life is doing what people say you cannot do.
  —*Walter Bagehot, British author and editor, 1826-1877*

- The Difficult is that which can be done immediately; the impossible that which takes a little longer.
  —*George Santayana, Spanish philosopher and author, 1863-1952*

- We need to be disturbed by God when our dreams come true because we dreamed too little. And when we arrive in safety because we sailed too close to shore.
  —*Bishop Bienvenido Tudtud, who served in the Philippines, 1931-1987*

- What we cannot comprehend by analysis, we become aware of in awe.
  —*Abraham Joshua Heschel, Rabbi and Jewish theologian, 1907-1972*

- Courage is often nothing more than the power to let go of the familiar.
  —*John C. Maxwell, contemporary author and speaker on leadership, born 1947*

- Courage does not always roar. Sometimes it is the quiet voice at the end of the day saying, "I will try again tomorrow."
  —*Anonymous*

- The worst trials are visited upon us by trivial things. They attack us daily, incessantly and tenaciously, and usually find us unprepared. Furthermore, there is no honor to be gained in such a battle. Moses and the 'Lord' knew what they were doing. They didn't plague Egypt with tigers but with grasshoppers.
  —*Multatuli, the pseudonym of Dutch author, Edward Douwes Dekker, 1820-1887*

Truisms:

- Prayer is the overflow of inner love.

- You can only live your life for love.

- Love turns the other cheek to our slaps. That is what love is, what love does, and what love receives, suffering. True love is willing to suffer. Love is the Cross. Love is self-sacrifice.

- Love can change an end into a beginning.

- The one who prays is not afraid of the future.

- We need to stop talking about prayer and start praying from our hearts out of love.

- The family that prays together stays together.
  —*Rev. Patrick Peyton, CSC, known as the Rosary Priest, 1909-1992*

- You will always find time for whatever you love or even just like. The problem is not having enough time—but having enough love. Let the Bible be in a visible place in your home.

- Our families must be a living church in which we pray and love one another so that we can reach out in Christian love to our neighbor.

- No matter what you have experienced of love so far, there is more beyond.

- The family and the church, both, are where Christians come together to be briefed, trained, and strengthened to see that each person you meet is one who either knows God or is seeking to know God, as everyone living moves toward love or away from love.

Some additional key points in this book are:

1. There are some things that we know to exist as self-evident truths from our own experience, but some people would have us believe that they do not exist, such as truth, love, goodness, and all of the other values, virtues, ideals, and principles, because their existence leads us to spirituality and a belief in God. Belief in God is rejected by secularists, humanists, and materialists.

2. We are transformed when we live with higher levels of thinking and with spirituality, which includes truth, love, goodness plus all of the other values, virtues, ideals, and principles.

3. A human being is made up of three qualities: a mind searching for truth, a heart searching for love, and a spirit searching for goodness and God.

4. There is something more that is beyond any categorizing of life into duality or trinity, and it is spirituality and God, which is transforming. And this realm of spirituality is our way out of the confusion of the horns-of-a-dilemma or the paradox of duality, as well as our way out of just trinity.

5. We can see with our inner eyes something invisible, like truth (mind), love (heart), and goodness (spirit) and other values, virtues, ideals, and principles. And the material world is always symbolically pointing these invisible things out to us, but some people are unable to see beyond the material symbols that point to the spirituality, or they don't want to see. There are three qualities—truth, love, and goodness—that make us human, and not just two out of three.

6. We have also seen that dualities are characteristic of our daily thinking, because we are always dealing with such terms as: them/us, either/or and but/also, the opposite is, in contrast, both, by comparison, then/now, two out of three, twins, twinning, etc.

7. And that even speaking symbolically by using numbers to represent invisible things, we know that there's always more than two, because there's three. Secular science wants us to think in terms of two—mind and heart, rational and emotional—to avoid dealing with the third quality of being human—namely, spirit—which leads us to goodness and God.

8. There is a benevolence in the world that is unexplainable by science. Science cannot explain many things, such as serendipity, God-incidences, miracles, clairvoyance, intuition, hunches, prophecy, etc. There is also an intelligent design or pattern of things that weaves everything together, and we are creatively participating in it.

9. Everything about the objective, outer-visible world contains a message about the subjective, inner-invisible world. As it is above, so is it below. What generations have found of the inner world and spirituality cannot be summarily discounted. That would be like saying that you think you've found something better than belts and shoes. I don't think so!

10. There is a realm of invisible things. These things are invisible to the outer eye but not to the inner eye, which can see truth, wisdom, double meanings, and the abstract. For example, when your plate is full of food and you say, "My eyes are bigger than my stomach," you are not talking about the size of your outer eyes being big, but the size of your invisible inner appetite. All the values, virtues, ideals, and principles are invisible to the outer eye but are known to the heart and visible to the inner eye.

11. Spirituality, ethics and morality deal with truth, love, goodness, and all of the other values, virtues, ideals, and principles. Recognizing what these are, and that they exist, is a wonder of revelation and awareness, which leads us to God and which leads us to worship. "Wonder is the basis of worship" (Thomas Carlyle, Scottish historian and essayist, 19th century).

12. The author of the book *Left to Tell: Discovering God Amidst the Rwandan Holocaust*, Immaculee Ilibagiza, said, "Where have you heard on earth (of) somebody killing 500 people and just living in peace? Have you heard it? Where is an example? There's always a bad end. They don't know what they do, oh my God! There's something they're lacking. It's the lack of love. The love in their hearts has died and has blinded them... [to the point] that where they are going is going to be bad for their children and for themselves."

13. You can't learn from someone you envy, only from someone you admire. *Parasites want what you've earned. Protégés (students) want what you've learned.*

14. There are times in your life when you do something good.

On Friday September 25, 1981, there was a picture of me in our local newspaper with the caption: "Surgeon Is Also Poet, Sunday School Teacher." I was pictured with the chaplain of the hospital where we both worked. The newspaper printed a copy of "A Doctor's Day Prayer" that I had written, and which I gave as a prayer at our hospital on Doctor's Day. Part of the words were: "Almighty God...Help us to really see this world we live in; where atom bombs make it easier to die, and birth control makes it harder to be born; where men speak of overkill, but never of over-love; where missiles are guided, and men are misguided; where men can reach the moon but fail to come closer to heaven."

Over the years, the second chaplain at our hospital invited me to give a sermon at three or four other Protestant Churches.

Here is part of a poem I wrote called "Go There by Car":

Life is a journey taking all of us far,
We can walk this distance, or travel by car.
I recommend going by automobile.
Keep looking for values, virtues and ideals.
Seek the lessons hidden in cars, if you're smart,
See with the insight of the mind and the heart...
Virtue is needed as a good set of brakes,
To prevent moral wrecks and other mistakes.

So many others have correctly condensed, into truthful sound bites, the truth into a nutshell—that it's worthwhile to listen to what they have been saying. And if you read enough of what so many others have found to be true, it's as if each represents one stroke of a brush that slowly reveals a truthful picture of ethics, morality and spirituality, which is our transformation beyond joy and sorrow, our transformation beyond consolation and desolation. It is our higher level of thinking and living. Some of you may see it for the first time in all its reality. It's as if each truth is a wave washing over the mind to clean it of what is not true and to open the inner eyes to see the invisible.

> All words, the wisest men have said…are always new, to those unread.
> —*Martin D. Buxbaum, Virginian poet, born 1912*

Robert Ellsberg (born 1955), a contemporary publisher and author, in his book *The Saints' Guide to Happiness*, notes that we are surrounded at all times by physical forces that remain invisible to our unaided eyes. Such forces include the following: ultraviolet rays from the sun, electromagnetic waves from the earth's rotation of magma, natural magnetism in magnetite rocks, electrostatic energy, radio signals, television images, cellular phone conversations, etc. If we could render these waves and forces visible to our eyes, we would find ourselves swimming in a sea of light, color, and sound, which are all dimensions of a reality that forms no part of our normal perception or consciousness. The saints were attuned to seeing, with their inner eyes, a similar reality, namely the invisible spiritual reality, which reveals that we are all connected in a *web of love* and a Communion of Saints. Scripture teaches us that human beings are created in the image of God; therefore, we are created in the image of love. When we use our inner eyes to see that web of love, we are astonished at the sight. We awaken from our illusion of being alone and separated. In other words, when we see with our inner eyes, we are, in some sense, healed by the sight.

> To the illuminated mind the whole world sparkles with light.
> —*Ralph Waldo Emerson, American philosopher, essayist, and poet, 1803-1882*

> We cannot live for ourselves alone. Our lives are
> connected by a thousand invisible threads, and along these
> sympathetic fibers, our actions run as causes and return to
> us as results.
>
> —*Herman Melville, American novelist and poet, 1819-1891*

When you are in the military, you can certainly feel a physical web of interconnection of each branch with every other branch and with all the units in your own branch. The military is a world within our world. I was Chief of Surgery at an Air Force base in Maine for two years of duty in compensatory military service, due to deferral from the draft, in order to complete my medical education. The first case I had was of a young child who went to catch a model airplane that was rotating on a cord held by another. I believe the other person was the child's father, who was bringing the plane in for a landing. The airplane hit the child in the forehead with the force of a sledgehammer with a projecting point, exposing damaged brain tissue. The child and the child's airman father and I were air-evacuated to another base for surgery on the child by a neurosurgeon. On the return back to my own base, I was on a crowded airstrip with other airmen awaiting boarding, when a superior officer turned around and saw me with my hat off, and my sad tired unshaven face with tears in my red eyes, as the child didn't live, but died near the end of surgery on the operating table. He at first looked shocked and angry that I didn't have my hat on and I was unshaven, but his features softened as he examined my countenance, and he didn't say anything, but he turned back to conversation with the other airmen. At that point, I could feel the spiritual web of connection that we all have as human beings, in addition to the military physical web of interconnection.

When you marry a spouse and have children, you know you're not alone, and that also helps you to see better with your inner eyes. To gain a spouse, or to have a child, is to recognize just how possible it is to love another person "as oneself." Poets have always sung of the power of love to make us feel more alive as we become so absorbed in the good of another as to lose all sense of a separate identity; to be willing "to bear all things, hope all things, endure all things" (1 Corinthians 13), for the sake of our beloved.

When we love, when we give, and when we share, we are no longer alone.

The world supports the illusion that happiness depends on attaining what we currently lack. Letting go of our attachments, however, frees us into a certain kind of poverty of the saints.

St. Francis of Assisi, in kissing a leper, was not only dispensing with his fear of death and disease, but also letting go of a whole identity based on status, security, and worldly wealth. Doctors, by self-sacrifice, have happy lives despite their ever-present fear and worry of contracting sickness and death. St. Francis of Assisi let go of everything that hindered his ability to love. He turned worldly values upside down. Where others saw security, he saw captivity and lessened freedom. There were no such things as possessions— but rather, things that possessed you. What others thought of as success was for him a source of strife, an "obstacle to the love of God and one's neighbor." Possessions only caused a need for arms for their defense and caused quarrels and lawsuits. Those who own much have much to fear (Rabindranath Tagore, Indian poet, 1861-1941). Spiritual poverty does not mean any particular standard of living but rather, a referral of us to where our treasure lies, for there our hearts will also be, as Jesus noted. The pursuit of happiness is inseparable from the call to holiness, which is the effort to conform one's life to the rule of God. Holiness is putting on the character of God. Your character in life is everything. If you lose your character, you've lost everything.

You can always tell when a person has good character, because they always try to tell the truth. And there is something about them that radiates love and goodness.

A preacher on television was explaining that there are four words for love in the Bible. One I had not heard before, it was *entrein*, if I have it spelled correctly, which is the natural love of a baby for its mother who it does not yet know, since you can only love someone who you know. And *agape* is the unconditional love of God; *eros* is reckless, erotic love; and *philio* or *phileo* is brotherly love, similar to Philadelphia, the City of Brotherly Love.

In the last chapter of John (John 21:15-19), Jesus asks Peter if he loves him—three times. And Peter answers that he loves Jesus—-three times. But the words that are translated as "love" are different words in both Latin and Greek for love, so the translation may be more properly translated as: "Peter do you have unconditional love for me?" And Peter says, "You know, Lord, that I am fond of you." This is repeated, and the third time Jesus changes the word for love to, "Peter are you fond of me?" and Peter answers as usual, "You know, Lord, that I am fond of you." Jesus then goes on to say that Peter will someday have his wrists bound to go where he does not want to go. The implication is that Jesus is telling Peter of Peter's martyrdom when Peter will love Jesus with *agape* or unconditional love, and not *philio*, or fond of you, kind of love.

And Peter, having denied Jesus three times, is now choosing his words truthfully and carefully when he answers Jesus. He remembers saying he would never deny Jesus. And perhaps then he was not as truthful or careful as he is now, because Jesus predicted that Peter would deny Jesus when the cock crowed, and Peter did deny Jesus, despite his earlier statement that he would never deny Jesus.

In the last book of the Bible, Revelation, in Chapters 2 and 3, there are seven letters to seven Churches. Some feel that this is a linear chain and that the last Church letter to Laodicea (Revelations 3:14-21) is a letter to the Church in the Last Days. And there are some who believe we are living in the Last Days, so the letter is addressed to us. The letter says that Jesus is standing at the door and knocks (Rev. 3:20). There is a classic painting of Jesus at a door. Many people think that behind the door are unbelievers. But it's clear, in this letter, that it is believers or the Church behind the door. In the letter, Jesus calls the Church "lukewarm" (Revelations 3:15). Perhaps our love has grown lukewarm. A preacher once pointed out that the only cure for being lukewarm is to open the door to let Jesus back into the Church. The letter ends by saying that those who have ears should hear what is being said to the Church in the letter.

Since a life without love is not worth living, and since you cannot love alone, the Ark is entered two by two. You cannot enter heaven without taking someone with you. It may only be you and Jesus. Love makes better persons of us all.

- Service is love made visible.

- Friendship is love made personal.

- Kindness is love made tangible.

- Giving is love made believable.

- Music is love made audible.

- Creativity is love made productive.

- Hospitality is love in action.

- Forgiveness is love made sacrificial.

- I want you to choose integrity and truth, because without it you can't even build anything or it will fall down.

- Liars can figure and figures can lie, but "Honesty is (still) the best policy"
  —*Mark Twain, American author, 1835*

- We are either problem describers or solution finders.
  —*Coleman McCarthy, American journalist and peace activist, born 1938*

- One always swims against the current to reach the source; it is trash that flows with the stream.
  —*Zbigniew Herbert, Polish poet, 1924-1998*

Mother Theresa of Calcutta read this prayer of St. Francis of Assisi for peace to the United Nations. Afterwards, she received a standing ovation. It's also a prayer used by Alcoholics Anonymous and others.

"Prayer of St. Francis of Assisi for Peace"

Lord, make me an instrument of Your peace,
where there is hatred, let me sow love;
where there is injury, pardon;
where there is doubt, faith;
where there is despair, hope;
where there is darkness, light;
and where there is sadness, joy.
O divine Master, grant that I may not so much
seek to be consoled as to console;
to be understood as to understand;
to be loved as to love;
for it is in giving that we receive;
It is in pardoning that we are pardoned;
and it is in dying that we are born to eternal life.

Truisms:

- Darkness cannot drive out darkness. Hatred cannot drive out hatred; only love can do that.
  —*Martin Luther King, Jr., clergyman, activist, civil-rights leader, and 1964 Nobel Peace Prize winner, 1929-1968*

- If you love peace then hate injustice, hate tyranny, hate greed—but hate these things in yourself, not another.
  —*Mohandas Gandhi, spiritual leader of India, 1869-1948*

217

- We must dare to be love in a world that does not know how to love.
  —*Charles de Foucauld, French Trappist Monk, hermit, martyr and beatified in 2005 toward becoming a saint, 1858-1916*

- Nobody cares how much you know, until they know how much you care. In a moment of decision the best thing you can do is the right thing. The worst thing you can do is nothing.
  —*Theodore Roosevelt, 26th President of the United States, 1858-1919*

If we want change, we must look to ourselves. We are the change we desire. The closer you get to the light the clearer you can see your own darkness. We all need to get closer to God, closer to light, closer to love, because we need to see our own darkness in order to remove it, which will be our change, our transformation. Our change is beyond both our joy and our sorrow.

A train is better than an ox-wagon only when it carries better men.
—*Olive Schreiner, South African novelist, aphorist and activist, 1855-1920*

Ignorance is a darkness. Every medical student in looking at bacteria growing on a Petri dish and seeing no bacteria growing around where the mold is growing realizes that they could have invented penicillin, because it was an idea coming of age. It is a matter of just being there at the right time and being prepared. Living a life without using defenses is an idea coming of age too, for us, and we are preparing to accept it at this time, because we are sick and tired of being sick and tired of living a life of defenses.

We have confused symbol with physical reality. For example, we use the time shown by our watches to tell us when our bodies are hungry. And at other times, we have confused money with true wealth, or the travel brochure with the landscape, or the guidebook with life, or the menu with dinner, and as a result, we feel empty inside and hungry for more. We are hungry for "more," and not just for more words.

Words point to something and say no more, but you must look at what's being pointed to and not at the pointing finger. Don't look at me, look at God. Keep a proper focus.

Keep a proper focus is a lesson that is repeated again and again in scripture.

1. We tend to focus on how great is the darkness in the world. Darkness is symbolic of evil and sin. But we should be focused on how dim is our own light as a believer.

2. The Pharisees, by focusing more on their traditions, were at the same time rejecting God (Mark 7:9, 13). They were taking their eyes off God.

3. The miracles that Jesus did had no repeatable method; otherwise, we would focus on the method and not on Jesus, and thereby take our eyes off God.

4. Peter, walking on water (Matthew 14:28-30), took his focus away from Jesus onto the water, and then Peter began to sink. He should have kept his focus on Jesus.

5. As in the days of Noah and Lot, people will be eating and drinking and marrying and giving in marriage, and buying and selling and planting and building until the day of destruction comes upon them (Luke 17:26-29). Their focus is not on God but on their own plans—similar to our own lukewarm world.

   As a face is reflected in water, so the heart reflects the person.
   —*Proverbs 27:19*

...wisdom is sweet to your soul. If you find it, you will
have a bright future, and your hopes will not be cut short.
—*Proverbs 24:14*

Pride ends in humiliation, while humility brings honor.
—*Proverbs 29:23*

I believe the first test of a truly great man is his humility.
—*John Ruskin, author, poet and artist, 1819-1900*

The best way to be right or wrong is humbly.
—*St. Arnold of Soissons, 1040-1087*

Henri Nouwen (Dutch author and priest, 1932-1996) said, "When
we honestly ask ourselves which person in our lives means the most
to us, we often find that it is those who instead of giving much ad-
vice, solutions, or cures, have chosen rather to share our pain and
touch our wounds with a gentle and tender hand. The friend who can
be silent with us in a moment of despair or confusion, who can stay
with us in an hour of grief and bereavement, who can tolerate not
knowing, not curing, not healing, and face with us the reality of our
powerlessness, that is a friend who cares."

If something explodes in outer space, it makes no sound, as there is
no air in outer space to transmit sound. This should give us a clue
that *some of the greatest things happen in silence*. Flowers grow in
silence, love blooms in silence, and supernovas occur in the silence
of outer space. And people get a change of heart and get transformation in the silence of their own heart.

In grammar school, I had to memorize Thomas Gray's (1716-1771)
old poem: "Full many a flow'r is born to blush unseen, and waste
its sweetness on the desert air." One symbolic interpretation is that
there are many people who live such ordinary lives that they're unknown and relatively unseen, and their thoughts never reach more
than the desert of their lives. But it's good to be yourself, if you are
always a first-rate version of yourself and not a second-rate version

or an attempted imitation of someone else. Because, just as there is a balance of nature that needs flowers in the desert, there is also a balance in life that needs everyone's existence right where they are planted, even if where they are planted is the silence of being relatively unknown and unseen. Great things come out of the silent desert. Jesus came out of the desert to start His ministry. One of the very first things God says in the Bible is that human beings aren't meant to be alone. We are never alone, because God exists.

Frederick Buechner (Presbyterian minister and American author, born 1926) said, "The life I touch for good or ill will touch another life, and that in turn another, until who knows where the trembling stops or in what far place my touch will be felt."

Life is not a mystery to be solved but an experience to be lived.

We are fearfully and wonderfully made. It's common knowledge that when you run a car, it breaks down, but when you move and exercise your body it gets better. Or to put it another way, in a duality way of speaking: Consider inactivity a form of illness from which the cure is to move around and exercise. It doesn't matter whether you have the joy of health or the sorrow of illness; there is transformation, and more, beyond trinity, that is found in God who has created you to be alive and fearfully and wonderfully made.

What is beyond God? What is beyond Love? Nothing, because love (God) encompasses all, and therein lies our transformation.

> If we ever forget that we're one nation under God, then we will be a nation gone under.
> —*Ronald Reagan, 40th President of the United States, 1911-2004*

> The purpose of life is not to win. The purpose of life is to grow and to share.
> —*Harold Kushner, American Rabbi and author, born 1935*

God doesn't need us to be successful but only to be faithful.
—*Mother Theresa of Calcutta, Albanian-born Indian Catholic nun, 1910-1997*

When you come to look back on all that you have done in life, you will get more satisfaction from the pleasure you have brought into other people's lives than you will from the times that you outdid and defeated them.
—*Harold Kushner, American Rabbi and author, born 1935*

As it is in sports, so it is in life. Being winner or loser is not as important as how you have played the game.

I don't know what your destiny will be, but one thing I do know; the only ones among you who will be really happy are those who have sought and found how to serve.
—*Albert Schweitzer, German medical missionary and theologian of the 20th century, 1875-1965*

If you want to be great, all you have to do is serve.
—*Martin Luther King, Jr., American clergyman, civil-rights activist, and 1964 Nobel Peace Prize winner, 1929-1968*

A life of service is a life of significance.
—*George Bush, 43rd U.S. President, born 1946*

The most beautiful flower or fruit of suffering is forgiveness, which is a plant that blossoms only when watered with tears.

It's hard to forgive, and it's also hard to say, "I'm sorry." To do either is to suffer. We must suffer the fight that it takes to have a better character for ourselves. There is a story in the Bible (John 5: 1-18) about a paralyzed man at the pool of Bethesda (also spelled Bethzatha in some manuscripts), who cannot get into the water fast enough for his cure whenever the waters are stirred up to give a cure. The story has a symbolic interpretation that whenever the baptismal waters of our soul are stirred up by an inspiration from the Holy Spirit, or from

Jesus during prayer, this stirring will help us to express the truth of what we know in our minds, and the truth of what we feel in our hearts, if we will only make the first move and ask for help, just like the unknown man at the pool asks Jesus for help. This is also what all alcoholics must do to start their rehabilitation. In order to have a miracle, there is something you must do first. You must pray, which is talking to God. And you must believe in miracles in order to have your miracle, because even if you were given a miracle, you wouldn't recognize it as a miracle, if you didn't you believe in miracles. And as the story shows, the second thing you must do is whatever Jesus asks you to do. It may seem like a hard thing to do, but it turns out to be as easy as simply getting out of your bed and walking.

Truisms:

- Wisdom is worth suffering for, because wisdom feeds our souls.

- Without wisdom we starve our souls.

- Wisdom is worth more than pleasure.

- Foolishness is worse than pain.

- Without wisdom, we are all fools, and no one more than the one who thinks he is not.

No one can give his or her faith to someone else; you have to get it on your own. Nevertheless, you can be guided to where to look. Some people, however, look at the pointing finger and miss what it's pointing at. I hope that is not the case with you, as I am pointing inside to your hearts and to what is inside there and inside the Bible, namely to truth, love and goodness.

God bless you. My final words of wisdom to you are:

Life may seem like a duality of predators and victims, or life and death, but there is more, a *third way* found in faith. "The power of faith is enormous. It is so great that it not only saves the believer: Thanks to one person's faith others are saved also (St. Cyril of Jerusalem, Bishop of Jerusalem and Doctor of the Church, c.315-c. 386)."

You are to live, love and laugh; trust God; carry your cross; and expect change, as it's the only constant in our world of ups and downs (consolations and desolations).

> To improve is to change. To be perfect is to change often.
> —*Winston Churchill, British Prime Minister, 1874-1965*

> Live so that when your children think of fairness, caring, and integrity, they think of you.
> —*H. Jackson Brown, Jr., American author, present day*

And keep your eye on the transforming invisible things of truth, love, goodness and all of the values, virtues, ideals, and principles, which you know do exist from the experience of truth in your mind, heart, and spirit.

And if you are searching for nuggets of truth, the Bible is a gold mine.

> Now this is not the end. It is not even the beginning of the end. But it is, perhaps, the end of the beginning.
> —*Winston Churchill, British Prime Minister, 1874-1965*

My dear wife, Margaret, died peacefully at home under hospice care on a sunny Tuesday afternoon in November 2008. All the leaves were at their peak of change into gorgeous colors. It was the kind of day in which she loved to be outside taking a walk, doing gardening, or feeding the birds.

Her last words to me were the same as mine to her, "I love you." I thank God for having given her to me. To love her is the greatest thing in my life. And the best thing that I have ever done.

We were able to celebrate our 51st Wedding Anniversary. But if you were to ask me, "How long have you known Margaret?" I would have to answer in love, "Not long enough!"

God gives us many gifts in our lifetime. Some we enjoy for a long time and others only briefly. But each gift has the power to change us, make us better people, and enrich us. In my sadness of grief, there is also joy that I had Margaret to love, and love is eternal. You can never lose what you have once loved.

Some persons may feel that cancer cuts short your time together, while others may feel that it gives you more time to say "Goodbye." Out of that duality comes the transformation of feeling that without this extra time that a slow death by cancer gives you, then you would have never known, without experiencing it, the depth of love and tenderness that are possible between two people on this earth.

I wrote on Margaret's cremation urn, which was made by our daughter: "Lovely and loving Margaret lived and died surrounded by love." This was followed by the dates of her birth and death. This urn was signed by all of our family before being glazed and fired.

I'm sad and lonely, and life will not be the same, but because of Margaret I'll be able to keep moving on. She would not want me to be sad too long. I can always find her in my heart, in my memories, in my prayers, and in this book, which is dedicated to her and published in her honor. She is in the love of each of our family members.

As a God-incidence, I accidentally found something from the Bible, Sirach 30:21-23, 25, that says: "Do not give yourself over to sorrow, and do not distress yourself deliberately. A joyful heart is life itself and rejoicing lengthens one's life span. Indulge yourself and take comfort, and remove sorrow far from you, for sorrow has destroyed many, and no advantage ever comes from it. Those who are cheerful and merry at table will benefit from their food."

In the Bible, the two thieves who are crucified with Jesus are each suffering. The question is: "What do you do with your suffering?" One thief uses suffering to gain friendship with Jesus and to gain Heaven, while the other thief dies alone.

In the Lord's Prayer, we ask for the Father's will to be done on earth. Love and mercy are the Father's will. Love and mercy were shown by God to Margaret in her peaceful death. One of our granddaughters, Christina, remarked that Grandma Margaret looked, in death, as if she were smiling. I could see it too, and it comforted us all.

We had a beautiful memorial service in Church for her with a Mass. The Bible readings and music, she chose ahead of time for herself. One was from Ecclesiastes in the Bible, where it points out that there is a time to laugh and a time to weep (Ecclesiastes 3:4). On the back of her memorial prayer card was a verse that is on a small sign in her garden: "The kiss of the sun for pardon, the song of the birds for mirth. One is nearer God's heart in a garden than anywhere else on earth" (Dorothy Frances Gurney, writer of hymns and poems, 1858-1932).

Her memorial service was facilitated by all of our children, many friends, and family. Afterwards, in her honor, in the school cafeteria of the Church, we had a catered, large gourmet meal for everyone in attendance. There we exchanged tears and laughter, and the truth that there is always more. There is eternal love. And light always follows darkness. Having Godly hope means that, even when things get worse, there is hope because God exists. It's the hope that was in the heart of Jesus at his arrest and crucifixion.

> Death is not extinguishing the light; it is only putting out
> the lamp because the dawn has come.
> —*Rabindranath Tagore, Indian poet, 1861-1941*

The duality, of being happy to see Margaret in the morning and of being blessed to sleep beside her at night, has been replaced by the transforming memory of how Margaret died with such quiet dignity, wisdom, and grace. And how she died with her faith, hope, and love, surrounded by all of ours.

> Our Lord has written the promise of resurrection, not in books alone, but in every leaf in springtime.
> —*Martin Luther, German Protestant reformer and scholar, 1483-1546*

> Oh heart, if one should say to you that the soul perishes like the body, answer that the flower withers, but the seed remains.
> —*Kahlil Gibran, Lebanese American author, poet, and philosopher, 1883-1931*

> Jesus revolutionized the meaning of death. He did so with his teaching, above all by facing death Himself. In this way, the Son of God wished to share our human condition to the end, to open it to hope. Ultimately, He was born to be able to die and in this way to free us from the slavery of death.
> —*Pope Benedict XVI, born 1927*

> When someone dies you don't get over it by forgetting; you get over it by remembering, and you are aware that no person is ever truly lost or gone once they have been in your life and loved us, as we have loved them.
> —*Leslie Marmon Silko, Native American author and poet, born 1948*

> Death is the end of a lifetime, not the end of a relationship.
> —*Mitch Albom, American journalist, author, screenwriter, playwright, born 1958*

> What we have once enjoyed, we can never lose. All that we love deeply become a part of us. The best and most beautiful things in this world cannot be seen, or even heard, but must be felt with the heart.
> —*Helen Keller, American author and activist, 1880-1968*

> Life is eternal, and love is immortal, and death is only a
> horizon; and a horizon is nothing save the limit of our sight.
> —*Rossiter Worthington Raymond, American mining
> engineer, author and novelist, 1840-1918*

When two persons are spiritually bonded together in true love, they each intuitively know this highest of truths, that their bond of love is eternal, immortal, constant and changeless, and that it can never be severed. That truth, which they have mutually collected, they know will last forever. The Russian author, Fyodor Dostoyevsky, (1821-1881), said, "Beauty will save the world." If you wonder what kind of beauty that would be, I would like to offer a suggestion that seems especially resonant from Cardinal Carlo Maria Martini, S.J., Archbishop Emeritus of Milan: "The beauty that will save the world is love that shares pain."

God bless you. Love always,   Dad/Ron

Postscript

After the death of my dear wife, Margaret, I went to Griefshare, which is a type of group therapy, which offers help for the grieving. Support groups for those in grief are given by various churches of different denominations and by Hospice. These workshops may have different groups of support separately for adults, children, teens and/or survivors of suicide. I attended a meeting once a week for 13 weeks. My son and his wife and my daughter also attended. During Griefshare every week, various people in their various stages of grief are shown in a movie, where they express their ideas, suggestions and reactions to their grief. Afterwards there is a group discussion, along with questions relating to the movie. These questions are presented by the facilitator in order to have the group open up with their feelings about the answers. Opening up is key to venting your grief.

Science tells us that matter can neither be created nor destroyed, and we begin to learn over the weeks in Griefshare that love, grief and sorrow are forces that don't go away, either, but all of these forces become transformed. When a loved one dies, two people die. But eventually the living partner has to have a resurrection from their death. They have to realize eventually that only one person died. And the remaining person has to survive to carry on for the both of them.

I chose to go to a church sponsored Griefshare, because I knew it would share the hope of everlasting life with Jesus after death, which is the difference between Christians and other groups as they relate to death. Jesus showed the conquest of death by his Resurrection, and He reinforced this conquest by showing himself to many after his Resurrection (Mark 16:14, 1-Corinthians 15:5-7), and by His promises in Scripture (John 14:2). Becoming a Christian is likened to getting engaged with all the excitement and anticipation of the eventual upcoming wedding, symbolized by your death and entrance into heaven to be with Jesus. Christian Resurrection is not Hindu and Buddhist Reincarnation, because the Bible points out that we are appointed once to die (Hebrews 9:27).

Everyone recovers from their grief in their own way and in their own time. Some need to be alone, others need to be with people. If you are with people you have to guard against being a people pleaser where you bend to their expectations and to their pressure for you to get back to life. No one can take your memories away from you. And you can't rush through grief.

In Griefshare we are taught that there are five tasks in grief:

1.) Accept the loved one's death, and that he or she will never return.

2.) Release all of your emotions.

3.) Store memories into the past.

4.) Separate your identity from that of your lost spouse, and accept that you are single.

5.) Move past what was your past life, and invest in the future life of your own.

In grief you are exposed to comments from people trying to care and help, but who are unaware of how careless and hurtful their remarks are. For example:

"*I know how you feel.*" No you don't. Each loss and grief is unique.

"*The same thing happened.*" No, it can't be the same.

"*It was a blessing.*" Letting go does not feel like a blessing.

"Let me know if there is anything that I can do." Don't add to my "to do" list in my bereavement.

"He/she is in a better place." It's the bereaved who are hurting.

"Everything happens for a reason." What is the reason for this loss?

"God doesn't give us more than we can bear." Our hurt is unbearable and unique.

"Buck up" "Keep a stiff upper lip." Grief needs time and tears.

"He/she lived a long life." Longevity means deep bonds and deep grief.

"Your holding up so well." The grieving should not have to take care of the non-grieving.

"You've got to be strong." The grieving should not have to take care of the non-grieving.

"At least you've got one left." This discredits the uniqueness of the deceased.

"I thought you'd be over this by now." We will always continue to miss the deceased.

"God needed another angel in heaven." We are not rewarded by death.

"You're the man/woman of the house now." Don't encourage adult behavior in children. Let children be children.

Instead of careless comments in grief we should share that we care and that we remember, and that we will share our presence and be there to help take off some of the burdens.

Grief and sorrow are a force. Forces change form, they do not get destroyed. We pass from the deep pain of loss to a deeper sympathy, a deeper love and a deeper insight. We pass into the knowledge that we have a right to our use of ritual, and we have a right to embrace our spirituality. We have a right to our memories, and a right to our unique grief. And we have a right to our grief attacks and a right to our emotions. And we have a right to our physical and emotional limits. And we have the right to talk about all of it, as we search for meaning and try to heal.

You do not outlive your sorrow and become who you were at the start before your grief. That would be a poor result. Our old selves had blind spots in our love, and our old selves didn't fully appreciate human suffering. Our old selves thought too superficially about tragedy and loss. Our old selves had too feeble a sense of God's presence and we made weaker prayers. And our old selves were too self oriented.

It's said that the Bible was written by those on their knees in tears, and it can only be understood by those who are also on their knees and in tears. Grief, then, is our opportunity to understand scripture more fully. That opportunity should not be wasted.

It's possible that each of us in our grief has received a message from the other side, but we have failed to recognize it as a message, because it came simply as an insight, or a God-incidence, or a comfort, etc.

Death and grief are a great barrier. When you love someone you'll find a way to be with them when all sorts of barriers are placed between you. Love finds a way. In the Bible in Mark 16:3-4, the women who loved Jesus (They are named in Matthew 28:1 to be: Mary Magdalene and the other Mary; and they are named in Mark 16:1 to be: Mary Magdalene, Mary the mother of James, and Salome; and they are named in Luke 24:10 to be: Mary Magdalene, Joanna, and Mary the mother of James; and John 20:1 simply names: Mary Magdalene) they ask. *"Who will roll away the stone for us from the entrance to the tomb? (It was a very large stone.)"* These women who had known and served Christ for years we wouldn't expect to have to face such a cruel situation. How could God allow these things to happen to those who had served His Son so well? It is the age old question of, "Why do bad things happen to good people?" We need to notice that the women, who perhaps knew the Lord Jesus Christ the best, did not ask, "Why?," they simply asked "Who?" They didn't even ask "who" had rolled the problem in front of them in the first place. We tend to blame everyone, even God, and they didn't. The women had every right to believe that Jesus, who could have helped them, was sealed by death into ineffectiveness by the very stone with which they were now confronted. When we fear an immovable object that neither our strength nor that of our friends can move, we do not run away, because love doesn't give up and run away even when it believes the object of its love is dead. Love finds something to do with its love. Jesus in his perfect love did not run away from being in that tomb, because He knew about Resurrection and life everlasting. The God you think may be dead may just be alive forevermore, and you will not have your own proof of Resurrection if you give up or if you turn back. Walk right up to your problem with every intention of walking right on through it or around it, and take someone with you if you can, for friendship helps. Find your way to Jesus on the other side of your problem. Jesus may or may not move or intervene on your behalf. The women waited until they got there to deal with what was concerning them, because their love was not dead even though the object of their love was. Love is eternal. And love tackles the insurmountable and faces the impossible. Love can lay down its life and not expect a reward. Love that is like that finds sepulchers to be empty of their dread reality of despair and death, with soldier asleep at its feet. Love that is like that is met by life, instead of finding anticipated deadness, because no stone can shut Jesus away from his disciples. Jesus can come through the locked doors of our doubt, and rise out of the sepulchers of our sorrow, because he cannot be contained within the limitations of any tomb or any obstacle. The stone is just a symbolic reminder of the reality of all the problems we have to live with, but Christ can move them aside for us to be together with Him. Eventually, you will be telling His disciples the good news of the gospel that "The stone is rolled away."

You never truly get over grief, you only get to a place of feeling better with time. When you are in grief you think things that you have never thought before. For example, I was reading an article in a magazine stating that when things go the way we want we're thankful, but thankfulness is us-centered. But praise is God-centered, and the article stated that *praise is the beginning of healing.* Because when you get away to God, it is not running away, it is caring for yourself. When you are smothered in grief you need to come up for air. Part of getting over grief is praising God a symbolic 10,000 number of times. The Bible says that God inhabits the praises of His people (Psalm 22:3), and that when two or three are gathered together in His name, He is there in their midst (Matthew 18:20). Going to God is going to "The Great Physician" (Luke 5:31-32). There is no better time to start healing than now. So why not praise God this very moment by saying: "Praise God, from whom all blessings flow; praise Him, all creatures here below. Praise Him above, ye Heavenly Host; praise Father, Son, and Holy Ghost. Amen. (This doxology hymn was written in 1674 by Thomas Ken, a priest in the Church of England.)"

Every human being consists of:

1.) a physical <u>body</u>,

2.) an intellectual <u>mind</u> that seeks truth,

3.) an emotional <u>heart</u> that seeks love and

4.) a <u>spirit</u> (or soul) that seeks goodness and God.

In order to get over grief:

1.) Your <u>body</u> needs to do the symbolic 10,000 simple and ordinary things we all have to do, even though they are harder to do in grief.

2.) Your <u>mind</u> needs to go to scripture a symbolic 10,000 number of times, because in grief you will see there what you have never seen before, as you get new and deeper insights.

3.) Your <u>heart</u> needs to release its emotion and cry a symbolic 10,000 times.

4.) Your <u>spirit</u> needs to praise God a symbolic 10,000 number of times, even if you don't feel like doing it at first. An old Irish saying is that you can believe in the sun even though it's not shining

It's one thing to think positively, and it's another thing to recognize the truth about ourselves. We may even have to have others tell us what they see about ourselves that we cannot see. You may not recognize your denial, or your anger, or that you are stuck in your grief. You may not recognize your defenses of fight, flight fright, fun and falsity, which you are unwilling to let go.

Psychologists did an experiment where they gave two groups each an impossible puzzle and the first group ate cookies while the second group ate radishes, which most people don't want to eat. This radish eating group gave up trying to solve the impossible puzzle eight minutes before the cookie eating group. This suggested that the energy of will that it took to eat the radishes depleted the will for other things. The psychologists called this "ego depletion." If you can deplete something, then you can replete something. Psychologists did that by asking people to do something easy, different, and new by eating with their left hand if their right hand was their dominant hand. Perhaps grief is a severe case of ego depletion and doing the easy everyday things that need to be done, which may seem different and new without the beloved, is what causes repletion of will to accomplish return to ordinary living again. But it is not just doing the symbolic 10,000 number of things with the physical body, there is also the mind, heart and spirit that needs to do its 10,000 things.

Suppressing our tears only makes us sick and we will cry later over being sick if we don't cry now in grief. There is a benefit in reliving memories and reviewing the funeral and the cards afterwards if they make you cry. You need a release for your emotions of grief in tears. In addition to tears an outlet for your grief occurs in: willingly embracing your cross, getting insights from reading scripture, recognizing God-incidences, encountering truths, and accepting the balm of going to Jesus in prayer. Some find release in writing a journal or a grief letter to their relatives or in making every day count.

In the Bible is a story (Matthew 8:1-4) of a man with a dreaded skin disease who goes to Jesus and says "Sir, if you want to, you can make me clean." Jesus says: "I do want to. Be clean" And Jesus touches the man and he is instantly healed. Grief may be our hidden leprosy. The book of Leviticus Chapter 13 says that we are to isolate (do not touch) a leper, but Love transcends the law.

Jesus is always going around saying: "Don't be afraid" (John 6:20 and Luke 8:50) or "Fear not." Love casts out fear (1 John 4:18). So in effect, Jesus is saying: "Love." "God is love, and whoever lives in love lives in union with God and God lives in union with him" (1 John 4:16). What you have once loved you can never lose. The love that a person in grief has is a spiritual bond that death cannot sever. "Grief is the price of loving" or to put it another way "You would not hurt so much now if you did not love so deeply."

I was listening to a preacher on television and he was talking about Luke, 5:17-26, the story about the friends with faith breaking a hole in the roof to lower a paralyzed man to Jesus. The preacher pointed out that Jesus was amazed at their faith and he cured the man. The paralyzed man didn't even have to say anything or ask for anything. The faith of others caused God to give this paralyzed man something wonderful that made the crowd praise God.

There were obstacles to get the man and Jesus together that the faith of others overcame. It gives new meaning to the old expression, "Keep up the faith!" It gives us hope that because there are people of faith all around us in the Church, with enough faith already, that grief will not be an obstacle preventing God from giving to us something great. And no obstacle will keep us from getting together with Jesus, and no obstacle will prevent the crowd from eventually praising God.

Just like the women at the tomb (Mark 16:3-4) wondering who will roll the stone away, we know that obstacles will roll away if we will just show up. Just like the disciples on the way to Emmaus who were out of hope, and saying, "We had hoped..." (Luke 24:21), Jesus (The "Hound of Heaven") finds them and reminds them of what they were slow to believe by reviewing what was said about himself in all of the Scriptures, beginning with the books of Moses and the writings of all the prophets, and that made their hearts burn (Luke 24: 25, 27, 32).

And like the woman (Matthew 26:6-13) who lavishly broke open her alabaster jar of expensive perfume to pour on the head of Jesus, we can give Jesus what we secretly hoard and prize, which may include our lost beloved and our grief, for His recognition and for the glory of God.

God can use broken things to bless us. Our grief makes us a broken thing upon our cross of grief. In the Bible Jesus feeds thousands with seven broken loaves of bread after blessing it (Mark 8:1-9). The broken form of Jesus upon the Cross sets souls free. There is a loneliness and a testing of faith in grief. Love is triumphant in victory and strongest in loss, but love is also a sacrament made for a Cross. That is when love does not feel like a victory march. Those in grief may feel angry at love. God is love, and so they may feel angry with God. Love in grief finds its faith to be different than the joy of when it first believed. Love is to suffer. Faith is to suffer. And grief is impatient and can't wait for Jesus to come a second time with the cry of the Archangel (1 Thessalonians 4:16). There's a song called "Hallelujah" (a song written by Canadian singer-songwriter Leonard Cohen, originally written and released in 1984) with some of the words written by Welsh singer-songwriter John Cale. And

Cales' version was featured in the 2001 animated film Shrek, with some of the words being: "Love is not a cry you can hear at night; It's not somebody who's seen the light. It's a cold and it's a broken, Hallelujah."

There is a deeper meaning to all of scripture when you are in grief, because grief is our obstacle, grief is our stone that needs someone to roll away, and grief requires us to give to God what we secretly hoard and prize and have previously not wanted to give to Him. Like the Blind man, Bartimaeus, who shouts out when he hears that Jesus is passing by (Mark 10:47), those in grief know that it is their moment to call out to Jesus. Wisdom is discerning the difference between one moment and the next. Like the woman who touches the edge of His garment (Luke 8:44; see also Matthew 14:36), because she knows that this is now her moment. Those in grief know that this is their moment to interpret scripture with the eyes of grief. That they should not waste their grief, because like the nuns that I had at school used to say, "God must love you very much to give you so much grief." I bring all of this up to you, because it may help you to understand that it's in times of grief when friends of faith mean more than ever. I want you to know that you and your thoughts and prayers are appreciated. And because of you I look forward now to something wonderful happening to eventually make the crowd praise God.

The Bible shows that God never does anything without first telling his prophets. And I heard a sermon in which the preacher pointed out the third rider on a dark horse in Revelation, 6:5-6, where the rider says, "a Denarius for a loaf of bread" which implies a prediction of future severe inflation. (Revelation 6:6 GNB says: "A quart of wheat for a day's wages, and a quart of barley for a day's wages.") At the time the Bible was written a Denarius was a day's wages. It is obviously like now, a time of financial crisis for the world, but with a high inflation rate. But just as the Jews were saved from the angel of death when they were passed over by having the blood of the lamb of sacrifice on their door posts (Exodus 12:13), so too, believers may be protected at that end time, because the Bible is not meant to scare us but to share hope and good news, because the preacher said that the dark horse rider says, "Do not hurt the wine and the oil." (Revelation 6:6 GNB says: "But do not damage the olive trees and the vineyards!") The Jews were symbolically olive trees and they were anointed by oil. Oil also represents in the New Testament a symbol of the Holy Spirit. And the Gentiles (Christians) have the wine used in the Mass. And Jesus is represented in the New Testament as the vine with all true believers as his branches (John 15:5). This suggests that God wants to protect you because He loves you very, very much.

Additionally, in the Bible the last letter of seven letters is sent to the Church of Laodicea in Revelation, Chapter 3, in which Jesus calls believers lukewarm (Revelation 3:16) and knocks on the door for entrance saying, "If you have ears, then, listen to what the Spirit says to the churches!"(Revelation 3:22). The way to get over being lukewarm is to let Jesus back into the Church. At that point Jesus is *outside* the door.

But in John 20:19-29 Jesus is *inside* the door. The Bible says, "*Now a week later his disciples were again inside and Thomas was with them. Jesus came, although the doors were locked, and stood in their midst and said, "Peace be with you"* (John 20:26). Thomas, called Didymus, one of the Twelve, a week earlier had said that he will not believe until he has physical proof (John 20:25). That sounds angry and disappointed to me, like a person in grief. In a time of grief our only comfort is to believe in a life ever after. But in grief some of us become paralyzed in our faith like the man being put down through the roof by his friends to Jesus (Luke, 5:17-26). But the faith of others has *already done* something that will give to us something that we just have to lay back and accept. Jesus is able to overcome not only the locked door of the room where Thomas is, but also *Jesus is able to overcome the locked door of Thomas's hope.* Jesus says, in effect, that Thomas should physically see and touch what love has *already done* for Thomas, "and do not be unbelieving, but believe. Blessed are those who have not seen and have believed" (John 20:27-29). Jesus is knocking in our grief on the door of our locked hope, asking us to open up to Him. And to open up to hope. First

Jesus gets rid of our fear, such as our fear that there may not be life after death, by saying "Peace be with you" (John 20:26). Thomas was afraid to put hope in his heart as he didn't want to be disappointed again, because he used to have hope before he lost it when Jesus died. *Incredulity was like a defense mechanism for Thomas, because his love for Jesus became mixed with fear.* We know that perfect love casts out all fear (1 John 4:18), and that Jesus is perfect love. Thomas in his love wanted to see the hands of Jesus again, and in his love for Jesus, Thomas wanted to see Jesus' body again. In the same way that we in our grief wish to be together with our lost beloved. We must first heal our fear before we can heal our faith, and in order to do that we need love.

Jesus loves you and wants to heal you and wants to be with you, and wants to say to you, "Fear not!" so that you can cry out: "My Lord and my God" (John 20:28). We must allow those who love us, even Jesus, to love us not as we want them to love us, but to fearlessly accept love as it comes in ways mysterious to us. In order to receive we have to let go; in order to receive we have to open our fists. And in order for our love to be perfect we have to remove all fear by unlocking our hearts, opening up to hope and trustingly releasing everything there to Jesus in faith. "Love increases by means of truth, and love draws near by means of truth" (Pope John Paul II, Polish priest, 1920-2005). And that is why I added this Postscript so that I could share with you the truth that I was able to collect while I was attending Griefshare, so that you could have an increase in your love And in your faith and hope.

God bless you all.

Love always, Dad/Ron

240

If I overlook giving credit for any quotes that I have collected over the years, please let me know so I can correct it in the next edition. —Ron

Index

69, 72, 73, 74, 75, 77, 80, 82, 83, 84, 88, 91, 95, 97, 98, 102, 103, 107, 112, 114, 120, 121, 122, 123, 124, 126, 131, 134, 135, 143, 144, 145, 147, 149, 150, 155, 156, 157, 159, 160, 167, 169, 170, 172, 180, 182, 189, 190, 198, 204, 205, 206, 208, 209, 210, 211, 212, 214, 215, 218, 219, 221, 222, 223, 224, 225, 226, 227, 228, 231, 232, 233, 234, 235, 236, 237, 238, 239, 240

Goddess 134, 135

God-incidences 33, 54, 209, 236

Goethe, Johann Wolfgang Von 59, 112, 135

Gogh, Vincent Van 12, 75

Goldilocks principle 57

Good viii, xviii, 1, 13, 14, 19, 22, 23, 31, 35, 36, 49, 62, 65, 79, 84, 87, 90, 94, 98, 99, 107, 114, 118, 121, 122, 124, 125, 130, 131, 136, 141, 145, 151, 152, 156, 158, 162, 164, 167, 172, 173, 176, 183, 184, 187, 190, 192, 195, 198, 200, 205, 211, 213, 214, 220, 221, 233, 238

Goodness xiii, xvii, xix, 2, 9, 11, 12, 13, 14, 16, 18, 25, 35, 37, 38, 40, 45, 47, 48, 55, 59, 60, 61, 62, 63, 64, 66, 67, 72, 76, 80, 81, 82, 84, 103, 104, 107, 108, 113, 114, 116, 117, 120, 124, 131, 144, 149, 150, 152, 200, 204, 208, 209, 210, 214, 223, 224, 234

Gorgeous 6, 224

Gray, Thomas 220

Greatest 1, 21, 22, 76, 79, 87, 173, 187, 206, 220, 224

Grief 8, 9, 16, 53, 220, 225, 229, 230, 231, 232, 234, 235, 236, 237, 238, 239, 240

Griefshare 229, 230, 240

Griffith, Joel 136

Growing 2, 32, 35, 36, 54, 73, 92, 104, 125, 151, 152, 167, 187, 188, 218

Gunshot 15, 99, 125

Gynecology 24

H

Haiku 30

Hair 7, 18, 35, 68, 168

Hamilton, Scott 41

Hansen, Mark Victor 20

Happiness xvi, 10, 14, 20, 21, 28, 42, 87, 123, 149, 150, 160, 161, 162, 163, 164, 169, 170, 182, 214

Happy xvi, 18, 20, 29, 41, 68, 80, 84, 87, 114, 117, 123, 125, 127, 158, 161, 163, 164, 165, 167, 169, 170, 171, 214, 222, 226

Healed 25, 30, 33, 45, 58, 75, 128, 205, 212, 236

Healing 9, 25, 42, 44, 45, 205, 220, 234

Healthy xviii, 45, 170, 194

Heard 4, 31, 32, 33, 39, 40, 161, 162, 176, 187, 210, 214, 227, 238

Heart xiii, xiv, xvii, xix, 1, 2, 5, 7, 8, 12, 13, 14, 18, 22, 24, 26, 27, 28, 30, 33,

J

K

M

N

O

P

Q

Quadruple 131, 134, 135, 137
Quenching 16

R

Radiotherapy 7, 17, 18, 37, 80
Raleigh, Sir Walter 75, 124
Rational 8, 18, 48, 58, 84, 103, 106, 107, 114, 170, 209
Raymond, Rossiter Worthington 203, 228
Raytheon Company 54
Reading xiii, xv, xvii, xx, 8, 9, 10, 14, 30, 41, 46, 49, 104, 146, 185, 187, 234, 236
Reagan, Ronald 21, 26, 221
Recovery 6, 18, 19, 65, 176, 192, 193, 197, 205
Reflection 10, 93, 117, 134, 137, 165, 181, 182
Rehabilitation 6, 192, 193, 197, 223
Religion 36, 41, 44, 53, 58, 86, 93, 112, 113, 115, 144
Repplier, Agnes 168
Research ix, 146
Residency ix, 38, 99, 117
Respect 55
Responsibility 55
Reverend viii
Review xiv, 149
Rhythms 57, 116
Rigid 9, 17, 190
Risk 17, 65, 77, 116, 196
Robotic 2
Rock Hound 8, 100
Rocks xvi, 8, 100, 212
Rocky Mountain Spotted Fever 5, 6
Rohn, Jim 136
Roosevelt, Theodore 218
Rorschach test 10, 11
Ross, Leonard Q. xiv, 123
Rosten, Leo Calvin 123
Rotten xviii
Runbeck, Margaret Lee 170
Ruskin, John 220

S

Sacrament 8, 237

LaVergne, TN USA
29 March 2010

177497LV00003B/2/P